D0889829

PYTHAGORAS REVIVED

B243
O46
1989

Pythagoras Revived

Mathematics and Philosophy in
Late Antiquity

DOMINIC J. O'MEARA

DISCARDED
URI LIBRARY

CLARENDON PRESS · OXFORD
1989

18350053

Oxford University Press, Walton Street, Oxford OX2 6DP

Oxford New York Toronto
Delhi Bombay Calcutta Madras Karachi
Petaling Jaya Singapore Hong Kong Tokyo
Nairobi Dar es Salaam Cape Town
Melbourne Auckland
and associated companies in
Berlin Ibadan

Oxford is a trade mark of Oxford University Press

Published in the United States
by Oxford University Press, New York

© Dominic J. O'Meara 1989

All rights reserved. No part of this publication may be reproduced,
stored in a retrieval system, or transmitted, in any form or by any means,
electronic, mechanical, photocopying, recording, or otherwise, without
the prior permission of Oxford University Press

British Library Cataloguing in Publication Data

O'Meara, Dominic J.
Pythagoras revived
1. Mathematics. Philosophical perspectives,
100–500
I. Title
510'.1
ISBN 0–19–824485–1

Library of Congress Cataloging-in-Publication Data
O'Meara, Dominic J.
Pythagoras revived.
Bibliography: p.   Includes index.
1. Pythagoras and Pythagorean school.
2. Mathematics—Philosophy—History.   I. Title.
B243.046   1989   119'.09'015   88–25246
ISBN 0–19–824485–1

Set by Joshua Associates Ltd., Oxford
Printed and bound in
Great Britain by Biddles Ltd.
Guildford & King's Lynn

PATRI DILECTISSIMO
SACRUM

PREFACE

Research begun many years ago with the support of a Junior and Visiting Fellowship at the Dumbarton Oaks Center for Byzantine Studies brought me to the texts and theses explored in this book. A sabbatical grant and generous leave of absence from The Catholic University of America and a grant provided in ideal circumstances by the Alexander von Humboldt-Stiftung allowed me to develop these theses. Completion of the book was made possible by the support made available by the Université de Fribourg. I am also much indebted to friends and colleagues for their assistance. Henri-Dominique Saffrey made many helpful suggestions and corrections for which I am grateful, as I am to Oxford University Press's reader for constructive and detailed comments. Ilsetraut Hadot also proposed improvements to the book, which is indebted to her research as it is to the work of Pierre Hadot, a longstanding source of inspiration for me. Leendert Westerink and John Duffy were unfailing in their expert assistance. I am particularly grateful to Werner Beierwaltes: he put me on the track of Iamblichus and gave me invaluable advice and help during my stay in Freiburg-im-Breisgau and Munich. The deficiencies that remain in the book are of course mine. My wife Carra gave my work her full encouragement and support throughout many years. Amy Eiholzer-Silver prepared the typescripts of the final revisions of the book with intelligent care.

In an effort to simplify footnotes as far as possible, I have adopted the practice of referring to modern works by the name of the author and the year of publication: further details may be found in the second part of the Bibliography. The texts of ancient authors are cited by page and line in the editions listed in the first part of the Bibliography (for fragments, by fragment number and line). In cases where this seemed appropriate, I have added a chapter number before the page reference (e.g. I ch. 2, 3 = vol. I, chapter 2, page 3). Translations are mine, unless otherwise noted. The following standard abbreviations are used:

CAG *Commentaria in Aristotelem Graeca*, Berlin, 1870 ff.
DK   H. Diels, W. Kranz, *Die Fragmente der Vorsokratiker*, Berlin, 1952.

LSJ   Liddell, Scott, Jones, *Greek—English Lexicon.*
RE   Pauly, Wissowa, Kroll, *Realencyclopädie der classischen Alter-tumswissenschaft.*
SVF   *Stoicorum veterum fragmenta*, ed. H. von Arnim, Leipzig, 1905–24.

This book was completed early in 1986. I have tried to include mention of what has been published since, but have only been able to take account to a limited extent in particular of the important Paris colloquium on Proclus: *Proclus, lecteur et interprète des anciens*, ed. J. Pépin, H.-D. Saffrey, Paris 1987.

D.J.O'M.

Fribourg, Switzerland
Christmas 1987

TABLE OF CONTENTS

PART II

IAMBLICHEAN PYTHAGOREANISM IN THE ATHENIAN
SCHOOL

Introduction

PLOTINUS had been dead some thirty years when his pupil Porphyry published on the threshold of the fourth century AD the definitive edition of his master's works. Porphyry's edition opened with a biography of Plotinus, the *Vita Plotini*, that was intended, among other things, to introduce the reader to Plotinus as the figure of the ideal philosopher. Inspired by this model and by the wisdom and otherworldly serenity that it promised, the reader would move on to read the Plotinian tractates that followed. These tractates Porphyry divided and grouped in six sets of nine works ('Enneads') and arranged the sets in such a way that their sequence led the mind of the reader up from the material world, through ever higher levels, to the source of all reality, the One. Thus Porphyry's edition, taken as a whole (*Vita* and *Enneads*), constituted a systematic introduction, initiation, and path to the highest truths of philosophy.

Porphyry's edition could give his contemporaries every reason to feel confident in the strength and promise of their ancient philosophical culture: Plotinus had brought together with considerable success the many philosophical tendencies of preceding centuries into a whole that came astonishingly close to Plato, if not always in doctrine, certainly in emotional and spiritual power, in intellectual depth, and in the promise of a comprehensive understanding of reality. These qualities in Plotinus' philosophy had already attracted the attention and admiration of many important men of letters and of action, pagan as well as Christian. Greek philosophy, it seemed, had acquired in Plotinus and in his school new vigour.

This was indeed the case. Philosophical schools sprang up and developed throughout the Eastern part of the Roman Empire under the direct and indirect inspiration of Plotinus' fundamental ideas.[1] Porphyry's pupil Iamblichus set up a school in Syria which in turn contributed to a revival of Platonic philosophy at Athens in the fifth

---

[1] Cf. Blumenthal (1981); much remains to be investigated concerning the ways in which Plotinus was read and criticized by later Neoplatonists such as Iamblichus (a subject I hope to discuss elsewhere) and Proclus, who wrote a *Commentary on Plotinus*.

century. The first major figures of the Athenian school, Syrianus and
Proclus, had among their pupils philosophers, in particular Ammonius, who would be responsible for an important period in the life of
Platonic philosophy at Alexandria, producing influential commentators on Aristotle such as John Philoponus. Even when the Athenian
school was closed by imperial decree in 529[2] it included two major
philosophers, Damascius and Simplicius. And the Platonic school at
Alexandria managed to carry on, thanks, it appears, to its having
reached an understanding with church authorities.

This last, extremely dynamic and fruitful period in the history of
Greek philosophy has in recent years been receiving the attention it
deserves. The philosophical and scientific interest of the ideas of
Iamblichus, Philoponus, Simplicius, and others has been stressed.[3]
The important role late Antique Platonism (or 'Neoplatonism') played
in the development of philosophy in the Islamic, Byzantine, and
Western Medieval worlds is better known. However, much remains to
be investigated. In particular the development of Neoplatonic philosophy in the period between Plotinus and the Athenian and Alexandrian schools of the fifth and sixth centuries is very far from being
understood. This has to do primarily with the fact that, if the works of
Plotinus and of late Neoplatonists such as Proclus and Simplicius
have in large part survived, the same is not true of the philosophers
who came between them. In particular almost all the major philosophical works of Porphyry and Iamblichus have disappeared: all that
remains as evidence for their ideas are some minor works, fragments,
and quotations and reports to be found in later authors such as
Proclus. From such bits and pieces a reconstruction must be
attempted, without which the history of Greek Neoplatonism cannot
be written.[4]

A particularly difficult problem in this regard is posed by the case of
Porphyry's pupil Iamblichus. Both the later Neoplatonists and
modern research agree that Iamblichus was largely responsible for
changing Plotinus' philosophy so that it would take the form it has
later, for example, in Proclus.[5] Significant progress has been made in

---

[2] Cf. Blumenthal (1978).   [3] Cf. Sorabji (1983), (1987); Sambursky (1962).
[4] For Porphyry cf. P. Hadot (1968), Smith (1974); the task of reconstruction is made
all the more difficult in that the reports in later authors cannot be treated uncritically,
i.e. as if their precise source need not be identified and as if these authors do not report
in terms of their own philosophical perspectives: on this problem cf. Steel (1978), 12–13;
Gersh (1978), 7–8.
[5] Cf. Praechter's pioneering work (1910), (1932); Steel (1978), 12.

the study of Iamblichus in recent years. In particular the fragments remaining of his commentaries on Plato have been collected, translated, and discussed by Dillon (1973) and a first synthesis based on a large body of evidence has been presented by Larsen (1972). However, much remains unclear about the *precise* ways in which Iamblichus altered the course of Neoplatonic philosophy. To understand this we would need to find out more about Iamblichus' philosophical ideas and the ways in which they were conveyed to, and used by his successors.

In this book I propose some answers to the question of Iamblichus' place in the history of late Greek philosophy, using evidence that has, in this regard, never been exploited. Besides playing a pivotal role in later Neoplatonism we also know that Iamblichus attempted to revive Pythagoreanism (in some sense) as a philosophy.[6] Indeed the first four books of a work he devoted to Pythagoreanism are still extant. Iamblichus' work *On Pythagoreanism* was furthermore, as I shall show, known to and used at Athens by Syrianus and Proclus. This work then not only allows us access to some of Iamblichus' philosophical ideas. It also provides a concrete link between him and his philosophical successors. As yet, however, Iamblichus' revival of Pythagoreanism has not been examined, his work *On Pythagoreanism*—for reasons to be noted later—not given much weight, and the importance of this work and more generally of his revival of Pythagoreanism for the history of later Neoplatonism largely ignored. In discussing this evidence I hope to show that it can serve to shed new light on a number of specific areas in the history of Greek philosophy after Plotinus.

Ever since Plato and his Academy Platonists have shown great interest in the figure of Pythagoras and a strong inclination to 'Pythagoreanize'. In order then to assess properly Iamblichus' attempt to revive Pythagoreanism as a philosophy it will be necessary first to survey various Pythagoreanizing tendencies among his immediate philosophical predecessors (Chapter 1). The analysis of Iamblichus' Pythagoreanizing programme will then begin with a study of the first four extant books of the work (*On Pythagoreanism*) he devoted to the subject (Chapter 2). Although the remaining books of this work no longer survive, it has recently been possible to recover excerpts from Books V–VII preserved in a Byzantine author, Michael Psellus. These excerpts are examined here for the first time (Chapter 3). This new

---

[6] Cf. Praechter (1910), 173; Harder (1926), xvi ff.; Burkert (1972), 98; Szlezák (1979), 35.

material makes possible a better evaluation of the importance of *On Pythagoreanism*. It will be shown furthermore (Chapter 4) that what we know of Iamblichus' other works indicates that there also he Pythagoreanized Platonic philosophy, an important consequence of which was a strong mathematizing of this philosophy.

In Part Two of the book the impact of Iamblichus' Pythagoreanizing of Neoplatonism will be discussed with reference in particular to the Athenian School at its beginnings in the fifth century (Chapter 5), as represented by Syrianus (Chapter 6) and by Syrianus' brilliant and very influential successor Proclus (Chapters 7–10). In these chapters I shall show that Iamblichus' work *On Pythagoreanism* and more generally his Pythagoreanizing programme were familiar to Syrianus and Proclus and may be used as providing an approach to their thought in which the extent to which they were inspired by and also moved away from Iamblichus' programme may be measured. Most emphasis will be given to Proclus, not only on account of his historical importance and of the fact that much of his work survives, but also because he seems to have reacted critically and rejected in certain respects Iamblichus' revival of Pythagoreanism, a response that throws light on the constitution of his philosophy.

The reader will infer from the above that what follows is limited in its ambitions. My purpose is to bring out what information can be found in some unexploited and in some new evidence concerning a particular theme and period in the history of later Greek philosophy. One perspective will serve as guide, namely the revival of Pythagoreanism viewed as a claim both about the origins and about the nature of Platonic philosophy. Only the works of a few, selected philosophers will be discussed. There are of course other themes, other philosophers that would need to be considered also, were a comprehensive history of later Neoplatonism to be attempted.[7] This book is limited furthermore in that it touches on mathematics only in so far as mathematics, under the pressure of Pythagoreanizing tendencies, became a subject of increasing interest to philosophers in late Antiquity and came to mark their theories. The history of mathematics *per se* in late Antiquity is not therefore considered. Nor is the question of the origins and original doctrines of Pythagoreanism. Yet a better appreciation of how Neoplatonic philosophers appropriated Pythag-

---

[7] One important theme that would require discussion is the role played by 'Chaldaean' oracles and theurgy, on which cf. Lewy (1956), Saffrey (1984), Shaw (1985), for example.

orean ideas, making them express much later philosophical develop-
ments, may be of use in the critique of modern tendencies to confuse
Pythagoreanizing Neoplatonism with ancient Pythagoreanism. And in
the sense that the history of Pythagoras and of his thought is essentially the history of his legend in later times, one might consider as
part too of that history the account of how philosophers in the last
centuries of the Roman Empire found in Pythagoras an authority and
a stimulus for the development of theories of considerable sophistication and originality.

PART I

The Revival of Pythagoreanism in the Neoplatonic School

I

Varieties of Pythagoreanism in the Second and Third Centuries AD

A COMPLETE account of Pythagoreanism and of Pythagoreanizing tendencies in the second and third centuries AD would require a treatment going far beyond the scope of this chapter. One would need to discuss questions such as these: Did there exist during this period Pythagorean or Neopythagorean 'sects'? Who belonged to these sects, if indeed they existed? Was Ammonius, Plotinus' teacher, a member? Or should he be considered, along with others such as Eudorus and Moderatus, as merely a Platonist who was inclined to Pythagoreanize? What are we to make in this context of such 'Pythagorean' figures as Apollonius of Tyana and Alexander of Abonoteichus? What is the relation between the Pythagoreanism of this period and earlier forms of Pythagoreanism? Does anything of ancient Pythagoreanism still survive at this time? An adequate approach to these matters would require the collection and analysis of an extremely varied and widely scattered body of evidence, both literary and archaeological, pagan and Christian.[1]

The purpose of this introductory chapter is by comparison very limited: to supply some points of reference in relation to which Iamblichus' programme to Pythagoreanize Platonic philosophy can be better understood. I propose to select four thinkers who provided immediate precedents to what Iamblichus attempted in this programme, two of them well known to Iamblichus through their works, Numenius and Nicomachus, and two of them his teachers, Anatolius and Porphyry. In discussing these four predecessors of Iamblichus, I shall attempt to sketch their ideas concerning two general issues that will emerge as central in Iamblichus' programme: (i) the role of Pythagoras in the history of philosophy and more generally in man's search for wisdom, and (ii) the relation between the Pythagorean

---

[1] Cf. e.g. Burkert (1961); Dörrie (1963); Armstrong (1967), 90–106 (Merlan); Dillon (1977), ch. 7. On Eudorus cf. Burkert (1972), 53; Cherniss (1976), 164–5, 170–1; Dillon (1977), 115 ff. On Ammonius cf. Schwyzer (1983). On Moderatus cf. nn. 8, 46, 52 below.

mathematical sciences (arithmetic, geometry, astronomy, and music) and philosophy (and its parts).

I. NUMENIUS OF APAMEA

If we know little about the life of Numenius—just enough to date him to the second century[2]—we know a good deal more about his ideas, thanks to the interest taken in him by the Neoplatonists and by Christian authors. He was read and discussed in Plotinus' lectures; he was quoted by Porphyry; and Iamblichus thought him important enough to accuse Neoplatonic colleagues—Porphyry, Harpocration, Theodore of Asine, and perhaps Amelius—of parroting him.[3] He is referred to as a 'Pythagorean' both by Porphyry and by the Christians Origen and Eusebius.[4] This may have been Numenius' own description of himself, since it corresponds, as will be seen, to his original views about the history of Greek philosophy and to the purpose he wished his work to accomplish in that history. And yet if he is placed in the context of his own time, he is best understood as part of a widespread and varied effort in the first centuries AD to interpret Plato's dialogues so as to reach a systematic Platonic dogma.[5]

Numenius wrote a remarkable book on the history of philosophy some extracts of which are quoted by Eusebius (frs. 24–8). The title of the book, *On the Dissension between the Academics and Plato*, introduces the dominant theme, that of dissension, conflict, war. The theme of a 'war' between philosophers is conventional.[6] But Numenius develops it in interesting ways. It has first a political significance. It refers to the disputes that increasingly tore apart Plato's school, the Academy (frs. 25, 27). Such strife—a characteristic of those disputatious materialists and most bellicose of philosophers, the Stoics (fr. 24, 37 ff.)—produced a malfunctioning and unhappy Academy to which Numenius opposes the fidelity to the Master and unity of mind of the Pythagoreans and of

---

[2] Cf. Numenius, *Fragments*, p. 7; Dillon (1977), 362.

[3] Cf. Leemans (1937), *Test.* nos. 18–20, with Lewy (1956), 503 n. 23; Iamblichus is exploiting an old charge made against Plotinus (Porphyry, *Vit. Plot.* 17, 1–6).

[4] Numenius, frs. 1 a, 1 b, 1 c, 4 b, 24, 29, 52 (the texts in Calcidius and Nemesius probably derive from Porphyry, cf. Waszink [1964], 11, 25).

[5] Waszink (1966), 37–9; O'Meara (1975), ch. 1.

[6] Cf. Maximus of Tyre, *Or.* 26, 310, 4–15. The term διάστασις in Numenius' title refers more technically to the distancing and confrontation preparatory to battle (cf. Numenius, frs. 24, 41; 25, 86 and 104).

the Epicureans (fr. 24, 18–36). Numenius is reluctant to refer to the
latter (notorious and ignoble materialists that they are!), but he must:
their peaceful unanimity produces a true, ideal community which
stands as a constant reproach to the squabblings of Plato's successors
(cf. fr. 24, 33–6). All this is reminiscent of the contrast depicted in
Plato's *Republic* between the peaceful unity of mind of the correctly-
functioning good state and the self-destructive dissensions and conflicts of the malfunctioning evil state.[7] Numenius in his book is thus
proposing a critique of the history of the Academy based on the
criteria of the ideal state in Platonic political philosophy. These
criteria provide him with the means for both understanding and criti-
cizing that history.

When and how did the evil arise? Although Numenius is elusive on
this point, it seems that he is prepared to find the seeds of conflict in
Plato himself (cf. fr. 24, 62–4), in the secretive way, between clarity and
obscurity, in which Plato communicated Pythagorean doctrines.
Numenius is not willing to ascribe this secretiveness to envy or
maliciousness on Plato's part. He will not therefore go as far as that
Pythagorean theory, reported by Porphyry, which alleged that Plato,
Aristotle, and Plato's pupils plagiarized the best of Pythagorean
doctrines, admitting as Pythagorean only those trivialities that would
later become a subject of mockery.[8]

The theme of dissension also has deeper, metaphysical connotations in Numenius' book. As he showed in his interpretation of
Platonic ontology in his dialogue *On the Good*, change, flux, disintegra-
tion are characteristics of the material world, whereas stability,
unchangingness, self-integrity are proper to the world of true, immaterial being.[9] This ontological contrast is applied by Numenius to
his history of Plato's Academy. Plato's successors increasingly failed
to maintain intact and unchanged the philosophy of their Master (fr.
24, 5–18), so much so that the doctrine now in their hands has woefully
disintegrated.[10] Indeed the successors themselves begin to look very

---

[7] Cf. the ὁμόνοια and ὁμοδοξία of Plato's just state (*Rep.* 432 a, 433 c), and the
μεταβολή, πολυπραγμοσύνη, and στάσις in the evil state (cf. 434 b). Numenius refers
to the Epicurean school as a 'true state' (fr. 24, 34 πολιτεία . . . ἀληθεῖ) in the sense of
'true' (i.e. ideal) used by Plato (cf. *Rep.* 372 e 6).

[8] Cf. Porphyry, *Vit. Pyth.* ch. 53, 61, 20–7. It is usually assumed that this passage
derives from the first-century AD Platonist/Pythagorean Moderatus of Gades. It should
be noted, however, that the section in which Porphyry cites Moderatus ends just before
(ch. 53, 61, 13, closing the passage beginning in ch. 48, 58, 21). Cf. Burkert (1972), 95.

[9] Frs. 2–4 a; cf. O'Meara (1976).

[10] Compare fr. 24, 11 παραλύοντες (of Plato's successors) with fr. 4 a, 24–5

much like the fluid, changing material world.[11] This assimilation suggests that the changeability and disputatious behaviour of Plato's followers is testimony to their error, and that the unchanging integrity of Plato's doctrine is a sign of its truth, a truth which, despite the distortions inflicted on it in the history of the Academy, remains intact and unaffected, just as the Platonic Forms transcend and are independent of the fragmentary images of them reflected in matter.

Numenius' critique, on Platonic political and metaphysical grounds, of what happened in the history of Plato's school points to the remedy he proposes: the restoration of Plato's doctrine to its pristine integrity, an operation involving 'separating it off'[12] from its subsequent history, i.e. the interpretations of Plato to be found in the immediate successors, Speusippus and Xenocrates, in later members of the Academy, Arcesilaus and Carneades, and in such more recent Platonists as Antiochus of Ascalon. They must all be rejected (fr. 24, 68–70). All innovation and change must be removed from the pure unchanging doctrine of Plato.[13] This curious study of Plato's Academy, which progressed by rejection of the history it described, seems to have been preceded by a similar attempt at purification, this time 'separating' Plato off from Aristotle and from the Stoics, a task all the more pressing in Numenius' time when much use was made of these philosophers in the interpretation of Plato.[14]

What then is Plato thus purged? Pythagoras! (fr. 24, 70). If then Numenius described himself as a Pythagorean, he understood this in relation to his programme of rejecting an adulterated and disintegrating Platonic tradition and restoring Platonic doctrine to its original, i.e. Pythagorean, integrity. His view of the relation between Plato and

παραλυόμενον (of material body). The phrase in fr. 24, 72–3 ὅλος δ' ἐξ ὅλου ἑαυτοῦ μετατίθεταί τε καὶ ἀντιμετατίθεται οὐδαμῶς (of Plato) echoes Plato, Rep. 380 d 5–e 1, which is understood by Numenius, fr. 6, 11–12, as describing the unchanging nature of true being (cf. O'Meara [1976], 125). Cf. Puech (1934), 767.

[11] In his edition of Numenius des Places has noticed (76) that the same expression is used (fr. 27, 11) for Carneades and (fr. 3, 11) for matter. Cf. also παλινάγρετος in fr. 25, 31 (of Arcesilaus) and in fr. 3, 5 (of material objects).

[12] χωρίζειν, fr. 24, 68: perhaps another parallel with the metaphysical separation (χωρισμός) of the Forms.

[13] Numenius thus has metaphysical and political grounds for rejecting innovation (καινοτομία); cf. frs. 24, 30–1; 28, 14–15.

[14] Fr. 24, 67–8 (note the critical references to the Stoics in fr. 52). Another second-century Platonist, Atticus, wrote against the adulteration of Plato with Aristotelianism (possibly under Numenius' influence; cf. des Places's edition of Atticus, 19–20 and fr. 1), a theme also treated in a lost work by yet another contemporary, Calvenus Taurus.

Pythagoras differs from Aristotle's account (*Metaphysics* A, 6): far from simply combining Pythagorean and Socratic ideas, Plato joined Socrates and Pythagoras by humanizing in Socratic fashion the 'lofty' Pythagoras (fr. 24, 73–9). The difference then between Plato and Pythagoras is primarily one of style rather than doctrine.[15] Thus pure Platonic philosophy can be referred back to Pythagoras; pure Platonism is Pythagoreanism.

Numenius also refers to Egyptians, Persian mages, Indians, Jews. One might wonder if he is here taking up the old idea—popular since at least the time of Plato and Aristotle—of an ancient and superior wisdom possessed by Pythagoras, by other ancient Greek sages, and even by some barbarian nations.[16] Numenius refers to these nations as corroborating Pythagorean doctrines; Jewish scripture is appealed to because it shares with Pythagoreanism the idea of an immaterial deity.[17] It is not clear however on what grounds Numenius explained the corroboration and agreement between Pythagorean truths and barbarian ideas. Did Pythagoras learn these truths from various barbarian, e.g. Egyptian, teachers? Did Numenius have in mind rather the (Stoic) theory that there are some fundamental 'common conceptions' shared by all nations and peoples? The surviving evidence is not adequate to permit of an answer.[18] We do not know how Numenius thought Pythagoras came in possession of philosophical truth. There is a suggestion in fr. 14 that knowledge is a divine gift to man. Numenius here refers to Plato *Philebus* 16 c, where Prometheus is said to have conveyed knowledge as well as fire from the gods to men. Did Numenius find in Plato's reference to Prometheus an allusion to Pythagoras, an obvious and likely enough interpretation? Would he then have thought of Pythagoras as a mediator of truths revealed to him in some way by the gods? We simply do not know how Numenius read the passage of the *Philebus* in its possible bearing on the attainment of knowledge by Pythagoras and (to some degree, at least) by barbarian nations.[19]

Little also can be said about Numenius' views on the Pythagorean mathematical sciences and their relation to philosophy. He did not

---

[15] Cf. frs. 24, 77–9; 52, 2–4 (a somewhat diffident attitude is adopted in fr. 7, 5–7).

[16] Cf. Festugière (1950–4), I 20–6; Dörrie (1955), 328–9; (1973a), 99 ff.; Waszink (1966), 47–8; Aubenque (1962), 71–2; P. Hadot (1987), 23 ff.

[17] Cf. frs. 1 a; 1 b, 5–8; 8, 9–13; 30, 5–6; Waszink (1966), 46. Note ἐπικαλεῖσθαι (fr. 1 a, 5): appealing to, as a witness. Homer is also used as a witness in fr. 35, 16.

[18] Cf. Whittaker (1967), 200–1.

[19] See below, Ch. 2 n. 22.

neglect mathematics: we know that he wrote a book concerning numbers (fr. 1 c, 4). In the extracts from his dialogue *On the Good* (fr. 2, 20–3), it appears that he adopted Plato's indication in the *Republic* (527 d ff.) that the mathematical sciences serve to lead the mind's eye away from the material world, preparing it for contemplation of pure immaterial being. Did Numenius' Pythagoreanizing bring him so far as to soften the distinctions Plato makes here between mathematics and its objects, on the one hand, and the 'highest study' (called 'dialectic') and its objects (pure being, or the Forms, and the source of the Forms, the Good), on the other? Did his Pythagorean programme prompt him to identify mathematics with dialectic, numbers with Forms? The language of the passage in fr. 2 is not entirely clear on this point. Numenius refers elsewhere (frs. 11, 15; 52, 6) to matter as a 'dyad' and to god as a 'monad' (fr. 52, 5) and a vague report (fr. 39) has him and many others seeing soul as a mathematical entity, the product of monad and dyad. Is this simply the adoption of a supposedly Pythagorean nomenclature that had been popular ever since its exploitation in Plato's Academy?[20] Or should we speak of a profound mathematization of Platonic metaphysics in Numenius? There is at any rate no sign of such a mathematization in the fragments that survive of the dialogue *On the Good*, a work that appears to be an attempt to develop systematically the science of being and its source that Plato calls dialectic, a science that starts from, but that goes beyond mathematics.[21]

2. NICOMACHUS OF GERASA

In the case of Nicomachus (roughly a contemporary of Numenius)[22] the situation is almost the reverse: little is known of his views on Pythagoras, but a good deal can be discovered about his theories concerning the mathematical sciences and their relation to philosophy.[23]

---

[20] The best account of Pythagoreanizing tendencies in Plato's Academy is Burkert (1972); cf. also Krämer (1964), 63 ff.

[21] Cf. fr. 2, 22–3. The question Numenius sets as the theme of *On the Good* I, τί ἐστι τὸ ὄν (loc. cit.; fr. 3, 1), reminds one of Aristotle's formulation of the subject of 'first philosophy' or metaphysics (*Met. Γ* 1); however, Numenius develops his highest science in a quite different, Platonic direction: cf. O'Meara (1976).

[22] Cf. D'Ooge *et al.* (1926), 71–2. On Dillon's argument (1969) for 196 as a date for Nicomachus' death cf. Tarán (1974), 113.

[23] Cf. I. Hadot (1984), 65–9.

Nicomachus won a reputation for himself in his own life-time as a great mathematician. Iamblichus' very high opinion of him—as a 'true Pythagorean' (see below, Chapter 2)—assured the presence of Nicomachus' introductory mathematical writings in the curriculum of Neoplatonist schools and was what prompted Proclus' particular attachment to him (see below, Chapter 7). The works that will be discussed here are his elementary *Introduction to Arithmetic* and a book known by the title *Theologoumena arithmeticae* that survives only in a summary of it produced by the Byzantine Patriarch Photius in the ninth century and in excerpts preserved in an anonymous compilation also entitled *Theologoumena arithmeticae*.[24]

Had Nicomachus' *Life of Pythagoras* survived, much more might be known about Nicomachus' understanding of the place of Pythagoras in the development of science and philosophy.[25] As it is, we must rely primarily on indications given in the *Introduction to Arithmetic*. In the introductory section of this work Nicomachus presents Pythagoras as the first to establish science. Before him could be found various sorts of wisdom—some technical skills are given as examples—but Pythagoras first restricted the application of the word wisdom (σοφία) in order to make it refer only to the 'science of being', that is, an unshakeable grasp of the unchanging immaterial realities which are true being, as contrasted with the changing fluid material world whose existence imitates and derives from true being (1, 5–2, 19). Nicomachus uses (3, 9–4, 5) the same passage in Plato's *Timaeus* (27 d) as is used by

---

[24] The anonymous *Theol. arith.* has been attributed to Iamblichus on the basis that Iamblichus' *On Pythagoreanism* VII was thought to have covered the same ground (for a critique cf. already Tannery [1885a], 181–2). Oppermann (1928) has made the strongest case for this attribution. He provides a careful analysis of the excerpts from Nicomachus' *Theologoumena* and from Anatolius' *De dec.* that make up the anonymous and argues (i) that it is in turn excerpted from a larger unitary work in which the texts of Nicomachus and Anatolius were assembled, and (ii) that this larger work is Iamblichus' *On Pyth.* VII. In support of the latter claim he notes that the references in the anon. to an 'Introduction' (to arithmetic) correspond to Iambl. *In Nic.* (= *On Pyth.* IV) rather than to Nicom. *Intro. arith.* (compare anon. *Theol. arith.* 1, 10–18 with Iambl. *In Nic.* 11, 15–24; however, compare also anon. *Theol. arith.* 3, 2–7 and Nicom. *Intro. arith.* 111, 17; 113, 2–6). He who assembled the excerpts, it is assumed, is also the author of the 'Introduction': Iamblichus. It is not excluded, however, that the anon. is simply using Iambl. *In Nic.* for what he takes to be the content of Nicom. *Intro. arith.* (cf. 83, 4–6 for the title). At any rate the newly recovered excerpts from Iambl. *On Pyth.* VII (below, ch. 3) show it reflected a developed stage of Neoplatonic metaphysics absent from the anon. *Theol. arith.* This suffices to show that the anon. *Theol. arith.*, whoever its compiler might be, is not based on *On Pyth.* VII.

[25] Cf. D'Ooge, 79–87, and Tarán (1974) for a list and discussion of Nicomachus' works. Burkert (1972), 98 ff., discusses material originating from Nicomachus' *Life of Pythagoras*.

Numenius (fr. 7) to express this ontological distinction common in Platonic authors of the period. As in Numenius, the distinction is assumed to be Pythagorean. In Nicomachus it is fundamental, since it serves as the ground for Pythagoras' achievement of a strict definition of science and its isolation from technical expertise.[26] If the ontological distinction is conventionally drawn in Nicomachus, there are some novel aspects to it which will be considered shortly. At any rate it can be concluded that Nicomachus identified Platonism with Pythagoreanism. How Pythagoras is supposed to have elaborated what *we* would describe as 'Platonic' philosophy is not clear. In his *Theologoumena*, Nicomachus referred to the Babylonians and the Persians Zoroaster and Ostanes,[27] but we do not know how Nicomachus understood the relation between them and Pythagoras.

The *Introduction to Arithmetic* reveals much more about Nicomachus' views on the relation between the mathematical sciences and philosophy. His position seems to be at first glance, however, inconsistent. On the one hand, he develops Plato's view in the *Republic* that the mathematical sciences prepare for a higher pursuit. They act as 'ladders' and 'bridges' to pure being, purifying the mind's eye, turning it away from material reality, and facilitating its access to true immaterial being (7, 21–9, 4). Such ideas suggest that Nicomachus conceived of a region of pure being and its science different from and higher than the mathematical sciences and their objects. However, as one reads more of the *Introduction*, it becomes less clear that Nicomachus really would wish to dfferentiate mathematics and its objects (in particular, number) from a higher science (dialectic) and its object (being). At 12, 6–9, for example, he identifies number with pure being. It seems possible then that, in spite of his introductory claims, Nicomachus in fact tends to consider mathematics, and especially the highest mathematical science, arithmetic, as the first and highest form of knowledge, and number as the first and highest form of being.

This inconsistency can be analysed further in relation to the various accounts that Nicomachus provides in the *Introduction* and in the *Theologoumena* of the production of the material world. The standard second-century Platonic cosmology is given: a divine craftsman, or 'demiurge', models matter after ideal patterns (the Forms) in his mind. There are, however, some unusual elements in Nicomachus' version

[26] For Nicomachus' high claims for Pythagoras' scientific achievements in music, cf. Levin (1975), 46 ff.
[27] Cf. anon. *Theol. arith.* 56, 13–15.

of the cosmology. For instance, the patterns used in the ordering of matter are listed in the *Theologoumena* as 'quality, quantity, and the other categories'; according to these 'categories', and 'from number', matter is ordered.[28] More information can be found in the *Introduction* about the 'categories' and their relation to number. They include (2, 21–3, 5) qualities, quantities, shapes, sizes, equalities, relations, activities, dispositions, places, and times. In themselves they are incorporeal and unchanging, sharing only *per accidens* in the materiality and flux of bodies. It has been suggested that Nicomachus' 'categories' are not categories at all (in the Aristotelian sense), but rather Platonic Forms.[29] This is the case inasmuch as their ontological character, in particular their transcendence, is that of the Forms. Indeed, they represent Nicomachus' interpretation of the Forms. At the same time, however, his choice of the term 'category', and the particular categories he names, indicate that he views these Forms in close relation to the general structuring of matter.

The way in which Nicomachus relates his Forms (or categories) to number is also unusual. In his *Theologoumena* he describes the Forms of things, quantity, quality, relation, as number, or rather as properties or 'characters' (ἰδιώματα) of number.[30] The categories are all virtually present already in the monad and are shown forth actually in the first ten numbers, the decad.[31] The intention of Nicomachus is, I think, clear: to reduce the Platonic Forms, the models of the universe which he identifies with Aristotelian categories, to the formal properties of number; the universe is organized according to the various properties of number.[32] We can conclude then that Nicomachus does indeed distinguish between number and true being (the Forms), but in a way that *reverses* the situation in Plato's *Republic*, that is, that subordinates Forms to number. This conclusion reinforces rather than resolves the inconsistency detected above. Not only does it not appear to be true that mathematics prepares for and leads up to a higher (non-mathematical) science of being, but if there is to be such a science at all—and it is not clear what would be left for it after the mathematical study of number and its properties—it must be subordinate to mathematics.

[28] Cf. anon. *Theol. arith.* 44, 7–13 (=Nicomachus; cf. D'Ooge, 85 n. 5).

[29] D'Ooge, 94–5.

[30] Anon. *Theol. arith.* 20, 15–21, 4 (=Nicomachus; cf. D'Ooge, 86–7, and the reading given by the important MS E for 20, 1); 44, 8–13.

[31] Anon. *Theol. arith.* 3, 1–11; 21, 18; 23, 4–6.

[32] Cf. *Intro. arith.* 12, 1–8; 9, 10–15; 114, 17–18.

In the *Introduction* (12, 6–14) it looks as if a distinction is made between 'intelligible' and 'scientific' number.[33] Could this offer a resolution of the inconsistency? Could there be for Nicomachus a conventional, 'scientific' mathematics concerned with 'scientific number' and constituting an intermediary leading the mind's eye up to a higher study corresponding to dialectic in the *Republic*, a contemplation of the 'intelligible', 'divine' numbers presiding over all reality?

More clues can be found in Nicomachus' discussion of the implications of mathematical principles and theorems for non-mathematical subjects. He shows himself to be interested in such implications, particularly for physics and ethics, in his *Introduction*, and the *Theologoumena* was largely devoted to the matter. I shall discuss first the references to physics and ethics in the *Introduction*.

Nicomachus' view of the relevance of number to the physical universe can easily be inferred from his cosmology: number is namely the model, or paradigm, of the universe. Thus the mathematical principle which permits of deriving forms of inequality from equality[34]—a derivation which, Nicomachus insists (66, 1–2), is not of human contrivance, but a natural, i.e. 'divine' process—'proves' that inequality in the physical world also derives from equality.[35] The paradigmatic relation between the world and numbers is such that what is true of numbers and their properties is also true of the structure and processes of the world.[36]

Nicomachus also points out parallels between mathematical and ethical principles. In particular he compares 'perfect', 'superabundant', and 'deficient' numbers with the (Aristotelian) analysis of virtues as 'means' and of vices as 'excesses' and 'deficiencies'. From the context and the language of such comparisons, it appears that the relation between numerical and ethical principles is again paradigmatic. One important passage (65, 8–16) introduces ethical considerations in the context of a comparison between numerical principles and the making of the world. The virtuous life is described as an 'organizing'

[33] The distinction is not as clearly made as D'Ooge, 98–9 (under the influence of Philoponus, *In Nic.* I 12, 5–8), and Bertier (1978), 21–2, imply.

[34] Cf. D'Ooge, 225 n. 1.

[35] *Intro. arith.* 65, 17 ff. τὸ εἰς τὰ φυσικὰ ταῦτα (not D'Ooge's 'universal matters', but the objects of φυσιολογία at 64, 23–5) συντεῖνον θεώρημα. Porphyry's reference, *Vit. Pyth.* 45, 14–15, to the 'tetractys' as πρὸς πολλὰ διατεῖνον φυσικὰ συντελέσματα may come from Nicomachus (named at 45, 4).

[36] Cf. 64, 23–65, 8; 114, 4–9 and ff. (another example).

by the rational of the irrational, which produces good order.[37] This ethical cosmology echoes in the soul that achieved by the divine demiurge in the universe. Not only do numbers then hold the keys to understanding the organization of the world; they also contain principles which constitute standards for the ethical life.[38]

The implications of number were more fully explored by Nicomachus in his *Theologoumena*. As this work was, as I hope to show in the following chapters, of considerable importance and yet has scarcely been examined as a work in itself in modern research, it calls for some attention here. A report going back to late Antiquity refers to it as follows:[39] 'You must first read this book (i.e. the *Introduction*) because it is introductory. For Nicomachus produced another arithmetic entitled *The Major Arithmetic* or *Theologoumena* in which he refers[40] to the present work'. Leaving aside for the moment the interpretation of the second title, *Theologoumena*, one might note that the first title tends to support the suggestion in this text that the *Introduction to Arithmetic* was intended, as a 'minor arithmetic', to lead and introduce the reader to a major work, the *Theologoumena*. Nicomachus' own practice in the *Introduction* goes to some degree in this direction[41] as does Photius' summary of the *Theologoumena*, in which it is stressed that a long training in mathematics is necessary as preparation for Nicomachus' curious arithmetical theology.[42] The passage in Photius reminds us again of the theme in Plato's *Republic* of mathematics as a preparation for 'dialectic', and, as applicable to the relation between the *Introduction* and the *Theologoumena*, strengthens the supposition that Nicomachus could with consistency speak of the mathematical sciences as intermediary (in the sense of Plato's *Republic*) and yet consider number as the highest reality, calling for a study

---

[37] 65, 9-12 (note τὸ τῆς ψυχῆς ... κοσμητικόν and εὐτακτηθήσονται); cf. anon. *Theol. arith.* 35, 15-36, 1 (=Nicomachus; cf. D'Ooge, 85 n. 4).

[38] See the long 'mathematical' account of justice excerpted from Nicomachus' *Theol. arith.* in anon. *Theol. arith.* 37, 1 ff.

[39] Anon. *Prol. in Nic.* 76, 20-4 (the editor, Tannery, xiii, regards this work as Byzantine; it resembles the *prolegomena* produced in Alexandria in late Antiquity); roughly the same details are found in Philoponus, *In Nic.* I 1, 1-2.

[40] Cf. above, n. 24. Nicomachus refers in his *Intro. arith.* 122, 20-123, 3 to his *Theol. arith.* (=Photius, *Bibl.* III 47, 145 a 6-7).

[41] The physical and ethical applications in the *Intro. arith.* come at the *end* of discrete mathematical sections which are described as a necessary method of approach (ἔφοδος, 64, 23-4) to these applications.

[42] *Bibl.* III 41-2, 143 a; Photius at 142 b 23 describes Nicomachus' *Intro. arith.* as 'prior' to (πρὸ) his *Theol. arith.*: this may indicate the order of the works in the manuscript he used; cf. Hägg (1975), 160-1.

crowning mathematics and concerned with the first numerical principles of all reality, a study such as was presented in the *Theologoumena*.

What did this supreme study consist of? What does 'Theologoumena' mean here? We depend for hints of Nicomachus' intentions in
the *Theologoumena* on Photius' report, and Photius is both informative
and frustrating. He tells us Nicomachus' work consisted of two books
dealing with each of the first ten numbers, Book I with the first four
numbers, Book II with the remainder.[43] Each number was discussed
(i) in relation to its specific mathematical properties and (ii) in relation
to various non-mathematical subjects, physical, ethical, and in particular theological. In reporting on this last aspect of the work—it
involved references to many pagan deities—Photius adopts the stance
of righteous indignation appropriate for such heathen nonsense.[44]
This helps to obscure things considerably. Yet what he says, if combined with some extracts preserved in the other source of information
about Nicomachus' book, the anonymous *Theologoumena*, is enough to
yield some clues about what Nicomachus was trying to do.

Photius indicates (142 b 35 ff.) that Nicomachus assimilated various
gods and goddesses to each of the first ten numbers, the specific
quantity of each number (ἰδιάζουσαν... ποσότητα) being the basis
of such identifications. Photius attacks Nicomachus' method of
assimilation (ἀναφορή), charging that he tampered with the specific
properties of the numbers in order to achieve his identifications
(142 b 22 ff.). Be that as it may, it is clear that Nicomachus' approach
involved two phases: (i) setting forth the specific mathematical
characteristics of each number (such as had been at least partially
introduced already in the *Introduction*), and (ii) using these character-

---

[43] For the Pythagorean there are really only the first ten numbers, since all other
numbers are constructed out of the first ten; cf. Nicomachus in anon. *Theol. arith.* 27, 10–
15; 80, 10; Theon, *Exp.* 99, 17–19; Anatolius, *De dec.* 29, 7–8. Treatises on the first ten
numbers are common in Pythagorean-type literature, e.g. Anatolius, *De dec.*, Theon,
Exp. 99, 17–106, 11 who refers to a *De decade* by (Pseudo-) Archytas and to Philolaus, *De
natura* (also a source for Nicomachus; cf. anon. *Theol. arith.* 74, 10 ff.). One should add
also the (Pseudo-) Pythagoras' *Sacred Discourse*. Cf. Tannery (1885a), 182–9; Delatte
(1915), 233–4; Robbins (1921); Staehle (1931), 15–17, 19–75; Mansfeld (1971), 157–9;
Thesleff (1965), 164–6; and below, n. 52.

[44] Appropriately enough Photius' ecclesiastical censure has been renewed by the
modern rationalist. Delatte's description of this sort of subject, which he terms
'arithmology' (1915, 139), as a mixture of 'la saine recherche scientifique' and 'les
fantaisies de la religion et de la philosophie' echoes Photius' judgement of Nicomachus'
work as a mixture of the truth about numbers with fictions dreamed up by an impure
mind (143 a 22–4, 142 b 25–6).

istics in order to relate various divinities to each number. Notwith-
standing his repugnance for such things, Photius concentrates on the
second phase, listing some of the divinities named by Nicomachus
and neglecting the first phase almost completely. A more coherent and
balanced view of Nicomachus' method can be gathered from the
excerpts in the anonymous *Theologoumena*. For example, on the
subject of the monad, a summary of the mathematical characteristics
of the monad is first given (1, 4–2, 17). Various features are stressed:
the monad's capacity to generate other numbers without changing in
itself (1, 6–8); its possession in potentiality of all that appears in
actuality in the following numbers, e.g. odd and even (1, 9 ff.; 3, 2 ff.);
its unificatory property.[45] These features, demonstrated in mathematical fashion of the monad, allow Nicomachus then to identify it with
god (3, 1 ff.), with intellect, and with the demiurge as an organizing,
productive principle (4, 1–2; 4, 9–12). The rationale of Nicomachus'
work disappears in Photius' irate enumeration of pagan divinities. In
his *Theologoumena* Nicomachus attempted then, it seems, to deepen
and justify, through exploration of the mathematical properties of
numbers, the simple assimilations and identifications common in the
Pythagorean tradition between various numbers and assorted gods
(and other objects) whose naïveté had long since exposed Pythagoreanism to ridicule.[46] Thus the Pythagorean saying that 'Justice is
five' entailed for Nicomachus a long exploration of the mathematical
characteristics of the pentad in which the basis of the identification
would emerge.

As the Pythagorean tradition had related numbers not only to
deities, but also to other subjects—indeed a venerable Pythagorean
saying has it that 'all is likened unto number'[47]—so in his *Theologoumena* Nicomachus is concerned with ethical and physical (see above,
nn. 37–8) as well as with theological assimilations. It seems then that

---

[45] 2, 18–19. These first pages of the anon. *Theol. arith.* include some glossing by a
Neoplatonic editor of material which is however essentially Nicomachean; cf. Burkert
(1972), 98, and above, n. 24.
[46] See the decadic works listed above, n. 43. In an interesting passage quoted from
Moderatus in Porphyry, *Vit. Pyth.* ch. 48, 58, 21 ff. (cf. above, n. 8), it seems Moderatus
claimed that the Pythagoreans used the numbers of the decad διδασκαλίας χάριν, to
convey higher, more difficult ideas, namely the Forms and first principles. This
suggests that by the first century AD Pythagorean decadic literature had fallen into such
disrepute that Moderatus felt obliged to defend it as being designed for simpler minds
and as symbolic of higher realities. Nicomachus' *apologia* is quite different and more
faithful to this Pythagorean literature.
[47] ἀριθμῷ δέ τε πάντ' ἐπέοικεν; cf. Delatte (1915), 14–15.

the title *Theologoumena* refers, not to a specific study or science which Nicomachus called 'theology', but very generally to the ancient, mysterious, and wise utterances of the Pythagorean tradition concerning mainly but not exclusively the gods.[48]

As has been shown above, the physical and ethical assimilations indicated in these utterances are understood by Nicomachus on the basis of a paradigmatic relation between mathematical and physical or ethical principles. But what is the relation between numbers and deities? To judge by the approach he takes, it seems that Nicomachus regards the proliferating Greek pantheon as a manner of referring to numbers; *his* gods and goddesses are the monad, dyad, triad. Or, as Photius expressed it, Nicomachus sought to make the numbers gods.[49]

The conclusion that I believe emerges from all this as regards the problem of consistency raised towards the beginning of this section is the following: mathematics, in particular arithmetic, functions for Nicomachus, as for Plato's *Republic*, as an introductory and mediatory study. In contrast to the *Republic*, however, Nicomachus does not regard the *objects* of arithmetic, numbers, their properties and laws, as intermediary between sensibles and Forms. Numbers are, on the contrary, the principles of the Forms, the Forms being no more than the properties or characters of numbers. There then seems little room for the 'highest study', dialectic, of the *Republic* in Nicomachus' system. Is it replaced by another ultimate science? What does the study of arithmetic lead to? To a command of the theory of numbers, one must suppose, such that the numerical structure underlying physical laws, ethical principles, and religious systems becomes clear. Such command, to the degree that it approximates to the numbers which produced the universe, could appropriately be described as a divine science.[50]

In comparison then with Numenius, it appears that Nicomachus, as a Pythagoreanizing Platonist, did go so far as to mathematize Platonic philosophy completely, replacing dialectic and the Forms with some

[48] Note the 'they' in Photius' report (e.g. 143 a 39, 143 b 23, 144 a 4), i.e. the Pythagoreans as referred to by Nicomachus.

[49] Cf. Photius, 142 b 32–7; 143 a 10.

[50] One wonders what the relation might be between the divine demiurge and the decad that he uses as model (cf. anon. *Theol. arith.* 57, 21–58, 7; 32, 11–12), especially in view of Nicomachus' identification of the monad as demiurge. One suspects that the craftsman metaphor in cosmology must yield to the mathematical flux of everything from the monad.

sort of higher arithmetic concerned with the divine numbers that constitute and control everything.

3. ANATOLIUS

Our third case of Pythagoreanism brings us into the third century and concerns Anatolius, a contemporary of Plotinus and Porphyry and a teacher of Iamblichus.[51] Doubts have been raised about whether this Anatolius is the same as the Anatolius mentioned by Eusebius, a professor of Aristotelian philosophy in Alexandria made bishop of Laodicea in the last quarter of the third century who composed ten books of *Arithmetical Introductions* and as a bishop continued to show mathematical inclinations.[52] In particular, it has been thought that chronology required that, if only one Anatolius were concerned, then Iamblichus would have had to have studied with Anatolius acting as bishop of Laodicea, which seems very improbable. However more recent studies have suggested an earlier date for Iamblichus' birth (245 or before), which would make it possible to have Iamblichus working under Anatolius before the latter became bishop in the 270s.[53] 'We should not multiply Anatolii unnecessarily': Dillon's Plotinian principle seems reasonable. Perhaps some slight support in favour of the identification of Iamblichus' teacher with the future bishop—and there are no strong arguments against it—is the fact that both Iamblichus and the future bishop had Pythagorean mathematical interests. For similar reasons we may suppose that it is again the same Anatolius to whom is attributed a work *On the Decad* which has survived both independently and in the form of excerpts included with extracts from Nicomachus' *Theologoumena* in the anonymous *Theologoumena arithmeticae*.

In view of their common Pythagorean mathematical interests, one would like to know much more about Iamblichus' teacher than can be gathered from the little evidence about Anatolius that we have. The excerpts from the *Arithmetical Introductions* edited by Hultsch show

---

[51] Eunapius, *Vit. soph.* 363; Porphyry dedicated a work to an Anatolius (*Quaest. Hom. ad Il.* 281, 2; cf. Schraeder's discussion in his edition, 347–8).

[52] Eusebius, *Hist. Eccles.* II 726, 6–9; ten books: a good Pythagorean number; Moderatus' work on the Pythagoreans may also have been in ten books; cf. Buecheler's reading at Porphyry, *Vit. Pyth.* 59, 1.

[53] Cf. Dillon (1973), 7–9; Larsen (1972), 37–8; I. Hadot (1984), 257–8; and already Tannery in Heiberg's edition of Anatolius, 56.

that Anatolius used Aristotelian sources. He also stressed the scientific character (τὸ ἐπιστημονικόν) of Pythagorean arithmetic and geometry, a character achieved through restricting the objects studied to those that are eternal, immaterial, and unchanging.[54] The similarities with the opening pages of Nicomachus' *Introduction to Arithmetic* are striking and point either to a dependence of Anatolius on Nicomachus or, more likely, to a source concerning Pythagoreanism used by both. Anatolius notes furthermore the importance of number to the Pythagoreans and quotes the saying that 'All is likened unto number' (279, 20–2). But from such meagre remains it is not possible to extract anything certain about how Anatolius himself viewed Pythagoras, Pythagoras' place in the history of philosophy, and the relation between Pythagorean mathematics and philosophy.

Anatolius' work *On the Decad* offers only slightly more scope. Each of the first ten numbers is treated with respect to its mathematical characteristics and to the various epithets associated with it in the Pythagorean tradition. In the latter part of his treatment Anatolius does little more than list the various items by which each number was 'named', or to which each number was 'likened' (εἰκάζοντες, ὁμοιοῦντες) by the Pythagoreans. For example, the monad is likened to 'The One, the intelligible god, the ungenerated, the beautiful itself, the good itself'.[55] Anatolius does not explore however what the basis or significance of such assimilations might be. Is the monad 'like' the One because it produces all numbers, or is it rather itself the ultimate source of everything, which is also referred to as 'god' or 'the One'? The very close verbal parallels between this and many other passages in Anatolius' work and the section on the decad in Theon of Smyrna's *Exposition of mathematics* (written in the second century AD) show that Anatolius is merely summarizing the traditional Pythagorean decadic literature also used by Theon[56] and which Nicomachus had tried, in his *Theologoumena*, to clarify and deepen. Anatolius does refer several times to Plato's *Timaeus* (33, 13 ff.; 36, 28 ff.; 40, 1 ff. and 14 ff.), thus introducing the notion that the universe and the soul are produced from number. But this is not used as a general basis for justifying the Pythagorean assimilations of numbers to other items. The impression conveyed by the assimilations is rather one of fairly arbitrary and

---

[54] *Excerpta* 277, 8–14.
[55] 29, 19–22 (cf. Theon, *Exp.* 100, 4–6).
[56] The parallels are listed by Heiberg in his edition of Anatolius, 27–8 (add the parallel above).

specious pairings. The work represents then a regression compared to the writings of Nicomachus and even (two centuries earlier) of Moderatus. It is possible, however, that Anatolius' *On the Decad* is in fact a version of a much earlier Pythagorean writing[57] which came, in some way, to be associated with Anatolius. At any rate it would be imprudent to use it alone (and there is not sufficient evidence otherwise) as a basis for attempting a reconstruction of Anatolius' own philosophical views.

4. PORPHYRY

In the final section of this chapter it will hardly be possible to do much more than note some aspects of the work of Plotinus' great pupil Porphyry. Porphyry's interests and learning were so wide, and so little of his work has survived, that it is in any event hardly possible to produce an adequate account of him. The necessary scholarly work has yet to be done, namely an exhaustive collection of, and critical commentary on, the surviving fragments and *testimonia* relating to Porphyry.[58] Yet he cannot be omitted. Iamblichus studied under him.[59] They became involved in polemics with each other. Porphyry criticized Iamblichus in his book on the Delphic oracle 'Know thyself';[60] Iamblichus replied at length in his *On Mysteries* to Porphyry's *Letter to Anebo* and also appears to have accused Porphyry of being 'full of Numenius'.[61] This difficult relationship indicates the importance of Porphyry to Iamblichus and makes one suspect that perhaps they were, after all, closer to each other in their ideas than either of them would be prepared to admit.

An incomplete *Life of Pythagoras* by Porphyry is still extant. The *Life* was once part of the first book of a *Philosophical History* in four books beginning with Homer and ending with Plato which is otherwise, apart from some short extracts, lost.[62] It is therefore not easy to see

---

[57] From which the names of pagan gods have been purged; cf. above, n. 43.

[58] For Porphyry's range cf. Beutler (1953), 278–301 (an edition of selected fragments of Porphyry is to be published by A. Smith). Problems in the reconstruction of Porphyry's intellectual development cannot be treated here.

[59] Eunapius, *Vit. soph.* 363; cf. Dillon (1973), 10–11.

[60] In Stobaeus, *Anth.* III 579, 6–580, 1.

[61] Above, p. 10; Dillon (1973), 10, and Saffrey (1971), who show how much of Iamblichus' work consists of responses to specific writings by Porphyry.

[62] Cf. Porphyry, *Opuscula*, 4–7; for a full discussion cf. A. Segonds in Porphyry, *Vit. Pyth.*, 162–97.

what place the *Life* occupied in the larger work. Nor is it even clear what Porphyry's own attitude to Pythagoras is in the *Life*. The *Life* reads like a learned compilation of source materials concerning Pythagoras. The stories about Pythagoras' education among the Egyptians and Chaldaeans are repeated. The Jews, Arabs, Phoenicians, and Zoroaster are also named as educators. Pythagoras' philosophy emerges as an elementary sort of Platonism involving the search for wisdom, namely knowledge of immaterial realities, through liberation of the mind from its imprisonment in the body.[63]

More can be learnt about Porphyry's views on Pythagoras from the remnants of some of Porphyry's other books. In his *Philosophy from Oracles*, Porphyry expressed the intention to present philosophical doctrines, as these had been divinely communicated to man in oracles. Such a book, he felt, would be welcomed by those who, 'in labour'[64] after truth, have prayed for the rest from intellectual perplexity (ἀπορία) that a divine revelation could give (110, 1–7). The 'philosophy' expounded by Porphyry on the basis of the oracles he had collected seems to have been primarily religious: it concerned the nature and order of the gods and the rites and objects appropriate to their cult.[65] In his *Letter* to an Egyptian priest, Anebo, Porphyry sought from Egyptian doctrines about the divine a broader philosophy. He had no doubts about the existence of gods,[66] but found the Egyptian doctrines logically inconsistent and was also unclear about their views on the structure of reality:

What do the Egyptians think the first cause is? Is it Intellect or above Intellect? Is it alone, or with another or others? Is it incorporeal or corporeal? Is it identical with the demiurge, or prior to the demiurge? Are all things derived from one or from many? Do they know of matter or primary qualitative bodies, and is matter ungenerated or generated?[67]

It would not be easy to give a more concise list of the major questions debated by Platonists in the second and third centuries AD. What is more relevant here is that Porphyry expected the divinely revealed

---

[63] Chs. 46–7, 57, 22–58, 20; cf. Segonds in the edition, 162–8.

[64] ὠδίναντες: Plato's metaphor (e.g. *Symp.* 206 e 1).

[65] Cf. Wolff (edition), 42–3; Bidez (1913), 17 ff. Cf. also, however, J. O'Meara (1959), 29–31. Porphyry's introductory words lead one to expect a philosophy broader in scope than that found in the fragments preserved in Eusebius.

[66] Porphyry, *Ep. ad An.*, Sodano's introduction, xviii.

[67] 22, 11–23, 3 (= Iamblichus, *De myst.* 260, 4–10); I have put the passage into direct speech.

teachings of the Egyptian priesthood to provide a Platonic philosophy that was logically consistent and complete.[68] This expectation, it appears, was not fulfilled, at least at the time the *Letter* was written.

It looks also as if Porphyry expected to find such a philosophy in other religions and in the sayings of ancient sages, if we can judge by his interpretation of a Homeric passage in *Of the Cave of the Nymphs*. Porphyry here attempts to recover the views of the 'ancients' (*Op. sel.* 57, 17–24), not only those of Homer, but also those of Zoroaster, Orpheus, and other ancient 'theologians',[69] and of philosophers such as Pythagoras and Plato. What is found is again a basic Platonic philosophy: Homer's cave of the nymphs symbolizes the sensible world into which the soul has descended and from which it must escape. Pythagoras is thus a member of a great assembly of ancient prophets, theologians, sages, philosophers, and poets in whom Porphyry sought to discover the same, namely Platonic, philosophy. According to the *Letter* to Anebo, this philosophy was communicated through such channels to mankind by the gods.

Certain conclusions follow from this with respect to Porphyry's view of Pythagoras. As in Numenius (who is cited by Porphyry in *Of the Cave of the Nymphs*), Pythagoras is regarded by Porphyry as essentially a Platonic philosopher whose views can be corroborated by reference to various oriental religions. However, and here I believe Porphyry differs from Numenius, Pythagoras loses some of his prominence as he joins a vast chorus of voices from the past and from different religions and cultures all giving expression to a divinely revealed philosophy. Porphyry, then, is not a Pythagoreanizing Platonist, i.e. one who singles Pythagoras out as the fountainhead of all true (Platonic) philosophy, but rather a universalizing Platonist: he finds his Platonism both in Pythagoras and in very many other quarters. These conclusions are consistent with what emerges from the most extensive work of Porphyry to have survived, *On Abstinence*.

Towards the beginning of this work, Porphyry refers to a certain Clodius of Naples who had criticized vegetarianism.[70] Clodius found Pythagoras at the origin of vegetarianism and saw the Pythagorean theories of the kinship and transmigration of souls as arguments

---

[68] Iamblichus, *De myst.* 96, 5–10, criticizes Porphyry for having an approach that is φιλοσόφως μᾶλλον καὶ λογικῶς.

[69] Orpheus (68, 1), Homer (78, 15–16); Plato is distinguished from the 'theologians' at 71, 17 (cf. 77, 22).

[70] Cf. Bouffartigue and Patillon's introduction to their edition, I 25–9 (Clodius: a teacher of Mark Antony?).

supporting the abstention from eating meat.[71] It is noteworthy, however, that Porphyry, in setting out to argue for abstention, does not confine himself to a defence of Pythagoras and of Pythagorean doctrine.
His approach is far broader in scope, bringing into play an extraordinary command of the history of Greek philosophy and of the literature
on oriental peoples in order to establish a general context in which
abstention from meat can be seen to be desirable. This context, not surprisingly, is the plight of the soul imprisoned in the body and whose
desire for knowledge and felicity can only be satisfied in a liberation
from the body and an ascent to the immaterial and divine. All distraction, all drawing away of the soul's concentration on the immaterial
world, must be avoided. The vegetarian diet is therefore desirable: in
contrast to a diet of meat, it demands the minimum of attention from
the soul, since it is inexpensive to procure, simple to prepare and un-
exciting![72] (Porphyry would prefer that we do away with food
altogether, but this conflicts (I 72) with his disapproval of suicide.)
Pythagoras, various sages, and Plato are identified with these views,[73]
as are Egyptian, Jewish, Persian, and Indian sects whose practices, as
documented in Book IV, support Porphyry's thesis. Thus Pythagoras,
in *On Abstinence*, tends again to be integrated into a very large group of
authorities and nations, and Pythagorean vegetarianism becomes part
of a philosophy assumed to be attested in all these sources, namely a
Platonic metaphysical and ethical otherworldliness.[74]

If these inferences about Porphyry's views on Pythagoras are
correct, we might be led to conclude also that he would not have felt
any need to give particular stress to the Pythagorean mathematical
sciences. The evidence, such as it is, tends to bear this out. In the *Life
of Pythagoras* Porphyry does refer to the mediatory role that can be
played by the mathematical sciences: they can bridge the gap for us
between the material and the immaterial (Ch. 47, 58, 12–19). Their
possible purificatory function is mentioned very briefly in *On Abstinence* (I ch. 29, 64), where Porphyry also provides a short summary
of Pythagorean 'arithmology' (II ch. 36, 102). None the less, what
survives of Porphyry's writings gives the impression that in general he

[71] I ch. 15, 3, 55; ch. 18, 1 and 19, 1, 56.

[72] I chs. 30–2; 46. With some irony Porphyry notes that those arch-hedonists, the
Epicureans, followed the simple diet suitable to the Platonic soul (I chs. 48 ff.).

[73] I ch. 36; Clodius had tried to dissociate Socrates and his followers from Pythagorean vegetarianism (I ch. 15).

[74] Porphyry returns in Book III to the kinship of souls, which is understood in a
Platonic way.

is more concerned with ethical and religious than with mathematical means of ascending to the immaterial. A good example of this can be found in his *Life of Plotinus*. Dörrie has attempted (1955) to construct a Pythagorean personality for Plotinus' teacher Ammonius from aspects of Plotinus' life as presented by Porphyry. It is more prudent however to take Porphyry's account as constituting to some degree a portrait of the ideal philosopher. Indeed in the *Life* Plotinus shows many of the features of the true philosopher sketched in *On Abstinence*:[75] he abstains from meat,[76] indeed eating hardly anything, such is his rapt concentration on the higher world;[77] he demonstrates extraordinary purity and freedom from distraction by this world (23, 1 ff.); he turns people away from political life (7, 32–5); he has, or at least seeks, relations with oriental peoples, priests, and even gods and demons, so much so in fact that his work, Porphyry asserts, is divinely inspired.[78] Most significantly for us, however, he concerns himself little with arithmetic and geometry, although Porphyry is anxious at the same time to claim that he is not ignorant of such matters (14, 8–10). It is to some extent true that Plotinus had no special devotion to mathematics. But it is noteworthy that this trait persists in a portrait of Plotinus which Porphyry tends to paint in the image of an ideal philosopher who exhibits otherwise a number of 'Pythagorean' features.[79]

[75] *De abst.* I chs. 27–28; II chs. 49–52, 114–16; Bouffartigue and Patillon's introduction I 33; II 48–9 (noting the Plotinian themes in these passages).

[76] *Vit. Plot.* 2, 5 (note the implied contrast between corporeal and intellectual food that is important in *De abst.* IV, *Opuscula* 264, 20 ff.).

[77] *Vit. Plot.* 8, 20 ff. (note προσοχή here and in *De abst.* I ch. 39; Bouffartigue and Pataillon's introduction I 34–5).

[78] *Vit. Plot.* 23, 20–1 (see Armstrong's note ad loc. in his transl.). I do not wish to deny that *some* of this may have been true of Plotinus. But what is significant for us here is what Porphyry chose to record and the way he recorded it.

[79] Porphyry's breaking up and arrangement of Plotinus' treatises into six sets of nine ('Enneads') is the most striking example of his imposition of Pythagoreanism on Plotinus. To some of the Pythagorean traits already noted might be added the vow of secrecy made by Plotinus and some fellow-pupils of Ammonius (*Vit. Plot.* 3, 24–7). Cf. L. Brisson *et al.* (1982), 254–6. Further traces of 'Pythagoreanizing' in Porphyry may survive in Augustine's *De ordine*. Having shown (II ch. X, 28 ff.) the numerical basis of the seven liberal arts and the role of the mathematical sciences in leading the soul to philosophy, Augustine relates this to Pythagoras, who is praised quite emphatically (xx, 53). I. Hadot (1984), 101–36, argues that Augustine is using a Neoplatonic source which she identifies hypothetically as Porphyry's *De regressu animae*. If she proves the Neoplatonic character of Augustine's theory of the liberal arts and the presence in particular of Porphyrian themes, it would also be necessary to show that Porphyry was Augustine's *only* source before Augustine could be used with confidence as a witness for Porphyry. For Augustine's interest in Pythagoras and in Pythagorean number-theory cf. Solignac (1958), 124–6, 129–37 (who argues that Augustine read Nicomachus).

2

Iamblichus' Work *On Pythagoreanism*:
Title, Plan, The First Four Books

THE various Pythagoreanizing tendencies reviewed in the preceding
chapter converged in the programme to Pythagoreanize Platonic
philosophy elaborated by Porphyry's former pupil and frequent rival
Iamblichus. This programme surpassed its predecessors in its comprehensive and systematic quality and succeeded, as I shall attempt to
show in Part Two, in playing a decisive role in the history of later
Greek philosophy. It will be necessary, however, first to examine
Iamblichus' Pythagoreanizing programme in some detail. Traces of it
can be found in reports concerning Iamblichus' lost commentaries on
Plato and on Aristotle and in the surviving remains of other more
systematic writings. But the most accessible expression of the
programme is the multi-volume work Iamblichus devoted specifically
to the theme, *On Pythagoreanism*. When Iamblichus wrote this work, or
when more generally his Pythagoreanizing programme was developed, is unclear. I shall give grounds below (pp. 91 ff.) for not accepting
an early date for the work. It and the programme to which it belongs
and which appears also in the commentaries on Plato and Aristotle
ought to be dated in all likelihood to the time when Iamblichus had
already left Porphyry (probably well before the end of the third
century) and had set up his own philosophical school in Syria, in
Apamea, and/or in Daphne.[1]

In Chapter 4 the traces of a Pythagoreanizing programme that
can be found in what little has survived of Iamblichus' many other
philosophical writings will be examined. An obvious point of departure however is provided by the work *On Pythagoreanism*. This work
has been transmitted to us by one manuscript, 'F' (fourteenth
century), from which all of the later manuscript copies derive.[2] Manu-

---

[1] On the evidence and problems concerning Iamblichus' biography cf. Dillon (1973),
4–14; although the evidence that Iamblichus was Porphyry's pupil is not conclusive, so
much points in this direction that Dillon simply assumes this (correctly, I believe) as a
fact.

[2] The importance of F (Florence, Laur. 86, 3) has been demonstrated by Pistelli
(1888).

script F begins with a Table of Contents (*pinax*) listing the titles of nine books constituting the work. The *pinax* is followed, however, by the first four books only. The remaining books have since disappeared. We may suppose that this might easily have happened if the work had been transmitted bound in two volumes (codices) of which the second, containing the last five books of the work, came to be mislaid or ignored.[3] The loss of the last five books occurred at any rate after the eleventh century, when the Byzantine polymath Michael Psellus was still able to read and make excerpts from Books V–VII. This process of dismemberment of Iamblichus' work, begun thus negligently enough, was completed with true philological furor in the last one hundred years. The surviving first four books of the work were published as if separate, independent works; and Deubner, in his edition of the first book, *On the Pythagorean Life* (1937), even neglected to print the *pinax* for the work as a whole, which helps us relate *On the Pythagorean Life* to the following books making up the work. The dismemberment was carried out most diligently, however, within each of the first three books: each was ransacked for what could be extracted from it of lost writings by (or on) Pythagoreans, Aristotle, Speusippus . . . A silent decapitation finally resulted from a lack of serious interest even in what the title of the work as a whole might be.[4]

In this chapter I shall try to restore some unity to Iamblichus' work, beginning with its title and overall plan and proceeding through the first four books considered to the extent to which they relate to an overall plan. In Chapter 3, the excerpts in Psellus from Books V–VII of the work will be analysed and will lead to some general conclusions in the following chapter concerning the purpose and significance of Iamblichus' work, its relation to traces of a Pythagoreanizing programme in his other works, and to the varieties of Pythagoreanism presented in Chapter 1.

In examining below the first four books of *On Pythagoreanism* I shall be concerned more with the *ways* in which Iamblichus understood and used the Pythagorean (and other) materials he assembled in composing these books, than with the materials themselves; more with his intentions, than with his sources.[5]

---

[3] For other cases cf. Whittaker (1974), 354.

[4] Cf. the remarks of von Albrecht (1963), 7–8; Larsen (1972), 66.

[5] The following pages might be compared with Larsen (1972), 66–147, who has similar goals but reaches, I believe, somewhat deficient results.

I. THE TITLE AND OVERALL PLAN

Three possible titles for Iamblichus' work might be considered:

(i) *On the Pythagorean Sect* (Περὶ τῆς Πυθαγορικῆς αἱρέσεως), a title attested in the *pinax* preserved at the head of manuscript F.[6] This title is also given by Syrianus in the fifth century (*In Herm.* I 22, 4–5).

(ii) *The Collection of Pythagorean Doctrines* (ἡ τῶν Πυθαγορείων δογμάτων συναγωγή), a title found also in Syrianus (*In met.* 140, 15; 149, 30) that has been preferred by modern scholars.

(iii) *Pythagorean Commentaries* (Πυθαγόρεια ὑπομνήματα), a title which is found also in manuscript F.[7]

Which of these three titles should be used?

The third title has the least authority for it and in any case is not a formal title, but a loose description. This latter point is true also of the second title, as can be seen from the fact that Syrianus refers by means of it to the writings of Iamblichus and of Nicomachus (*In met.* 103, 6–7): again a loose description, not a title. The first title has the strongest authority for it, both manuscript F and Syrianus.

A possible objection to adopting the first title as the right one is that 'sect' (αἵρεσις) is too restrictive: Iamblichus' work covered not only the Pythagorean sect but also (and especially) its doctrines and sciences. If this point can apply to the English word 'sect', it cannot hold for the Greek term αἵρεσις which had already, some centuries before Iamblichus, come to signify, not only the members of a religious or philosophical movement, but also the doctrines and theories of the movement.[8] Such is the meaning of αἵρεσις also in Iamblichus[9] in a passage, for example, at the beginning of the *Protreptic* (i.e. the second book of the work under consideration) which also provides further authority for the first title:

In the preceding we have said what is appropriate about Pythagoras, about his kind of life and about the Pythagoreans. Let us begin our account as to the rest of his sect (τὸ λοιπὸν αὐτοῦ τῆς αἱρέσεως) . . . (6, 12–15)

---

[6] The *pinax* is found on fol. 1ʳ and is printed by Nauck (1884), xxxiv. The title is also found at the end of *Comm.*: τέλος τοῦ γ´ λόγου . . . τῆς Πυθαγόρου αἱρέσεως.

[7] F, fol. 47ᵛ (cf. *Pr.* 6, 10 ff., *app. crit.*).

[8] Cf. Glucker (1978), 166–92.

[9] Cf. *Pr.* 7, 14–15; 8, 3–6; 124, 24.

Thus the treatment of the Pythagorean αἵρεσις continues from the first into the second book, which treats of Pythagorean doctrines and which is itself, as will be seen below, introductory to the following books of the work which also concern Pythagorean doctrine.

Such then is the authority for the first title that there can be little doubt that it is the correct one. To avoid the misleading connotations of the word 'sect' I shall translate the Greek title as *On Pythagoreanism* so as to include both the personalities concerned and their theories.

It is less easy to determine whether Iamblichus' *On Pythagoreanism* was originally made up of nine or of ten books. The *pinax* in manuscript F lists nine books. However, at the end of the fourth and last surviving book (*In Nic.* 125, 19–24) Iamblichus mentions the subjects he will cover later, namely music (=Book IX), geometry (=Book VIII), and astronomy. As there is no book devoted to the last subject in the list of nine books given in the *pinax*, it is reasonable to infer that a tenth book was (or was to have been) devoted to it. In any case his work, written in true Pythagorean spirit, *should* have contained ten books, even if it did not. It probably once did.[10]

The titles of the books of *On Pythagoreanism* as given in the *pinax* are:

I *On the Pythagorean Life*
(Περὶ τοῦ Πυθαγορικοῦ βίου)

II *Protreptic to Philosophy*
(Προτρεπτικὸς ἐπὶ φιλοσοφίαν)

III *On General Mathematical Science*
(Περὶ τῆς κοινῆς μαθηματικῆς ἐπιστήμης)

IV *On Nicomachus' Arithmetical Introduction*
(Περὶ τῆς Νικομάχου ἀριθμητικῆς εἰσαγωγῆς)

V *On Arithmetic in Physical Matters*
(Περὶ τῆς ἐν φυσικοῖς ἀριθμητικῆς ἐπιστήμης)

VI *On Arithmetic in Ethical Matters*
(Περὶ τῆς ἐν ἠθικοῖς ἀριθμητικῆς ἐπιστήμης)

VII *On Arithmetic in Theological Matters*
(Περὶ τῆς ἐν θεολογικοῖς[11] ἀριθμητικῆς ἐπιστήμης)

VIII *On Pythagorean Geometry*
(Περὶ γεωμετρίας τῆς παρὰ Πυθαγορείοις)

---

[10] Cf. above, ch. 1 n. 52; Larsen (1972), I 44–5.
[11] Nauck's correction of the reading θεοῖς in F, supported by *In Nic.* 125, 14–25 quoted below.

IX *On Pythagorean Music*
   (Περὶ μουσικῆς τῆς παρὰ Πυθαγορείοις)

To this list we should probably add then a tenth and final book:

X *On Pythagorean Astronomy.*

It has already been noted that of the whole work only the first four books are extant, together with excerpts from Books V–VII.

The unity of plan underlying the sequence of books will be brought out below in a detailed examination of the surviving books and fragments. However, it will be useful at this stage to propose an overall scheme for *On Pythagoreanism* as this emerges from combining the book titles of the *pinax* with programmatic passages in Books II and IV.[12]

In the passage quoted above from the beginning of the *Protreptic* Iamblichus moves from his account of Pythagoras, Pythagorean life, and the Pythagoreans in *On the Pythagorean Life* to a general preparation, presented in the *Protreptic*, for 'all education, learning, and virtue' (6, 15–16). This general preparation is intended as a stage leading the reader to a more specifically Pythagorean philosophy and science introduced at the end of the *Protreptic* and in the following books:

As the soul progresses gradually from lesser to greater things . . . and finally finds the most perfect goods, thus the turning ⟨of the soul⟩ (προτροπή) must progress along a route starting from what is general and common (τῶν κοινῶν). (*Pr.* 7, 8–12)

The succession of books in Iamblichus' work is thus related to a pedagogical progression from the general and common to what is more difficult, higher, and specifically Pythagorean. The progression is a 'protreptic': it is designed to lead the soul up to 'greater things'. The protreptic function is not only evident in the *Protreptic* itself: it will also be seen below to be present already in the first book, *On the Pythagorean Life*.

A second programmatic passage is found at the end of Book IV. Having presented in this book an introduction to arithmetic based on Nicomachus, Iamblichus gives a foretaste of what is to come:

We will study such other consequences as arise from the numbers, from the monad up to the decad, ordering matters according to a physical (φυσικός),

---

[12] Cf. Tannery (1885a), 179–81.

an ethical (ἠθικός), and furthermore (and prior to these) a theological (θεολογικός) account, so that it will be easier to convey to you the teachings of the following three introductions, i.e. the introductions to music, geometry, and astronomy.[13]

Thus the introduction to general mathematical science in Book III is followed by introductions to each of the four specific mathematical sciences, first arithmetic, treated in itself and then in relation to physics, ethics, and theology, the latter treatment being helpful to the student embarking on the remaining three mathematical sciences.

The following general scheme for the work as a whole might be suggested on the basis of the evidence considered so far:

Protreptic to Pythagoreanism:
    Pythagoras and his School: *On the Pythagorean Life* (Bk. I)
    General and Pythagorean Philosophy: *Protreptic* (Bk. II)

Introduction to Pythagorean Mathematics:
    General Mathematical Science (Bk. III)
    Arithmetic in itself: Nicomachus (Bk. IV)
            in Physics (Bk. V)
            in Ethics (Bk. VI)
            in Theology (Bk. VII)
    Geometry (Bk. VIII)
    Music (Bk. IX)
    Astronomy (Bk. X)

This scheme may serve as a rough sketch, to be filled in as Iamblichus' project is examined in detail in the following pages.

2. PYTHAGORAS (BOOK I: *ON THE PYTHAGOREAN LIFE*)

The first chapter of the first book can be regarded as a prologue to the work as a whole and is introduced as such in the chapter-headings (κεφάλαια) preserved in manuscript F.[14] It is an invocation of divine help, a traditional motif in Platonic literature inspired by Plato's

---

[13] *In Nic.* 125, 14–25 (expanding on 118, 11–19); cf. 3, 13 ff. I shall return to this passage in the next chapter. The book on music is also referred to at 121, 13; 122, 12.

[14] Cf. *Vit. Pyth.* 1, 3. The κεφάλαια are very probably composed by Iamblichus himself: they are used by Syrianus, *In met.* 101, 29–102, 34 (= κεφάλαια for *Comm.* 3, 6–8, 4). Cf. Deubner (1935), 689–90; Proclus, *Theol. Plat.* I 129 n. 2 (add the κεφάλαια preceding Iamblichus' pupil Dexippus' *In cat.* 1–2).

Timaeus.[15] In this and in other Platonic allusions in the chapter, however, Iamblichus indicates his intention not only to follow, but also to
go beyond Plato in some respects. The invocation of the gods is all the
more necessary at the outset of his work in that the philosophy named
after Pythagoras is revealed by the gods and can only be grasped
through their mediation (5, 4–9): it is superior to a vision such as that
in Plato's *Symposium* (210 e 4) which can be 'glimpsed in a flash' (5, 10–
11), because it transcends (mere) human capacities.[16] Hence our need
to entrust ourselves (5, 14) to divine guidance through which, alone,
we can have access to Pythagorean philosophy. The divine guide that
Iamblichus proposes to adopt is Pythagoras himself. But what does
Iamblichus mean here by 'divine guidance'? How is it realized in the
chapters on Pythagoras' life that follow?

Iamblichus' biography of Pythagoras adheres fairly closely to the
guidelines for writing *encomia* prescribed by the ancient rhetoricians.
To praise a hero or prominent citizen one should extol his race,
fatherland, education, virtues, and the great deeds stemming from
these virtues; physical excellences should also be praised; transitions
between sections should be clearly marked.[17] Iamblichus follows all of
these prescriptions—he was after all a rhetorician in his own right[18]—
marshalling the various source-materials available to him so as to fit
them into the required compositional structure.[19] To discover, however, the relation between the encomium of Pythagoras and Pythagoras' function as 'divine guide', one must examine some significant
texts in detail.

Commenting on the story that Pythagoras was fathered by Apollo,
Iamblichus not only tells us that we ought not believe it (7, 26–7); he
also provides an interpretation of Pythagoras' divine parentage which
is far less corporeal in emphasis:

---

[15] *Tim.* 27c; compare Numenius, fr. 11, 9–10; Proclus, *Theol. Plat.* I 131 n. 4.

[16] On human weakness and the distance this creates between men and gods cf. the
texts cited by von Albrecht (1966), 59 n. 64.

[17] Hermogenes, *Prog.* 14, 17 ff.; Theon, *Prog.* 109, 20 ff.; Menander, *Laud.* 372,
14–18.

[18] Syrianus refers (*In Herm.* 9, 9–10) to Iamblichus' (lost) book Περὶ κρίσεως ἀρίστου
λόγου; cf. Bidez (1919), 34; (1928), 215; Kustas (1973), 7, 169. A critique of the style of
Pythagorean literature is found in *Vit. Pyth.* 88, 14 ff.

[19] Roughly: (i) Pythagoras' *genos*, fatherland, education, travels (chs. 2–6); (ii) his
teaching (chs. 13–25); (iii) his virtues and his corresponding deeds (chs. 28–33); (iv)
matters remaining and not fitting in the scheme (chs. 34–6; cf. 129, 11–15). Cf. von
Albrecht (1966), 52 ff.; Festugière (1937), 439. For physical excellences cf. *Vit. Pyth.* 7, 13;
8, 13 and 22; for clear transitions cf. 19, 19–22; 75, 25–8; 129, 11–15.

No one would dispute, however, that the soul of Pythagoras was sent down to men from Apollo's train (ἡγεμονία)—being either a companion (συνοπαδός) or otherwise yet more fittingly aligned (συντεταγμένη) with the god: witness such a ⟨noble⟩ birth and the universal wisdom of his soul. (7, 27–8, 4)

The interest of this text increases if it is noticed that Iamblichus is interpreting the divine origin and mission of Pythagoras in terms of the myth in Plato's *Phaedrus* (246 e–248 c), in which souls follow in the retinue or army (στρατία) of gods and demons, Zeus leading (ἡγεμών), around the rim of the heavens. Each soul is assigned as companion (συνοπαδός) to one of the gods in the retinue (which includes of course Apollo), a relation that marks the particular aspirations of the soul (253 b). By referring to the myth of the *Phaedrus* Iamblichus is providing a context for the understanding of the traditional beliefs in Pythagoras' divinity which attenuates considerably their literal, materialist point-of-view[20] by stressing the divine origin of Pythagoras' *soul*, Pythagoras' spiritual rather than bodily genealogy. Pythagoras' bodily origin is a sign of, but not identical with, his divinity.[21] At the same time the reference to the *Phaedrus* helps to distinguish Pythagoras' soul from other, ordinary souls. In the *Phaedrus* the soul is represented as struggling to keep its place in the celestial retinue and losing it through its own deficiencies. Pythagoras, however, is not a fallen soul, but a soul *sent down* into the material world. He is in fact, it is suggested some pages later, the bearer of a divine gift for the improvement of human life, i.e. philosophy, a gift such as 'none better has been or will ever be given by the gods' (18, 5–10)—the text is taken this time from Plato's *Timaeus* (47 b 1–2). Iamblichus' use of themes in the *Phaedrus* and in the *Timaeus* thus provides a Platonic framework for the explanation of the divine origin and mission of Pythagoras: in respect to his origin, the superior affiliation of his soul with the intelligible realm is stressed; as for his mission among men, it is to mediate Plato's 'divine gift' of philosophy, a mediation, one may infer, made possible by the superior intelligible nature of Pythagoras' soul (cf. 18, 16–19, 10).

The notion that certain wise men have been sent by the gods to enlighten mankind and that philosophy itself is a divine gift is by no

---

[20] Cf. also 54, 5–14; 79, 11–17.

[21] For another interpretation (showing little awareness of the philosophical background) cf. Cox (1983), 60–1. One can suppose that Pythagoras' noble birth is witness to his divine soul on the Platonic grounds that each soul is received in an appropriate body; cf. Proclus, *In Tim.* I 51, 20–30; *In Remp.* II 118, 5 ff.

means new in the third century.[22] The Platonic background to this
notion in Iamblichus' *On the Pythagorean Life* can be detected in the
way that the notion represents an interpretation of the *Phaedrus* and
Timaeus. More information on this interpretation can be found elsewhere, notably in the surviving fragments of Iamblichus' *De anima*. In
this work Iamblichus discussed, among other things, the reasons for
soul's descent into the material world. Plotinus had raised the issue
before, in connection with the interpretation of the two Platonic
dialogues (*Ennead* IV 8, 1). The dialogues seemed to disagree, the
Timaeus suggesting that soul had a constructive mission in the world,
to vivify, organize, and perfect it, the *Phaedrus* intimating, however,
that soul, due to some sort of moral failure, had fallen from the
heavenly retinue of the gods and was plunged in a life of misery in the
body. Plotinus attempted to reconcile these two ways of seeing soul's
descent to the material world, stressing initially the positive constructive view, but also allowing for a moral failure and fall of soul.
Whatever the degree of the fall, however, Plotinus insisted that soul
always retained in part its presence in the intelligible world from
which it came—an original and notorious theory often rejected by his
successors.[23] Iamblichus, in particular, chose instead in his *De anima* to
to distinguish between different *sorts* of soul: those souls who are in
close contemplative union with true intelligible being and are
companions of (συνοπαδοί) and akin to the gods, and those souls
who, already before the descent to the material world, are morally
corrupt. On descent to the body the former can preserve their freedom
and purity (ἀκήρατοι) from the body.[24] This type of descent corresponds to the first reason for descent that Iamblichus gives, namely to
purify, perfect, and thus 'save' the material world, a task that does not
seem to imply loss of purity (ἄχραντος) in the soul concerned. The
other reasons for descent, moral improvement and punishment,
correspond rather to the second kind of soul, that which is already
before the descent morally fallen. In this latter type of descent, the

---

[22] Cf. Hyldahl (1966), 130–6; van Winden (1971), 46, citing Lucian, Justin Martyr,
Origen. Especially close to Iamblichus is Atticus: Πλάτων, ἀνὴρ ἐκ φύσεως ἀρτιτελὴς
(cf. *Phaedrus* 251 a 2) καὶ πολὺ διενεγκών, οἷα κατάπεμπτος ὡς ἀληθῶς ἐκ θεῶν, ἵν'
ὁλόκληρος ὀφθῇ ἡ δι' αὐτοῦ φιλοσοφία (fr. 1, 33–5). Cf. also Numenius' use of
Philebus 16 c (above, p. 13 and ch. 1 n. 14 on Atticus' relation to Numenius).

[23] Cf. also V 1, 2; Rist (1967), 112 ff.; Szlezák (1979), 167 ff.; Blumenthal (1975), 132;
Finamore (1985), 91–4.

[24] Iamblichus, *De an.* in Stobaeus, *Anth.* I 380, 19–29; cf. Festugière (1950–54), III 223,
who points out the parallels with the *Phaedrus*.

soul loses its independence and becomes implicated in material existence.[25]

Whatever one may think of this reading of Plato, it helps to bring
out at least the general context in which Iamblichus interprets Pythagoras as a soul-companion of the gods 'sent down' to save mankind.
The general context is the problem posed by Plato's dialogues concerning the purpose of soul in the material world. In Iamblichus' view,
Pythagoras' soul is one of those pure souls that are companions of the
gods and that have access to knowledge of intelligible truths. Pythagoras' soul is sent down: his is a mission of salvation, through the
knowledge he can communicate, to the other sorts of soul, who have
fallen and, plunged in the illusions of material existence, have for-
gotten their origin and true nature.[26] For such souls, apparently
unable to save themselves, Pythagoras plays a reforming and saving
role, revealing to them the divine wisdom to which he is privy.

Iamblichus' interpretation of Pythagoras provides a means of determining the purpose of his encomiastic biography of Pythagoras, at
least in its earlier chapters. The wondrous stories of Pythagoras' birth,
education, and travels constitute, not a biographical narrative, but an
accumulation of evidences and signs, recognized by those that
witnessed them, of Pythagoras' unique relation to the divine, his
privileged access to intelligible truths, and his soteriological mission.
The Pythagorean legend, in serving to recommend to the reader
Pythagoras' special claim to divine insight, also promotes that insight,
namely the philosophy and sciences associated with Pythagoras. In
short, *On the Pythagorean Life* is a protreptic to Pythagorean philosophy
through an illustration of the spiritual credentials of the founder of
that philosophy.

The later chapters accomplish somewhat more. This can be
indicated by means of a passage concerning the speeches, so full of
trite moralisms, that Pythagoras is supposed to have made to the
youths of Croton.

---

[25] Iamblichus, *De an.* in Stobaeus, *Anth.* I 380, 6–14; Festugière, III 222. Iamblichus
also distinguishes between pure (ἄχραντος) and impure souls in *De myst.* 69, 12–19; 81,
8–10; 83, 2–8; 8, 15–9, 1, according to the alignment of soul (συντάττεται). Cf. Steel
(1978), 85, and more generally on Neoplatonic interpretation of the *Phaedrus*, Proclus,
Theol. Plat. IV, introduction, and on the problem of the descent of the soul Festugière
(1950–4), III 63–96; Vollenweider (1985), 162–3; and especially Finamore (1985), 94–111
for a useful and detailed discussion.

[26] Cf. Plotinus, V 1, 1. In contrast Pythagoras knew his soul, τίς ἦν καὶ πόθεν εἰς τὸ
σῶμα εἰσεληλύθει (Iamblichus, *Vit. Pyth.* 76, 3–5).

And he composed other such ⟨speeches⟩, some derived from history, some from doctrines, showing culture to be a product common to the first in each race ⟨or generation⟩. For their discoveries became the culture of the others.[27]

This can also be applied to Iamblichus' own book. The chapters on Pythagoras' speeches, virtues, and deeds are made up of 'history' and 'doctrines'. They point to the origin of the sciences and philosophy in Pythagoras' 'discoveries'. In so doing they begin already the initiation of the reader to Pythagorean knowledge, just as Pythagoras had begun the education of the youths by showing them the achievements of the founders of their culture.

3. PYTHAGOREAN PHILOSOPHY (BOOK II: THE *PROTREPTIC*)

In *On the Pythagorean Life* Pythagoras appears as the mediator of what seems to be the totality of human science and philosophy (cf. 88, 24–89, 7). Yet Iamblichus also claims a specific character for Pythagorean knowledge.[28] This tension between the universality and the specificity of Pythagoreanism is eased to some degree as the reader progresses through the successive books of *On Pythagoreanism*, following the pedagogical programme going from the general and common to the specific and Pythagorean. Yet it is already resolved in principle in the Platonic evaluation of the various forms of knowledge which Iamblichus introduces in describing Pythagoras' scientific achievements in the *Life* (18, 17–19, 10): thanks to Pythagoras, he says, the Greeks acquired a conception of the gods, heroes, and demons, of the world, of astronomical phenomena, and of all things in the physical universe; such a conception was correct and suitable (likely, ἐοικυῖα) for these things, not in conflict with appearances. But sciences also (μαθήματα) and contemplation (θεωρία) and all that which is scientific (ἐπιστημονικά), which opens the mind's eye, purifying it 'so as to be able to see the true principles and cause of all things'—all this too was mediated by Pythagoras. My paraphrase of this passage emphasizes the contrast Iamblichus is making between forms of knowledge which are 'likely' as to their truth (those having to do with material reality) and those that are scientific and true (those having to

---

[27] 24, 16–20. On these speeches cf. Burkert (1972), 115 n. 38.
[28] Cf. *Pr.* 7, 12–25; 8, 4–5; 24, 15–17; 104, 27–105, 1 and 17–18.

do with immaterial objects). This contrast, inspired by Plato's *Timaeus* (29 b–d), shows that not all that Pythagoras communicated is of equal scientific value. We can infer that what is specifically Pythagorean is what is most important and truly scientific, the study that leads the mind up to, and concerns unchanging immaterial reality. This is indeed how Iamblichus defines the philosophy of Pythagoras, following here, appropriately enough, Nicomachus.[29]

The same position, presented in greater detail, can be found in the *Protreptic*. Having treated of Pythagoras in the preceding volume, Iamblichus here begins his account of the rest of Pythagoreanism, i.e. Pythagorean philosophy and science. However, in order to introduce and 'turn' the reader's soul to this subject, a progression from the general to the specific must be observed. The progression is accomplished in the *Protreptic* in three stages: a protreptic to philosophy in general, not restricted to a specific system (chapters 2–3);[30] an intermediate protreptic mixing in the general with the Pythagorean (chapters 4–20); a final protreptic to the technical demonstrations of the Pythagoreans (chapter 21).[31] I shall discuss briefly the specific Pythagoreanism introduced in the second and third stages of the progression.

Of chapters 4–20, 5 and 13 are most clearly intended as specifically 'Pythagorean'. Chapter 5 begins as follows:

We must also use as a protreptic the Pythagorean distinctions themselves. Succinctly, indeed perfectly and quite differently from other philosophies did the Pythagoreans divide the argument exhorting to philosophy, in this following his ⟨Pythagoras'⟩ teachings, skillfully strengthening and confirming ⟨it⟩ with highly scientific and coherent demonstrations (ἀποδείξεσιν). (24, 14–21)

The distinctions that follow,[32] and the 'scientific demonstrations' that are based on them, are almost entirely derived from selected passages in Plato's dialogues: Iamblichus removes the dialogue form from the Platonic texts, isolating the premises and conclusions to be found in the texts, so as to produce a chain of arguments having the appearance

---

[29] *Vit. Pyth.* 89, 23–90, 11 (cf. the references to Nicomachus in Deubner's *app.*); cf. 32, 17–21; 40, 5–14.

[30] This stage can include Pythagorean materials, used however as a protreptic to philosophy in general (cf. 16, 7–10).

[31] Such at least is the programme announced in *Pr.* 7, 12–8, 9. We shall find that it changes somewhat when we reach ch. 21. For the transitions between stages cf. 16, 11–12; 104, 26–105, 5.

[32] Cf. 24, 23–25, 2; 27, 12–13; 27, 22–5; 28, 19–21; 29, 15–19; 30, 12–15.

of a rigorous logical demonstration.[33] The conclusion of the arguments is to call for a seeking of 'the most perfect wisdom', which
involves rule of the soul over the body, cultivation of the soul and its
highest part, intellect, whose wisdom brings us in relation to the
divine (cf. 36, 2–11 and 24–6). What is noteworthy, however, is not so
much the conclusions of the arguments, which are not unexpected, as
their form: they are a specifically 'Pythagorean' protreptic, because
they are 'scientific demonstrations'. The use of Platonic texts not only
presupposes that Platonism is Pythagoreanism; it also makes the
Platonic texts more truly 'Pythagorean' by giving to them a rigorous
logical structure. In the 'Pythagorean' protreptic in chapter 13[34]
Iamblichus again resorts to paraphrasing Plato, especially the *Phaedo*
whose emphasis on a duality between soul and body, on soul's need to
escape the body through purification and to rise to the immaterial
realm, makes explicit the otherworldly structure of reality[35] presupposed by the ethical arguments of chapter 5.

When the reader reaches chapter 21 and awaits the third, most
specifically Pythagorean initiation, he finds an interpretation of a
variety of Pythagorean cryptic utterances (σύμβολα), to which is
applied, all over again, the triple protreptic mode: general, mixed,
specific (104, 26–105, 18). And what is said to be 'more Pythagorean'
(Πυθαγορικώτερον)[36] adds little to what has already been found in
chapters 5 and 13.[37] There is, however, a passage that is worth noting.
In explaining the utterance 'Do not cut in two what is on the road',
Iamblichus says:

Philosophy indeed, it seems, is a road.[38] ⟨The utterance⟩ means then: choose
that philosophy and that road to wisdom in which you will not 'cut in two', in
which you will propound, not contradictions, but firm and unchanging truths
strengthened by scientific demonstration through sciences (μαθημάτων) and
contemplation (θεωρίας), that is, philosophize in the Pythagorean manner
(Πυθαγορικῶς). . . . That philosophy which travels through corporeal things
and sense-objects, which more recent thinkers immoderately adopt (thinking

---

[33] Cf. the juxtaposed texts in Larsen (1972), I 105–11 and Iamblichus' syllogizing
analysis of the *Alcibiades* as reported by Proclus (Iamblichus, fr. 2, 4–5). Syllogized
versions of Plato can be found already in Albinus, *Did.* ch. 6.

[34] Cf. κεφάλαια, *Pr.* 4, 25.

[35] Note Iamblichus' comments at 65, 18–20; 70, 9–15.

[36] A Nicomachean expression (cf. anon. *Theol. arith.* 56, 13).

[37] Cf. 116, 26–117, 6; 120, 19–121, 3.

[38] Cf. Nicomachus, *Intro.* 7, 17 (insertion in a quote from [Pseudo-] Plato, *Epinomis*
992 a 3); Theon of Smyrna, *Exp.* 7, 7–8.

god and the qualities and soul and the virtues and simply all the prime causes in reality are body), is slippery and easily reversible—witness the very different accounts of it—whereas the philosophy which progresses through immaterial eternal intelligible objects that always remain the same and do not admit in themselves of destruction or change, ⟨this philosophy⟩, like its subject-matter, is unerring and firm, producing grounded and unswerving proof. (118, 7–26).

One will recognize in this passage the Numenian assimilation between different philosophies and their corresponding (i.e. immaterial and material) levels of reality.[39] The contrast, however, is not between Pythagorean Platonism and the Academy, but between Pythagorean Platonism and materialist, especially Stoic, philosophy.[40] The contrast serves to bring out, yet again, Iamblichus' (Nicomachean) identification of the scientific character of Pythagoreanism as its specific characteristic, and his grounding of this scientific character on the specific (i.e. immaterial and unchanging) nature of the objects with which it is concerned.[41]

One more text must be quoted before this review of the nature of Pythagorean philosophy, as it is presented in the *Protreptic*, can be concluded. The passage is found in an earlier part of the book (23, 21–24, 3):

⟨Archytas the Pythagorean says he is wise who⟩ contemplates the one, the goal of all contemplation. And yet he introduced a greater good, that consisting in being able to see from here, as if from a watch-tower[42], god and all in the train (συστοιχίᾳ) of god. For if god presides over all truth, happiness, all being, causes, principles, we must seek especially to acquire that science, through which we will see him clearly and through which we will find a smooth road to him.

The metaphor of philosophy as a road occurs here in an ontological landscape that is a good deal more complicated than that in chapter 21: there appears to be an ultimate cause of 'being, causes,

---

[39] Cf. above, pp. 11–12.

[40] For the Stoic identification of soul, quality, virtue as body, cf. *SVF* Index vol. s. vv. ἀρετή, ποιότης, ψυχή, or, for example, Plotinus, IV 7, 8, 26 ff. Iamblichus is also alluding to the Stoic spirit that travels (χωροῦσα), implausibly for Aristotelians and Platonists, through passive matter. There may be an allusion to Epicureanism in 'unswerving' (ἀκλινής). Cf. 125, 4–8 for another contrast between materialist ('Ionic') and immaterialist ('Italic') philosophy.

[41] Cf. also 111, 15–16; 114, 24–8; 110, 25–111, 1; 119, 25–6; 120, 5–8 and 20–6.

[42] Plato, *Rep.* 445 c 4; Numenius, fr. 2, 5–10 (cf. des Places's edition, 104 n. 2).

principles', to which corresponds a science that does not appear to be
a science concerned just with true unchanging beings. The text gives
strong expression to the pre-eminence of devotion to the divine in
Pythagoreanism.[43] But one must progress further in Iamblichus' work
to find any clarification of the structure of reality (obviously not a
simple two-world, immaterial–material structure) and of the system of
sciences that it presupposes.

4. PYTHAGOREAN MATHEMATICAL SCIENCE (BOOK III: *ON GENERAL MATHEMATICAL SCIENCE*)

If Pythagoras communicated all sorts of knowledge to mankind, it is
only those sciences leading up to, and concerned with, unchanging
immaterial reality which are specifically Pythagorean. In this section I
shall discuss the specifically Pythagorean sciences, in particular the
four mathematical sciences, their distinction from the (other) parts of
philosophy, and their applicability outside the mathematical sphere,
as these subjects are broached in Book III of *On Pythagoreanism*.

The four mathematical sciences are distinguished from other
sciences in good Platonic fashion, namely by means of the difference
between their objects of study and the objects of other sciences.
Mathematics has to do with realities that are intermediary between
pure intelligibles (which are immaterial and indivisible) and sensibles
(material and divisible).[44] Mathematical objects are thus immaterial
and divisible, higher than sensibles and lower than intelligibles, a
bridge joining causes to their effects (10, 8–11, 7; 95, 5–14). In fact the
mathematical realm is a derivation from immaterial being (10, 24–11,
3); it is parasitic on immaterial being as shadows depend on the
objects casting them. Therefore it is to be conceived, not by
abstraction from material reality, but by reference to immaterial being
which it images. The inferior image status it has in relation to true
being is expressed in its properties of quantity and extension; its tendency to lack of mass (τὸ ἄογκον, a Plotinian neologism) and indivisibility indicates its orientation towards true being (34, 10–18). If
Iamblichus' identification of the realm of mathematical objects as

---

[43] Cf. 112, 9–17; 108, 19–20; 111, 1–3.
[44] Or, more precisely, forms divided in bodies (περὶ τὰ σώματα μεριστά), i.e.
enmattered forms; cf. Plotinus, IV 2, 1, 33 ff. On Iamblichus' 'realism' cf. Merlan (1960),
11 ff.; Wedberg (1955), 10–15, 99–109.

intermediary between the material world and immaterial being recalls the treatment of the ontological status of such objects in Plato's *Republic*, as well as in Aristotle's report on Plato (*Metaphysics A* 6), the details of his description of their derivation from and dependence on immaterial being remind one more of the way Plotinus presents the procession of soul from intellect (which is pure being) and its relation to intellect.[45] At any rate this ontological structure of three realms sets mathematics off from other sciences, notably the study of intelligibles, i.e. dialectic,[46] and that concerned with sensibles, i.e. physics (18, 13–20).

The general ontological differentiation between mathematical and other objects also helps to characterize the specificity of particular mathematical principles and theorems. Limit and the unlimited, for example, two principles (ἀρχαί) of mathematical reality (οὐσία), show the characteristic of their nature (ἰδίωμα τῆς οὐσίας 53, 13), i.e. divisibility, which distinguishes them from the equivalent principles in the intelligible realm.[47] Such also is the case for quantity, which must be distinguished in its mathematical form from quantity in pure intelligibles or in sensibles (52, 5–8).

Mathematical principles àre differentiated also from the principles of psychic reality (οὐσία) by virtue of their unchanging character (13, 9–15; 18, 16–18). Thus to our list of sciences should be added psychology, which treats of a realm of being parallel, it seems, to the mathematical realm, with important resemblances (as noted above) to the mathematical realm, but not to be confused with it.[48] Iamblichus also refers to sciences concerned with action (ethics, politics) and making.[49] The relation of mathematics, not only to these latter practical and productive sciences, but also to the theoretical sciences already mentioned will be considered below. For the moment the system of sciences portrayed in the *On General Mathematical Science* and

---

[45] Cf. Plotinus, V 1, 3, 7 ff.; 7, 36 ff. Merlan (1960), 13, notes a similarity with the making of souls in Plato, *Tim.* 35 a.

[46] Cf. 46, 7–13; 39, 23–6. It is not clear if a distinction between a science of intelligibles and a science of the divine is to be made; cf. *Vit. Pyth.* 88, 25–6; *Comm.* 55, 8–19; 63, 24–64, 4; 91, 13–18.

[47] 12, 25–13, 28; cf. 18, 13–20; 50, 14–26.

[48] Ch. 10; however the treatment of the relation between psychic and mathematical objects is far from clear in the work as a whole; cf. Merlan (1960), 15–23, on the inconsistencies of treatment.

[49] Cf. 56, 4–8; 57, 22–4; 74, 3–4; 88, 29–30; 91, 27–92, 4. It is clear that Iamblichus is using an Aristotelian division of the sciences such as had been used to articulate Platonism by some Middle Platonists and by Porphyry; cf. O'Meara (1986), 5.

the place of mathematics in that system might be represented as follows, with the proviso that certain aspects will require refinement at a later stage:

Structure of reality	*System of sciences*
the divine, pure intelligible being	Theology, dialectic
mathematicals, souls	arithmetic
	geometry psychology
	music
	astronomy
sensible objects	physics ethics/politics
	sciences of production

In this diagram I have represented the four mathematical sciences in descending order. This is how Iamblichus tends to treat them, namely as if they corresponded to four sub-realms of mathematical reality, each of which is derived from and inferior to the higher.[50] Thus numbers would be higher than, and the sources of, geometrical figures, and so arithmetic will be correspondingly fundamental and prior to geometry. Must we then conclude that the objects of astronomy derive from the objects of music? It must be admitted that Iamblichus offers, not one, but several principles for ordering the mathematical sciences, none of which are comprehensively applied and reconciled with other principles of order. For example, the subordinate status of music and astronomy can be measured in terms of their lesser relation to immaterial being, an ontological order that need not entail a derivation of the objects of music, for instance, from geometrical figures.[51] Similarly, although it is implied that pure intelligible being is the source of numbers, it also looks as if in one passage (15, 6–23) numbers derive directly from the cause of being, 'the One', and from a matter-like cause, and not indirectly through being. Iamblichus simply has not expressed himself clearly enough for a consistent picture to emerge on these matters.[52]

---

[50] 14, 23–15, 2 = Nicomachus, *Intro.* 9, 15–10, 22; 83, 7–11; note γεωμετρικὴ οὐσία in Iamblichus 18, 6–7.

[51] Cf. 95, 14–96, 3; Geminus in Proclus, *In Eucl.* 38, 1–12; Anatolius, *Exc.* 277, 13–278, 4. Iamblichus cites in ch. 7 Nicomachus' classification of the four sciences (*Intro.* 4, 15–8, 7) as dealing with absolute and relative ποσόν (arithmetic and music), absolute and relative πηλίκον (geometry and astronomy), an order that seems inconsistent with a simple direct subordination going from arithmetic down to astronomy.

[52] Cf. also 50, 14 ff. On the basis of such inconsistencies Merlan (1960), 98 ff., argues that 15, 7 ff. is an excerpt from Speusippus. Cf. Tarán (1981), 86 ff.

To return to the distinction between mathematical and other sciences, this distinction can also be made in terms of the method proper to mathematics as compared to the method of other sciences. Iamblichus characterizes mathematical method as discursive, using λογισμός. It corresponds to the calculative thought proper to soul in Plotinus (e.g. V 3, 3, 14–15) and to the discursive thinking, διάνοια, assigned to mathematics in Plato's *Republic*. In Plotinus and Iamblichus, discursive thought is considered inferior to a non-discursive intellectual 'intuition', νοῦς, of (and corresponding to) pure being. Thus for Iamblichus the study of intelligibles grasps its objects as if 'by touch' (κατ᾽ ἐπαφήν), whereas mathematical science must operate by means of a reasoning process (διὰ λόγου).[53]

Iamblichus describes the discursive reasoning of mathematical science as 'syllogistic' (35, 16–17). Such recourse to a term of logic raises the issue of the relation between mathematical method and logic, a question considered in chapter 29. The idea that mathematics may derive its method from logic is rejected outright: the mathematical sciences have a method or logic of their own. Elements of this logic are listed: division, definition, various kinds of syllogisms, modes of the possible, impossible, and necessary. A distinction is also made between heuristic and critical method.[54] Iamblichus does not go any further than a bare enumeration of such elements of mathematical logic, but an application of this idea can be found at a later date in Proclus' use of logical analysis to set forth the structure of Euclidean geometrical demonstrations.[55] The application of logic to mathematics was not implausible: Aristotle himself frequently refers to mathematics in explaining his logic. It seems indeed that Iamblichus considers that logic can be illuminated by mathematical method.[56] One might note finally that this chapter clarifies considerably Iamblichus' earlier emphasis on the 'demonstrative' character of Pythagorean philosophy: he has in mind the syllogistic logic that he finds in the mathematical sciences, which leads up to the non-discursive intuition proper to the study of intelligibles.

If mathematics is distinguished from other sciences in terms of its

---

[53] *Comm.* 33, 19–25; 35, 11–22; 39, 13–26. Cf. Merlan (1960), 12.

[54] Cf. 89, 16–90, 24; 73, 23–4; 46, 1–13; 65, 7–22. Iamblichus' treatment is too brief to permit of inferring what sort of logic (Aristotelian, Stoic, a mixture) he has in mind. For the heuristic/critical distinction cf. Atticus, fr. 1, 18, and the heuristic/demonstrative distinction in Aristotle (cf. Iamblichus, *In Nic.* 4, 24).

[55] *In Eucl.* 69, 8 ff.; cf. Mueller (1974); below, Ch. 8.

[56] 91, 18–23.

proper objects and method, it can also be extended beyond its specific domain to all parts of philosophy.[57] The same mathematical principles can be used to clarify many different, non-mathematical subjects (92, 18–24). The relation between the study of intelligibles, mathematics, and physics is particularly close: they are neighbours, sharing theorems in common, a continuity corresponding to the continuity in the structure of reality going from the realm of the intelligibles, through mathematical, to sensible objects (88, 17–26). At the same time the different sciences must not be confused with each other (88, 30–89, 2). In order to show how mathematics can be applied outside its proper domain and in a way that does not involve confusion between it and other sciences, I shall review briefly Iamblichus' account of the use of mathematics in each of the various non-mathematical branches of philosophy.

(i) Mathematics and pure intelligibles. According to Iamblichus, who is using here without acknowledgement a text taken from Plotinus, mathematics prepares the soul for the study of intelligibles by habituating it to the immaterial, purifying and strengthening it for the transition to pure being.[58] It also anticipates the study of intelligibles to some degree by dealing with pure beings according to various sorts of comparisons or assimilations (ἀναφοραί) listed as follows (61, 22–8):

(a) common rational principles (κοινωνία τῶν αὐτῶν λόγων);
(b) a dim imaging ⟨of pure beings in numbers⟩ (ἔμφασίς τις ἀμυδρά);
(c) similarity (ὁμοιότης), near or distant;
(d) resemblance (ἀπεικασία), between model (beings) and image (numbers);[59]
(e) causation (αἰτία), the relation between cause (beings) and effect (numbers).

It will be necessary to consider other non-mathematical applications of mathematics before the meaning of this classification is considered.

(ii) Mathematics and Soul. Iamblichus touches very little on this. An assimilation between mathematical theorems and soul's powers and conditions is mentioned (61, 15–20), but not explained.

(iii) Mathematics and sensible objects. Mathematics demonstrates

---

[57] Cf. 57, 7–9; 54, 25–55, 5; *In Nic.* 3, 13 ff.
[58] 55, 8–22 (= Plotinus, I 3, 3, 6–7); cf. 59, 13–18.
[59] Cf. 63, 23–9 for this mode in relation to gods and numbers.

truths in physics by showing them to hold for causes prior to physical objects (93, 11–18). This might be compared to Nicomachus' proof (above, p. 18), as holding also for the physical universe, of the mathematical derivation of all forms of inequality from equality. In this connection Iamblichus gives again a classification of the bases according to which assimilations are made in mathematics to sensible objects (93, 19–94, 10; I omit (*b*), (*d*), (*e*) above, which occur also in this list):

(*f*) abstraction (ἀφαίρεσις), enmattered form considered without matter;[60]

(*g*) 'joining' (ἐφαρμογή), where mathematical principles lead to, and touch, sensibles;[61]

(*h*) perfection (τελείωσις), where mathematics perfects the imperfections of sensibles;[62]

(*i*) participation (μετοχή), where sensibles participate in mathematical objects;

(*j*) division (διαίρεσις), where a mathematical object is seen as divided and multiplied in sensibles;

(*k*) comparison (παραβολή), between mathematical and sensible forms.

This classification embarrasses both by its richness, in the number of modes of assimilation listed, and by its poverty, in the explanation of each mode. If the list is longer for physical than for intelligible assimilations, it might be noted also that Iamblichus could well have included some of the modes of physical assimilations in the list of 'intelligible' assimilations.[63] This, together with the fact that both lists share modes (*b*), (*d*), and (*e*), encourages us to treat the lists together, at least as far as the interpretation of their general sense is concerned.

One striking feature of the lists of modes of assimilation is the lack of clear difference between some of the modes, between (*c*) and (*d*) for example. It looks as if Iamblichus has collected the various terms, e.g. ὁμοίωσις, ἀπεικασία, ἐφαρμογή, to be found in Pythagorean literature describing the pairing of numbers to various non-mathematical objects.[64] His lists then are not true classifications with clearly-defined

---

[60] Also 64, 8–17.   [61] Cf. 93, 7; 19, 1; 91, 13.   [62] Cf. 91, 25–6.

[63] For example, mode (*i*) is applied to theology at 91, 13–14; the list of modes for the intelligibles is in any case not presented as exhaustive (61, 28).

[64] Cf. above, pp. 20, 24, and Nicomachus, in anon. *Theol. arith.* 79, 6 (ἀφομοίωσις, cf. ἀπεικασία in Iamblichus' list, 93, 24–6); 73, 11 ἴχνος (= ἔμφασις in Iamblichus' list, 94, 1); 45, 10; 3, 2; 22, 14 (ἐφαρμόζειν).

and differentiated classes or species. Neither are they, however, mere inventories of terms: some of the modes seem to be interpretations of Pythagorean pairings, e.g. modes (*e*), (*i*), (*j*). I conclude then that Iamblichus is giving both a list of Pythagorean terms referring to assimilations between (primarily) numbers and other objects, and an interpretation of the basis of such assimilations. This interpretation emerges most clearly from modes (*b*), (*d*), (*e*), (*i*), and (*j*): it is on the basis of the causal or participatory relation (which in Platonism is also a relation between model and image) between intelligibles and mathematicals and between mathematicals and sensibles, that mathematical theorems apply to the other two realms. Because mathematicals are 'dim' images of intelligibles, what is true in mathematics 'shadows forth' what is true in the intelligible realm. And because sensibles are images of mathematicals, what is true in mathematics is paradigmatically true of the physical universe. In the latter (but not in the former) extrapolation of mathematics, Iamblichus is refining Nicomachus' approach.[65] Not surprisingly, given the unclear relation between the mathematical and psychic realms, the assimilations of mathematicals to soul remain obscure in Iamblichus' account.

Iamblichus also follows Nicomachus' lead when it comes to the relation between mathematics and the sciences of action, ethics and politics: mathematical principles have a paradigmatic function in ethics and politics (56, 4–13; 91, 27 ff.). But this is not all. Presumably because the objects of mathematics are not, as in Nicomachus, the ultimate realities, they are not the ultimate standards of action. They lead rather to insight into such standards, which are above them. Thus they also have a *protreptic* function in ethics and politics (cf. 74, 3–4), raising the mind to knowledge of principles which should guide and be the goal of action.

Politics, ethics, and physics do not, however, come within the ambit of specifically 'Pythagorean' science and philosophy. The four mathematical sciences and the study of the intelligibles do.[66] The mathematical sciences provide the scientific demonstrative reasoning which foreshadows and prepares the soul for the non-discursive intuitive intellection of pure immaterial being and especially of the highest divine principle, source, and goal of everything. Mathematics

---

[65] Cf. above, p. 18; in treating of mode (*i*), identified with mode (*d*), in *In Nic.* 74, 12–14 (κατὰ ... μετουσίαν καὶ ἀφομοίωσιν) Iamblichus is expanding on Nicomachus, *Intro.* 114, 17–18 (κατ' εἰκόνα).

[66] Cf. the combination of Pythagorean μαθήματα and θεωρία in the texts quoted above, pp. 40, 42.

then is ancillary to, but an indispensible preparation for, higher science. The character of this science (or sciences) and of its objects (being, gods, the One . . .)[67] is not clarified in *On General Mathematical Science*, where such a clarification in any case would be out of place, or, rather, premature.

5. ARITHMETIC (BOOK IV: *ON NICOMACHUS' ARITHMETICAL INTRODUCTION*)

It will not be necessary here to do any more than make brief note of some aspects of the fourth book of *On Pythagoreanism*. In line with the overall progression from the general to the specific, it follows the preceding general introduction to mathematics in Book III as a specific introduction (3, 5) to the first and most fundamental of the mathematical sciences, arithmetic. Having treated of number considered in itself, it will be followed by Books V–VII dealing with number in relation to nature, ethics, and intelligible being (3, 13–16), these to be followed in turn by introductions to the remaining three mathematical sciences.

The importance of Nicomachus, as traced in the above study of Books I–III of Iamblichus' *On Pythagoreanism*, is made explicit in Book IV. For the purpose of introducing the reader to arithmetic Iamblichus does not feel he can do better than reproduce Nicomachus' *Introduction to Arithmetic*. The reasons for his high esteem for Nicomachus are worth noting (4, 14–5, 13). Iamblichus admires Nicomachus' style: precision, brevity, the most basic and general matters presented in orderly fashion. The purity of Nicomachus' Pythagorean mathematics is also stressed. The scientific, demonstrative command of arithmetic in Nicomachus is praised. In short, Nicomachus embodies the highest literary and Pythagorean virtues in Iamblichus' eyes. For these reasons Iamblichus announces his intention simply to reproduce Nicomachus' *Introduction*, adding, subtracting, changing nothing.[68]

As a matter of fact this claim is not verified by what follows.

---

[67] Cf. above, n. 46.

[68] 5, 15–25, where Iamblichus also denies any intention to introduce foreign matters (καινά); he will reproduce only the opinions of the 'ancients'. This might be compared to Numenius' ban on καινοτομία. Numenius may also be the inspiration of Iamblichus' stress on the *purity* of Nicomachus' Pythagoreanism.

Iamblichus does add to, and subtract from, Nicomachus' *Introduction*.
One wonders consequently what to make of his protestations of
fidelity. I think these might be understood in relation to the Pythagorean charges, reported in Porphyry's *Life of Pythagoras* (cf. above,
p. 11), of fraud, false interpretation, plagiary, and malevolent quotation
perpetrated against Pythagorean writings. Porphyry himself, perhaps
mindful of such abuses, makes claims of adding and subtracting
nothing (*Philosophy from Oracles* 109, 4). It is in relation to such charges
that Iamblichus' profession of fidelity to Nicomachus should be
judged in comparison with his actual practice, which is indeed faithful
in this sense, if not in a modern literal sense requiring exact du-
plication.

The differences between Nicomachus' *Introduction* and Iamblichus'
'new edition' of Nicomachus in Book IV of *On Pythagoreanism* have
already been carefully determined.[69] A few of these may be briefly
noted here. Iamblichus fleshes out some of Nicomachus' statements,
e.g. his definitions of number, with information drawn from Pythagorean literature.[70] He includes at several points criticisms of Euclid
which help to bring out the difference between Nicomachus' numerical treatment of arithmetic and Euclid's geometrical approach to
numbers.[71] Finally, Iamblichus gives more emphasis to the ethical and
physical implications of number than that already given in Nicomachus' *Introduction*.[72] This last aspect of Iamblichus' additions to
Nicomachus will be discussed further in the next chapter, in the
context of a reconstruction of Books V–VII of *On Pythagoreanism*.

---

[69] By D'Ooge *et al.* (1926), 127–32; 'new edition' is the apt description of the book in
D'Ooge, 126.

[70] Cf. D'Ooge, 127; *In Nic.* 10–11.

[71] Cf. 20, 10–14 and 19–21, 3; 23, 18–24, 14; 30, 28–31, 21; 74, 24 ff.; Philoponus, *In Nic.*
I 16.

[72] Cf. 32, 20–33, 10; 77, 25–79, 8; 82, 19 ff.; 113, 15–16.

3
On Pythagoreanism V–VII:
The Excerpts in Michael Psellus

ALMOST nothing would be known of the later books of Iamblichus' work *On Pythagoreanism*, and we would in consequence have an impoverished and unbalanced understanding of the work as a whole, were it not for the industry of Michael Psellus (1018–78), a Byzantine teacher, man of letters, historian, and politician, who copied out excerpts from Books V, VI, and VII of *On Pythagoreanism* before they and the other later books of the work disappeared. In this chapter I shall present briefly the argument showing that certain of Psellus' writings are indeed excerpts taken from *On Pythagoreanism* V–VII, and shall attempt a reconstruction of these lost books in so far as this can be done on the basis of Psellus' excerpts. For these purposes it will be useful to consider first some aspects of Psellus' philosophical interests and writings.

I. MICHAEL PSELLUS, PHILOSOPHICAL EXCERPTOR

Michael Psellus had a long and, on the whole, brilliant career as a most influential member of the Byzantine court. He himself finds the origins of this success in his literary or rhetorical abilities and these, together with his philosophical ambitions, provide the occasion for unrestrained displays of vanity.[1] If scarcely appealing to us, such pretensions were no doubt well calculated to project the 'image' that Psellus wished and made for himself at the Byzantine court. In support of his claims he could point to an enormous body of literature that he somehow managed to produce under his own name and which, even today, has not yet been fully sorted out, printed, and examined. In this vast collection of writings[2] one can find many philosophical, theological, legal, medical, rhetorical, poetical treatises; a large

[1] Cf. *Chron.* I 138–9, for example.
[2] Cf. Renauld (1920), ix–xvii, 424–5; Kriaros (1968). There is as yet no adequate list of Psellus' works, nor shall I attempt one here.

number of letters; a small encyclopedia; a variety of formal pieces—panegyrical speeches—in which Psellus demonstrates his impressive rhetorical talents; and the *Chronographia*, an important history (often eye-witness) of the Byzantine rulers of his time. In what follows I shall be concerned only with those parts of Psellus' enormous literary activity that have to do with philosophy.

The *Chronographia* informs us about Psellus' philosophical studies and goals. Having mastered rhetoric he turned, so he tells us, to philosophy and learnt logic, physics, mathematics, and metaphysics. In philosophy he had to teach himself: he claims that he found 'wisdom expiring in those who partook of it' and that he 'could not find worthy teachers or a seed of wisdom in Greece or among the barbarians'.[3] Psellus would have us believe that he acquired his knowledge of philosophy through his own unsupervised reading of books, or rather that these books themselves guided him: the later Greek philosophers referred him back to Plato and Aristotle, after which he returned in his reading to later philosophers, Plotinus, Porphyry, Iamblichus, ending with Proclus, a 'great haven' in which he could find all knowledge (I 136). If Psellus attempts in this account to make his education in philosophy follow the progress of the soul from logic and physics towards 'higher mysteries' (metaphysics) as prescribed by later Neoplatonists such as Iamblichus and Proclus, it is not so much for the attainment of such mysteries that he wishes to be admired, as for his labour in drawing philosophy forth from wells long neglected and blocked up, and in distributing it freely to all (I 138). Anticipating Marsilio Ficino's undertaking, four centuries later in Italy, Psellus is claiming in fact to bring back to life and foster Greek philosophy which had long remained hidden and inaccessible.[4]

To judge by the number of philosophical works Psellus produced, his contemporaries must have been fairly flooded by the newly-opened fountains of philosophy. These works show that Psellus read not only Plato, Aristotle, Plotinus, Porphyry, Iamblichus, and Proclus, but also almost every other Greek philosophical author to be found in the libraries of his time: Alexander of Aphrodisias, Ammonius, Aspasius, David, Elias, Hermias, Nemesius, Philoponus, Plutarch,

---

[3] I 135; for a sceptical view of these claims, cf. Lemerle (1977), 200–1, 245.

[4] On the question of the originality of this claim, cf. Browning (1975), 6; Lemerle (1977), 244–5, who notes that Psellus' 'Renaissance' was superficial and short-lived. Psellus was also more circumspect about the compatibility of Greek philosophy with Christian doctrine than was Ficino; cf. Hunger (1978), 50–1; below, n. 12.

Simplicius, Synesius, Syrianus, and no doubt others.[5] His labours thus ranged over almost the whole corpus of Greek philosophy as it survived in his day. This corpus was somewhat larger than it is now, since he read and used some works which have since disappeared: Proclus' *Commentary on Plotinus*, his *Commentary on the 'Chaldaean Oracles'*,[6] Iamblichus' *On Pythagoreanism* V–VII, and in all likelihood other works which have not yet been identified.[7]

Not only do Psellus' philosophical works show very wide reading of the Greek philosophical manuscripts available to him. They are also largely excerpted from these manuscripts. The ways in which Psellus incorporated excerpts in his philosophical works might be described roughly as follows.

Some of his writings are little more than centos made up, no doubt, for use by himself and his pupils. An example of this is an eight-page series of passages, sometimes slightly rephrased, selected from over three hundred pages of Nemesius' *On the Nature of Man*.[8] A somewhat more elaborate case is the short work on the six definitions of philosophy, in which Psellus selects and combines passages taken (without acknowledgement) from the *Prolegomena to Philosophy* of David and of Elias. At the end Psellus indicates that the work is a synopsis designed for his pupils' use, taking account of their limitations by omitting more complicated and profound matters.[9]

With this work might be compared various other pieces in which excerpts are presented as explanations of certain questions, subjects or texts. *Philos. min.* no. 7, for example, explaining some phrases in Plato's *Phaedrus*, is compiled from Hermias' *Commentary on the Phaedrus*, to which Psellus adds introductory words. *Philos. min.* no. 11 nominally discusses Greek doctrines about soul, but consists in fact of selections from Proclus' *Elements of Theology*—Psellus again merely

---

[5] Cf. Psellus, *Philos. min.*, *index locorum*.

[6] Cf. Westerink (1959); Psellus, *Philos. min.* nos. 9, 38.

[7] Cf. also Diels (1879), 29–30; Benakis (1964); Gautier (1977), 194. We owe to Psellus information confirming the authorship of Iamblichus' *On Mysteries*: Sicherl (1960). In other fields too Psellus used works no longer extant: cf. Aujac (1975b), Wolska-Conus (1979).

[8] *Philos. min.* no. 12; cf. also no. 13 (= Philoponus, *De an.*). For full references to the sources excerpted by Psellus in these and in the works cited in what follows see the *apparatus fontium* of the edition of *Philos. min.*

[9] This work is to appear as part of vol. I of Psellus' *Philos. min.* (to be published in 1989). Psellus describes his excerpting on behalf of his pupils as follows: 'I work late into the night and am back again at my books at daybreak, as is my custom, not to derive something from them for myself, but to extract the gist of them for you', Boissonade (1838), 148–9. Cf. Wolska-Conus (1979), 65–6.

contributes some prefatory words. The short work *On the Forms* is an interesting case: the work survives both in the form of a bare cento of excerpts taken from Plotinus, *Ennead* V 9, and in a more elaborate form, addressed to a high-ranking friend, in which Psellus has added a short introductory paragraph to the Plotinian excerpts (again unacknowledged).[10]

Very much like this last case is a large number of pieces, usually quite short, in which the selection of excerpts (almost never declared as such) is preceded by a few introductory lines in which Psellus claims to be replying to a question put to him. Psellus also sometimes adds some concluding phrases. Not infrequently does the alleged occasion of the work, the question put to Psellus, appear in the Greek source from which Psellus is excerpting. We must suppose consequently that the alleged occasion of the work is fictitious, which is not to deny that in *some* cases Psellus is responding to a real inquiry or that Psellus has didactic purposes in mind when collecting questions to put to himself and to his pupils. Some pieces are presented as if they were letters. Let one example of this type suffice. In *Philos. min.* no. 8 Psellus reports that his questioner (or correspondent) is puzzled by the following 'wondrous' problem (θαυμάσιόν τι ἠπορήσας): why, if each of our senses is composed from each of the physical elements, are there five senses, but only four elements? One might admire the erudition and acuity both of Psellus' pupil or friend and of Psellus' answer if one did not find both the puzzle and the answer in some pages of Alexander of Aphrodisias.[11]

Not all of Psellus' philosophical works are simple centos of borrowed passages presented as synopses, explanations, or answers to questions. In some pieces his contribution goes beyond that merely of excerpting and appending prefatory and/or concluding phrases. He can, in some cases, compare the pagan Greek material he is excerpting with Christian doctrine.[12] In other cases he incorporates echoes, rather than passages, from various Greek sources in prose characterized by considerable philosophical imprecision and by greater recourse to rhetorical device. Such is the primarily ornamental use made of philosophical learning in Psellus' literary show-pieces: his formal letters and his panegyrical speeches.[13]

[10] *Philos. min.* no. 33.
[11] Other examples of this sort of work: *Philos. min.* nos. 4, 5, 6, 10, 14, 44. Cf. Westerink (1959), 23, for other cases of bogus questions.   [12] Cf. *Philos. min.* nos. 35, 38.
[13] Cf. Wolska-Conus' conclusions concerning Psellus' legal works (1979), 77–8. For assessments of Psellus as a philosopher cf. Hunger (1978), 21, and Lemerle (1977),

2. PSELLUS' EXCERPTS FROM *ON PYTHAGOREANISM* V-VII

Among Psellus' philosophical writings can be found two works which are made up almost entirely of excerpts from Iamblichus' *On Pythagoreanism* V-VII. I may be permitted here to summarize and expand at some points my argument published elsewhere (1981) in support of this identification of the source of the two works in question.

In 1892 Paul Tannery edited a small piece by Psellus entitled *On Numbers*. He also suggested that *On Numbers* made use of Iamblichus' *On Pythagoreanism* V-VII. Indeed *On Numbers* quotes a work of Iamblichus, an 'arithmetic of higher ⟨i.e. divine⟩ natures' which can be identified plausibly with *On Pythagoreanism* VII.[14] Tannery's suggestion was, however, largely ignored. In 1981 I showed that *On Numbers* is in fact a shortened version of *two* other works by Psellus entitled *On Physical Number* and *On Ethical and Theological Arithmetic*. I also published these two works[15] and pointed to new evidence in them confirming Tannery's suggestion about Psellus' source.

First, the very titles of Psellus' two works match, and in the right order, the titles of Books V, VI, and VII of *On Pythagoreanism* as they are reported in the *pinax* in manuscript F: *On Arithmetic in Physical Matters*, *On Arithmetic in Ethical Matters*, *On Arithmetic in Theological Matters*. Furthermore, Psellus' *On Physical Number*, which does not name Iamblichus, contains a passage (lines 90-2)—not found in the short version, *On Numbers*—that corresponds closely in language and content to a report on Iamblichus' *On Pythagoreanism* V to be found in the fourth/fifth century Neoplatonist Syrianus:

The more accurate accounts do not admit of a paradigm of the void (τοῦ δὲ κενοῦ παράδειγμα) in numbers since there is no void either in beings, as Iamblichus shows in Book V of his work on Pythagoreanism. (Syrianus, *In met.* 149, 28-31)	Neither in nature nor in physical number is there void. Its paradigm would be nothing other than lack of harmony and lack of symmetry (ἀσυμμετρία). But lack of symmetry is banished from numbers. (Psellus, *On Phys. Numb.* 90-2)

244-6. High claims for Psellus' philosophical ability have been made so far in the absence of reliable analysis of Psellus' sources.

[14] Cf. the *pinax* cited above, p. 33.

[15] Reprinted below (Appendix I). Psellus also produced a Christian sequel to these two works, published by Gautier (1977).

Of these two passages the one in Psellus is more informative and accurate. We are told what the paradigm of the void might be (if there were such) in numbers—ἀσυμμετρία—and why there could be no such paradigm in numbers: numbers do not admit of ἀσυμμετρία. Psellus also speaks of 'nature' rather than of 'beings' as does Syrianus. But by 'beings' Syrianus means 'natural beings' and this imprecision, together with the lack of detail as compared to Psellus' passage, is just what one would expect of a report on Iamblichus' text, just as the accuracy and greater information in Psellus show him to be following more closely the Iamblichean original. The notion that there are in numbers paradigms or models of features of the natural world is of course to be found in Nicomachus of Gerasa and has been seen above (pp. 49–50) to be applied by Iamblichus already in *On Pythagoreanism* III. It is an idea that can be expected to have been of considerable importance in Book V.

Although Iamblichus is not named in Psellus' *On Physical Number*, it is clear from Syrianus' report that Psellus is using to some extent *On Pythagoreanism* V. However, in *On Ethical and Theological Arithmetic*, roughly at midpoint (line 53) when moving from 'ethical' to 'theological' arithmetic, Psellus does name Iamblichus, referring to a specific work (an 'arithmetic of higher ⟨divine⟩ natures') from which he quotes. In view of the evidence presented so far, we are justified in concluding that Psellus is here using *On Pythagoreanism* VII and, in the first half of the piece, VI.

But to what extent do Psellus' two works reflect the contents of *On Pythagoreanism* V–VII? Are they excerpts from Iamblichus? Or do they contain no more than occasional echoes of Iamblichean themes, perhaps combined with a few quotations? The resolution of this problem can be found in a comparison between the compositional structure of Psellus' two works and the various sorts of philosophical compositions described in the preceding section (above): the two works in question resemble most, in approximate length and structure, those other works of Psellus which are compilations of excerpts presented as replies to questions or puzzles, as the following brief review of their structure will show.

On Physical Number begins as if it were written in answer to a question which looks fictitious. Psellus' questioner is said to have wondered much (ἐθαύμασας), on the occasion of a discussion the day before (τὴν χθὲς συνουσίαν), on hearing from Psellus that there is 'physical number' as well as mathematical number, and hence asks to know more about it.[16] So also did Critias behave—if not à propos the same subject—in Plato's *Timaeus* (25 e): he also wondered much (ἐθαύμαζον) on hearing Socrates' discourse the day before (λέγοντος ...χθὲς σοῦ) about the ideal republic. One may be permitted to doubt that Psellus and his friends adopted the practices of Plato's characters in any other area than that of literary conceit, and to suppose that Psellus must have found, towards the beginning of *On Pythagoreanism* V, a question raised about the various sorts of number, physical, mathematical, and intelligible.[17] The opening lines of *On Physical Number* are then followed by a series of paragraphs which read like a discontinuous series of bits of material relating number to a variety of themes. In a concluding paragraph Psellus, as is sometimes his practice,[18] subscribes, but with qualifications, to these doctrines of 'the ancients' (95–9). The series of bits of material continues in *On Ethical and Theological Arithmetic*, first relating numbers to ethical themes, and in the second half, marked by the reference to Iamblichus, dealing with numbers and theology. In two final sentences (87–90) Psellus concludes by recognizing that these matters will probably be unpalatable for his reader.

This compositional structure matches exactly that of those pieces described above in which Psellus can be observed to be assembling strings of excerpts in the guise of an answer to an often fictitious question. This allows us to conclude that, with the exception of some introductory and concluding words (roughly lines 1, 94–8 of *On Physical Number*; 53, 81, 87–90, in part, of *On Ethical and Theological Arithmetic*), all of Psellus' two works derives, in the form of brief excerpts, from Iamblichus' *On Pythagoreanism* V–VII. If it is assumed, by analogy with Books I–IV, that Books V–VII were each the equivalent of about one hundred printed pages in length, then the excerpts from Book V in Psellus' *On Physical Number* amount to about 1/25 of the book, and the excerpts in *On Ethical and Theological Arithmetic* amount to about 1/50 of Books VI and VII each.

With such meagre remains must the attempt to reconstruct Iamblichus' *On Pythagoreanism* V–VII begin. The situation is not unlike that in which ancient pots are reconstructed from some scattered sherds. We must try to recover Iamblichus' lost books from small signs, fragmentary indications of broader patterns. As with

---

[16] Lines 1–4 (the question is implied in line 4, ἀπήτησας).
[17] Cf. the parallel texts cited in the notes to lines 3–8 (below, Appendix I).
[18] Cf. *Philos. min.* nos. 29, 35.

sherds, Psellus' excerpts may be broken off and damaged in different
ways: when excerpting, Psellus may copy a passage word-for-word
and *in extenso*; he may omit words, phrases, even lines here and there
in the passage; he can transpose words and whole sentences, alter the
grammar, or pick out key words and phrases in such a way that the
source text is summarized in its own words rather than quoted.[19] Each
piece of evidence must be considered and a general pattern built up
gradually. It is clear that all that can be hoped for is results that are far
from complete and that must be largely tentative in nature. The task of
reconstruction is made somewhat easier however by the fact that
Iamblichus tells us a certain amount already in *On Pythagoreanism*
I–IV about his intentions in Books V–VII. Psellus' excerpts will also
point to various other methods facilitating reconstruction.

3. *ON PYTHAGOREANISM V*

(i) *General Plan*

Iamblichus indicates at various points in Book IV what he intends to
do in the following three books. Book IV discusses number in itself
and is to be followed by a treatment of number in nature, in ethical
behaviour, and in the Forms or beings (*In Nic.* 3, 13–16). Book V in
particular is referred to at *In Nic.* 118, 12–18, where Iamblichus
announces his purpose to deal next with the decad and with the
'implications'[20] of the other numbers from the monad to the decad.
This is then connected up with the first passage (3, 13–16) later, at the
end of Book IV (*In Nic.* 125, 19–22), when Iamblichus tells us he will
show the implications of number, from the monad to the decad,
'ordering matters according to the physical, the ethical, and furthermore (and prior to ⟨i.e. above⟩ these) the theological account (λόγος)'.
Physical, ethical, and theological 'accounts' will thus provide the
framework in which the 'implications' of numbers, from the monad to
the decad, will be treated. This programme, arranged according to
three different sciences, is reflected in the titles of Books V–VII. How
it is carried out can be determined to some degree thanks to Psellus'

---

[19] Cf. the analysis of Psellus' excerpting practices in Aujac (1975*b*), Gautier (1977),
196.
[20] ἐπανθήματα. Cf. LSJ s.v.: 'special properties'; what is involved is not so much the
special properties of numbers in themselves (ἰδιώματα), as what arises from these
properties for non-mathematical objects.

excerpts. I shall examine first what these excerpts indicate about the 'implications' of number for nature, according to the 'physical account', as these were set forth in *On Pythagoreanism* V.[21]

Psellus first distinguishes in *On Physical Number* (3–8) between different sorts of number, ideal or intelligible, mathematical and physical. He then relates numbers to formal (13–26), material (27–32), and efficient causation (33–6), to change (67–74), to the finite and infinite (75–80), to place (81–9), and to the void (90–3). One will recognize here roughly the agenda of topics of Aristotle's *Physics* I–IV, as listed for example by the later Greek Neoplatonists Proclus (*In Tim.* I 6, 24–6) and John Philoponus (*In Phys.* 2, 13–16). One major topic is missing in Psellus, time; no doubt it could be found in the Iamblichean original. That the topics of *Physics* I–IV only are represented can hardly be accidental. For Porphyry had argued for, and imposed on Aristotle's treatise, a division into two parts, I–IV concerning physics, V–VIII concerning change.[22] It seems then that in *On Pythagoreanism* V Iamblichus followed in general the agenda of Aristotle's *Physics* (I–IV) in dealing with the implications of number in physics.

One might wonder, however, if Psellus' excerpts in *On Physical Number* might have been taken from some introductory pages of *On Pythagoreanism* V, and thus that the sequence of subjects discussed might not after all reflect the overall plan of the work, which may, for example, have adopted the traditional plan of Pythagorean decadic literature—that also of Nicomachus' *Theologoumena*—dealing in succession with each number of the decad and with its various associations. The evidence, however, such as it is, does not support this supposition. Iamblichus' reference in *On Pythagoreanism* IV to an ordering of the implications of number 'according to the physical . . . account' (*In Nic.* 125, 19–22) supports, and is clarified by, a plan for *On Pythagoreanism* V in which number would have been discussed according to an order inspired by Aristotle's *Physics*. The manner of Psellus' excerpting points in the same direction: some excerpts consist merely of lines cited out of context, others are fuller and more intelligible.[23] This suggests uneven dipping in a wide span of text rather than excerpting from a small number of pages. This impression will be

---

[21] Of the issues raised by Psellus' excerpts I shall discuss only those relating to the reconstruction of Iamblichus' books in what follows.

[22] Simplicius, *In phys.* 802, 7–13; cf. Moraux (1985), 229.

[23] Cf. the division of the text proposed below, Appendix I.

strengthened later when the degree to which *On Pythagoreanism* V
came to terms with Aristotle's *Physics* becomes clearer. It will be useful
in the meantime to keep Aristotle's *Physics* in mind, so that traces of
the use of Aristotle's work may be recognized when they are encountered.

(ii) *Physical Number*

The sorts of number which Psellus presents at first to his puzzled
companion—intelligible or ideal (εἰδητικός) number, mathematical,
and physical number (*On Phys. Numb.* 4–8)—recall distinctions
between different sorts of number appearing already in *On Pythagoreanism* III: ideal number, self-moved number,[24] and the principles and
forms in bodies (*Comm.* 64, 2–19). These last are described in Psellus'
excerpts as 'physical number'. They correspond to (Aristotelian)
immanent forms and (Stoic) 'seeds' which organize matter and which
had been introduced into the Platonic universe by Plotinus and by
Platonists before him.[25] To call them 'physical numbers', however, is
unusual.[26] *On Pythagoreanism* IV points to the reasoning behind this:
the demiurgic god organized the world by means of numerical forms
and principles, εἴδεσι καὶ λόγοις τοῖς κατ᾽ ἀριθμόν (*In Nic.* 79, 5–8).
The numerical organization of the world allows one to describe the
immanent, organizing principles of physical bodies as numbers,
physical numbers to distinguish them from mathematical numbers,
which are the paradigms of such numbers. According to Psellus'
excerpts the philosopher should 'fit' these 'physical numbers' to the
causes in nature (*On Phys. Numb.* 11–12), which is indeed what is done
in the following excerpts.

(iii) *Formal and Material Causation*

Psellus' excerpts next speak of two sorts of cause and assign various
numbers and groups of numbers to each (*On Phys. Numb.* 13–32). In
particular, numbers related to the monad (odd numbers) are said to be

---

[24] Apparently relating to soul, which has some close but obscure relationship with
mathematicals.

[25] For these in Iamblichus, cf. *Comm.* 55, 26–56, 2 (εἴδη φυσικά); *De myst.* 169, 7 ff.; *In
Tim.* frs. 47–8; *In Parm.* fr. 2, 13–14. Cf. Proclus, *In Tim.* II 25, 1–3.

[26] The expression φυσικὸς ἀριθμός is found in Nicomachus, *Intro.* 52, 1; 88, 17. Cf.
Plato, *Rep.* 525 d 7–8; Plotinus, VI 6, 16, 45–6.

formal causes, and even numbers, associated with the dyad, are identified as material causes. This rapprochement between monad and form, dyad and matter, had already been made in *On Pythagoreanism* IV: the properties of number are said there to derive from monad and dyad, just as all in the physical universe is based on form and matter; matter has the indefiniteness and inequality of the dyad, just as the monad has a formal function in constituting numbers (*In Nic.* 77, 22–79, 8). Indeed Aristotle himself had suggested in *Physics* I (189 b 8–16, 191 b 35–6) that the Platonic theory of 'the one' and the dyad (the 'great and small') anticipated his distinction between formal and material causes. Yet Aristotle also felt that he had superseded the Platonic theory, the inadequacy of which he seeks to show in *Physics* I 9.

There is no trace in Psellus' excerpts of a response to Aristotle's critique of the Platonic theory of causes (presumably assumed by Iamblichus to be Pythagorean). One wonders consequently, on the supposition that Iamblichus used Aristotle's *Physics* in *On Pythagoreanism* V, if that use might have been very superficial, perhaps merely a naïve adaptation of the Aristotelian theory of causes to Pythagorean numerical lore, involving little effort to meet Aristotle's criticism of Platonic–Pythagorean speculations. Yet the later Neoplatonic commentators on the *Physics* Simplicius and Philoponus (both end of the fifth/early sixth century) show that Aristotle's critique in *Physics* I 9 was not thought by Neoplatonists to be justified. Aristotle's main point was that the Platonists failed to distinguish between matter and privation; their theory postulated only two of the *three* causes (form, matter, privation) required if difficulties in accounting for physical changes were to be avoided (cf. 192 a 3–12). Simplicius argues, however, that Plato did know of 'privation', defined as 'absence ($\dot{\alpha}\pi o v \sigma i \alpha$) of the forms to be produced in matter'; it is found namely in his concept of an all-receptive matrix. Such a cause, however, is only logically distinguishable from matter. Being a cause only as absence, it is not an element constitutive *per se* of physical bodies and thus is not included in the list of such elements.[27] This need not have been Iamblichus' assessment of Aristotle's critique in *Physics* I 9, but it shows at least that the critique need not have been felt to support Aristotle's claim to have gone beyond the Platonic–Pythagorean account of causation in the physical world.

---

[27] *In phys.* 245, 19–29; 246, 2–16 ($\dot{\alpha}\pi o v \sigma i \alpha$ is Aristotle's own term, 191 a 6–7). Cf. Philoponus, *In phys.* 182, 20–5; 183, 11–184, 8.

(iv) *Efficient Causation*

Psellus' excerpts next concern efficient causation (*On Phys. Numb.* 33–64). It is argued, for example, that the numerically defined rhythms of the heavens, of health, disease, birth, and death, show numbers to act as efficient causes. The instances of numbered rhythms given are banal enough in the Pythagorean tradition;[28] not so is the identification of numbers as efficient causes. Certain numbers, the 'generative numbers' (34) seem to do double-duty, since they have already been put in the class of formal causes (21–2). Psellus' excerpts suggest here too at most a superficial match between Pythagorean arithmetic and Aristotle's *Physics*. Again, however, the later Neoplatonic commentators on the *Physics* show that this need not be the case. Having dealt with formal and material causation in *Physics* I, Aristotle adds in *Physics* II two further causes: efficient and final causes. Already in I 6 he had intimated that the Platonists identified formal with efficient causation (189 b 14–16), as we have seen above in the case of 'generative numbers'. Indeed in *Physics* II 7 Aristotle himself finds that formal, efficient, and final causes in nature are often identical, in form at least, if not in number. The later Neoplatonic commentators went even further in identifying formal with efficient causes in nature. For them Aristotle's description of the efficient cause as 'the first cause of change' (*Phys.* 194 b 29–30) implied that only the *first* source of all change in the universe is properly speaking an efficient cause; all other immanent causes, or 'natures', are formal causes.[29] Thus Iamblichus' use of the same numbers for different causal functions need not imply a superficial treatment of Aristotle's *Physics*, if indeed he is using the *Physics* in *On Pythagoreanism* V.

(v) *Change*

The first *clear* evidence that Iamblichus attempted in *On Pythagoreanism* V a critical, 'Pythagorean', reading of Aristotle's *Physics* is found in Psellus' excerpts on the subject of change (67–74). In the corresponding section of the *Physics* (III 1–2) Aristotle formulates a definition of change presented as superior to those of his predecessors, in particular the Platonic–Pythagorean identification of change with

---

[28] Cf. the references given in Appendix I, ad loc.
[29] Simplicius, *In phys.* 315, 10–15 (quoting Alexander of Aphrodisias). Cf. Syrianus, *In met.* 82, 4–5.

difference, inequality, non-being, i.e. the dyad. Such an identification, he allows, is plausible in view of the relation change seems to have with the indefinite. Yet he rejects it:

Difference, inequality, non-being are not necessarily changed, whether they are different, unequal, or non-existent.[30]

Not only do Psellus' extracts retain, however, the association of change with the dyad—referring indeed to the relation noted by Aristotle between change and the indefinite (70–1)—but they add a qualification:

The causes of change ⟨are⟩ . . . difference and inequality (one ⟨sort of these⟩ is like a relation and property, which is rest ($ἠρεμία$), the other ⟨sort⟩ a 'differentiating' ($ἑτεροίωσις$) and 'unequalizing' ($ἀνίσωσις$), such that *it is not the different and unequal that are in change, but those made different and unequal*). (69–74)

The relevance of this qualification would not be clear if one did not have in mind the Aristotelian passage quoted just before. By comparing the two texts we can see that Iamblichus is defending the Pythagorean association of change with the dyad by making a distinction between difference as a relation and as a 'differentiating' intended to respond to Aristotle's criticism. We have thus discovered evidence in Psellus' excerpts showing that Iamblichus, in *On Pythagoreanism* V, attempted to come to terms with Aristotle's criticisms of Platonism-Pythagoreanism in the *Physics*.

But what exactly was Iamblichus' response to Aristotle? It is hard to reconstruct a complete answer from the meagre fragments in Psellus. The distinctions made and the language used are found again, however, in Simplicius' commentary on the passage of the *Physics*, and this suggests that Simplicius might give some idea of what might have been Iamblichus' position. Simplicius distinguishes between (*a*) difference as a Form; (*b*) what is different by sharing in the Form; and (*c*) 'differentiating' ($ἑτεροίωσις$). Plato and the Pythagoreans identified change with (*c*), whereas Aristotle took them, so Simplicius claims, to be referring to (*a*). Aristotle's criticism is misdirected (*In Phys.* 432, 35 ff.). 'Differentiating' expresses the fact that when something changes it becomes different from what it was before.[31] Thus

---

[30] *Phys.* 201 b 16–27: . . . $ἑτερότητα\ καὶ\ ἀνισότητα\ καὶ\ τὸ\ μὴ\ ὂν\ φάσκοντες\ εἶναι\ τὴν\ κίνησιν·\ ὧν\ οὐδὲν\ ἀναγκαῖον\ κινεῖσθαι,\ οὔτ'\ ἂν\ ἕτερα\ ᾖ\ οὔτ'\ ἂν\ ἄνισα\ οὔτ'\ ἂν\ οὐκ\ ὄντα$.

[31] Simplicius, *In phys.* 433, 35–434, 1 (almost identical to *On Phys. Numb.* 72–4).

some essential features of Aristotle's account of change are silently adopted in Simplicius' 'Pythagorean' theory of change: change, as a 'differentiating', involves a subject and two end-points, what the subject was and the something else it becomes.[32] The difference or inequality that *causes* change is the difference between cause and effect, the gap in perfection that moves what changes (the effect) from imperfection to the perfection represented by the cause (433, 20–34).

(vi) *Place*

Another, fainter trace of Iamblichus' attitude to Aristotle's *Physics* can be detected in the excerpts of Psellus concerning number and place (*On Phys. Numb.* 81–9). These excerpts follow some sentences on the finite and infinite (75–80). In his *Physics* Aristotle had listed form, matter, extension, and the boundary of the containing body as possible definitions of place (IV 4, 211 b 7–9). He prefers the last of these (212 a 2–6). In Psellus' excerpts, however, place is described as 'accompanying bodies', συνακολουθοῦντα τοῖς σώμασι (83). If this matches neither Aristotle's position nor the other possibilities he mentions, it is, we can now assume, for a good reason. Fortunately this is confirmed and the few words in Psellus clarified by Simplicius who quotes extensively from Iamblichus' *Commentary on the Timaeus* à propos the same subject:

Iamblichus writes: Every body inasmuch as it is body subsists in place. Place therefore comes into being connaturally with bodies (συμφυὴς ἄρα τοῖς σώμασιν ὁ τόπος συνυφέστηκε).[33]

In what follows in Simplicius, Iamblichus contrasts this view of place with other views, including that of Aristotle and another mentioned by Aristotle (place as extension).[34] Iamblichus is concerned here with the interpretation of Plato's *Timaeus*, not with Aristotle's *Physics*. Yet what he says implies criticism of Aristotle. He distinguishes a central from a purely extraneous role given to place. Aristotle's view of place assumes it is something peripheral to bodies. But if place is an essential part of

---

[32] The term ἑτεροίωσις recalls Aristotle's term ἀλλοίωσις referred to by Simplicius (*In phys.* 432, 35–433, 1), and is found in Aristotle, *Phys.* 217 b 26.

[33] Iamblichus, *In Tim.* fr. 90, 8–10 (Dillon's transl., modified).

[34] The third view mentioned by Iamblichus (*In Tim.* fr. 90, 13–15), place as χωρήματα διάκενα, recalls the Pythagorean concept of void discussed below.

what it is to be a body,[35] then it must be intimately involved in the existence of bodies. It is not a mere boundary, but rather a bond of bodies. If it encloses them, it does so, not as a circumambient limit, but as a power supporting, gathering, delimiting bodies.[36]

Simplicius does not inform us much more about Iamblichus' views on place. He does, however, consider them to be related to those of Aristotle's pupil Theophrastus and of Simplicius' own master Damascius. Theophrastus, as quoted by Simplicius (*In Phys.* 639, 15–22), saw place as the relative position of parts in a whole, position being closely tied to the nature of the whole. Damascius' theory of place is extremely complicated,[37] and I can only note some aspects of it here. He distinguished between a 'proper ordering' ($εὐθετισμός$) of parts, which is connatural ($σύμφυτος$), and an extraneous ($ἐπείσα-κτος$) local situation.[38] The connatural 'proper ordering' has an organizing, preserving function recalling that given to place by Iamblichus as reported by Simplicius.[39]

In Psellus' excerpts numbers are said to have place as 'containing' bodies in their power, a causal rather than a local 'enclosing'. If numbers 'contain' bodies in this sense, then they also 'contain' a connatural part of bodies, namely place (81–4). The excerpts also ascribe to numbers place in a different sense, that rather of Theophrastus: numbers, as constituting an ordered series, have 'places' in the order of succession of the series (84–7). This latter sense of place is applied elsewhere by Iamblichus, not only to numbers, but also to other immaterial realities.[40]

(vii) *The Void*

The excerpts in *On Physical Number* deal finally with a related topic, the void (90–3). Here Iamblichus seems as firm as Aristotle (*Phys.* IV 6–9) in denying the existence of a void. This is surprising, since Aristotle includes the void in Pythagorean doctrine,[41] and Iamblichus

[35] The ontological importance of place is already stressed by Plotinus; corporeal existence (as opposed to incorporeal being) depends on place (cf. e.g. V 9, 5, 44–9).

[36] Cf. also Iamblichus, *In Tim.* fr. 20.

[37] Cf. Hoffmann (1979) and (1980).

[38] Simplicius, *In phys.* 625, 15 ff.; 626, 3 ff.

[39] Simplicius, *In phys.* 639, 24 ff.

[40] Iamblichus, *In Parm.* fr. 313 (Larsen); cf. Galperine (1980), 334–5; Simplicius, *In phys.* 641, 10–15; 642, 1–4 and 25–7; 644, 15–17.

[41] *Phys.* 213 b 22–7; cf. DK I 420, 8 (Eurytus).

could hardly have ignored the divergence between Aristotle and Pythagoreanism on this point. In fact a qualification preserved in the excerpts (92–3) turns out to be an element of a resolution which can be found, again fully explained, in the later Neoplatonic commentaries on the *Physics*. Psellus' excerpts concede the existence of a void, 'if one wishes to speak of even number as a discontinuous gap ($\delta\iota\epsilon\chi\widehat{\eta}$ ... $\delta\iota\acute{\alpha}\kappa\epsilon\nu\text{o}\nu$)' (92–3). The meaning of this phrase emerges if it is compared to Simplicius' and Philoponus' comments on the corresponding section of Aristotle's *Physics*. Both commentators understand the Pythagorean concept of void reported by Aristotle as referring to the difference between Forms, the separation between bodies. Thus the Pythagoreans, in introducing the void, were speaking in fact of a principle of differentiation.[42] If we recall that in Pythagorean arithmetic the principle of differentiation is the first *even* number, the dyad, then the sense of Psellus' excerpt and its function in a reconciliation of the Aristotelian and Pythagorean positions emerges: Iamblichus was prepared to defend a Pythagorean concept of void, if by this is meant a principle of differentiation. This enabled him to take Aristotle's side on the question and yet to claim to be faithful to Pythagoreanism.

(viii) *Conclusion*

Psellus' excerpts in *On Physical Number* reveal finally a good deal about Iamblichus' *On Pythagoreanism* V. Iamblichus developed here a 'Pythagorean' arithmetical physics following the plan of Aristotle's *Physics* I–IV. One major topic is missing in Psellus, time. Yet we know from another source something about Iamblichus' theory of time, as it was presented in his *Commentary on the Categories* in the form of an interpretation of a text supposedly by the Pythagorean Archytas.[43] It is a fair guess that the treatment of time in *On Pythagoreanism* V would not have been very different. In his *Physics* Aristotle occasionally criticized the Pythagoreans and Platonists and regarded his own physical theory as superior. Psellus' excerpts contain some indications showing that Iamblichus, far from ignoring Aristotle's criticisms, attempted to

---

[42] Simplicius, *In phys.* 652, 7–19; Philoponus, *In phys.* 610, 7–21; cf. Aristotle, *Phys.* 213 b 24–6.

[43] Iamblichus, *In cat.* frs. 2 ff.; cf. Sorabji (1983), 37 ff.; Samburscky, Pines (1971); Hoffmann (1980). Archytas is cited in *In Nic.* 6, 20–2, and elsewhere in *On Pythagoreanism* (cf. above, p. 43).

come to terms with them. This involved, in some cases at least, interpretation of Pythagorean doctrine so as to render it defensible. This
may have led to some projection of Aristotelian physics backwards on
to Pythagoreanism. At the same time, however, Iamblichus did not
hesitate to go beyond Aristotle, in particular on the subject of place.
This he did elsewhere, in the case of time, by appealing to a
supposedly earlier, Pythagorean source, Archytas. Such advances
were a source of inspiration for the sophisticated theories of place and
time to be found in later Neoplatonists, Syrianus, Damascius, and
Simplicius. More generally, the instances in which Psellus' excerpts
have been found to anticipate specific arguments in Simplicius' and
Philoponus' commentaries on the *Physics* suggest that Iamblichus'
study of the *Physics* was of some importance for the development of
these commentaries.[44]

But what arithmetical physics emerges from the excerpts? In
general it appears that the physical universe is structured by
immanent forms, called 'physical numbers', which derive their
character and behaviour from the properties of mathematical
numbers. Mathematical numbers in fact exemplify, in paradigmatic
fashion, the organization of the universe. This means that physical
theory can be found pre-contained in mathematics and that the
elements of such a theory are instantiated in the various physical
expressions of different mathematical numbers. It is this last idea that
is predominant in Psellus' excerpts: the components of an (Aristotelian) account of physical causality are shown to be embodied in
different (physical) numbers or groups of numbers. The excerpts give
the impression of a multiplicity and variety of immanent forms
expressing the relative simplicity of physical theory. Although the
latter appears in general to be Aristotelian, there are differences, at the
very least in the case of place: place is an intimate part of the being of
bodies and is produced by numbers (mathematical here, it seems,
rather than physical), which possess their own immaterial 'places' in a
serial organization.

---

[44] Simplicius and Philoponus are probably not specifically dependent on the reading
of Aristotle's *Physics* given in *On Pythagoreanism* V. They would have had other sources,
in particular Iamblichus' *Commentary on the Timaeus*. (We know of no commentary,
properly speaking, on the *Physics* by Iamblichus.) Simplicius, however, would have
known Iamblichus' *On Pythagoreanism* well, if we can trust Renaissance reports of a
manuscript (no longer to be found) containing a commentary by him on Iamblichus'
book; cf. I. Hadot (1987*b*), 28–9. Cf. above, n. 31, below, n. 50, for close verbal parallels
between Simplicius and Iamblichus' *On Pythagoreanism* as excerpted by Psellus.

These results are no doubt incomplete. But to go much further in the attempt to reconstruct Iamblichus' *On Pythagoreanism* Book V on the basis of Psellus' excerpts would, I believe, involve speculations whose degree of reliability would be hard to measure.

4. ON PYTHAGOREANISM VI

(i) *General Plan*

Psellus' excerpts in *On Ethical and Theological Arithmetic* fall into two sections, the first having to do with 'ethical arithmetic' (2–52), corresponding thus to *On Pythagoreanism* VI, the second containing 'theological arithmetic' (53–90), i.e. the subject-matter of *On Pythagoreanism* VII. I shall be concerned here with the first section and with the extent to which it reveals something of the content of *On Pythagoreanism* VI. The task of reconstruction is yet more difficult here than in the case of *On Pythagoreanism* V: there is only half as much available in terms of quantity of excerpts, and no related, i.e. ethical, Neoplatonic commentaries survive which could help in elucidating obscure passages.

Since it turns out that Iamblichus' ordering of the implications of number 'according to the physical . . . account' means in fact that the plan of *On Pythagoreanism* V follows that of Aristotle's *Physics* I–IV, one wonders if the same sort of situation might obtain with respect to the ordering 'according to the ethical . . . account' (above, p. 60) in *On Pythagoreanism* VI. And indeed it does. The sequence of topics in the first part of Psellus' *On Ethical and Theological Arithmetic* (2–52) corresponds roughly—with larger omissions, as one would expect with fewer excerpts—to that of Aristotle's ethical treatises: the first principles of ethics (2–15); the parts or powers of the soul (16–23); virtue defined (24–30); virtues intellectual and moral discussed individually (31–52).[45] For the same reasons as those given above à propos the plan of *On Pythagoreanism* V, Psellus' excerpts appear to be taken, not from a limited section, but from a range of chapters in *On Pythagoreanism* VI. They thus give some idea, however fragmentary, of the structure of the work. It is not clear, on the other hand, if Iamblichus follows one particular ethical treatise of Aristotle. He is familiar, as will be seen later, with both the *Nicomachean* and the *Eudemian Ethics*. His attitude

---

[45] At least one omission in the excerpts is a treatment of friendship promised in *In Nic.* 35, 5–10.

to both may have been such that he did not feel bound to follow closely the one rather than the other.[46] At any rate it will be useful to keep Aristotle's ethics in mind as Psellus' excerpts are considered in more detail.

(ii) The First Principles of Ethics

Aristotle begins his ethics starting from principles, ἀρχαί. These principles are not 'absolute', i.e. those standing at the head of a science of ethics that is complete, but 'relative': they are what is at first best known to us, those facts that experience teaches and which only a mature student of ethics will possess.[47] Psellus' excerpts begin, however, with a list of first principles which are 'absolute' and on which ethics is grounded: measure, limit, perfection, order, unity. They are also mathematical. How they ground ethics can be illustrated from Aristotle's characterization of happiness as something perfect (τὸ δ᾽ ἄριστον τέλειόν τι φαίνεται), as an activity of the soul according to the highest and most perfect virtue, in a perfect or complete life.[48] Iamblichus seems to be thinking of this description of happiness when, on the subject of the perfect as first principle, he says: 'for perfection (τελειότης) unitarily completes the best (ἄριστον) measure of life' (Psellus' excerpts, 8).

It is not, however, the perfect, but measure, or rather 'measure itself' and what is measured that are most important among the mathematical principles of ethics according to Psellus' excerpts (2–6). Measure and what is measured are in fact what come first in the list of 'possessions' whereby the human good, i.e. happiness, is constituted according to Plato's *Philebus* (66 a 6–7). On the assumption then that the Platonic dialogues are Pythagorean in inspiration, an assumption clearly made in *On Pythagoreanism*, the first elements of the human good in Plato's *Philebus* can be considered by Iamblichus as the absolute first principles of a Pythagorean 'arithmetical ethics'.

In the preceding chapter it was seen that mathematics not only furnishes ethics with its first principles. It also has a paradigmatic role in ethics. An example of this appears in Psellus' next lines: the 'mean'

---

[46] Cf. Kenny (1978), 38–9 (similar situation in Simplicius and Philoponus). I shall refer to the *Eudemian Ethics* only when it is clear that it, and not the *Nicomachean Ethics*, is being used by Iamblichus.

[47] *Eth. Nic.* I 4, 1095 a 31–b 8; I 7, 1098 b 1 ff.

[48] *Eth. Nic.* I 7, 1097 a 28, 1098 a 15–18.

in numbers is like a model of the ethically good character which involves good harmonization of the soul (12–15), i.e. the virtue of temperance.

(iii) The Powers of the Soul

Having defined happiness in outline, Aristotle develops his account by means of a brief discussion of the soul which yields a distinction between rational and non-rational psychic parts or powers. This produces in turn a differentiation between intellectual and moral virtue (*Eth. Nic.* I 13). Psellus' extracts contain a corresponding section (16–23), in which psychic powers are assimilated to numbers. For this purpose Iamblichus uses a text to be found in Aristotle's *On the Soul* (404 b 22–4), which he takes elsewhere to refer to Plato,[49] and here, presumably, to refer to the Pythagoreans. This text identifies intellect with the number one, science with two, opinion with three, and sense-perception with four. Iamblichus explains each identification and his explanations correspond exactly to those, given at slightly greater length, of Simplicius commenting on the same text of Aristotle.[50] The psychic powers mentioned in the excerpts relate only to the cognitive functions of the soul, and one must suppose that Iamblichus also treated of other psychic powers relevant to a 'Pythagorean' ethics, such as those he lists in his work *On the Soul*:

> The Platonists, Archytas, and the other Pythagoreans declare the soul to be tripartite, dividing it into reason, spirit, and desire. For these ⟨parts⟩ are useful for the constitution of the virtues. But they reckoned the powers of the soul to include nature, imagination, sense-perception, opinion, the thought that moves bodies, the desire of the fair and good, and intellections.[51]

This last list contains three of the cognitive powers mentioned in Psellus' excerpts, and the passage illustrates how these powers might have been brought into a discussion of psychology with reference to ethics in *On Pythagoreanism* VI. It is at any rate clear that Iamblichus substituted for Aristotle's account of the soul a 'Pythagorean' psychology based, in part at least, on reports found in Aristotle himself.

---

[49] Iamblichus, *De an.*, in Stobaeus, *Anth.* I 364, 15–18.

[50] Simplicius, *In de an.* 29, 2–9 (Simplicius refers in the plural to ἄνδρες, which must mean the Pythagoreans; cf. 28, 17 ff.). Such is the closeness of Simplicius to Psellus' excerpts (lines 17–19) that he can help clarify the condensed phrases of the excerpts.

[51] Iamblichus, *De an.*, in Stobaeus, *Anth.* I 369, 9–15; cf. Festugière (1950–4), III 194.

(iv) *Virtue*

Aristotle's ethics next lead to a definition of moral virtue as the excellence of that rational aspect of soul which obeys reason. On the analogy of natural excellence or virtue[52] and with much recourse to mathematics, Aristotle defines moral virtue as a 'mean' between two extremes, excess and deficiency (*Eth. Nic.* II 6). Psellus' excerpts recall this definition,[53] comparing virtue to 'mean' and 'perfect' numbers, and vices to 'superabundant' and 'deficient' numbers. Such a comparison had already been made by Nicomachus. Psellus' excerpts, however, concern natural, rather than moral virtue (26). They appear to derive from a section on natural functioning and excellence which may have introduced, as it does in Aristotle, an account of ethical functioning and virtue.[54]

Psellus' excerpts continue with a passage (27–30) putting the unmeasured, the unlimited, etc., in 'the column' of vice. A preceding passage might be missing, in which measure, limit, etc., may have been put in a 'column' of virtue such as that alluded to in Aristotle.[55]

Having defined moral virtue, Aristotle next gives examples of virtues as means and vices as extremes (*Eth. Nic.* II 7–8). Although there is nothing corresponding to this in Psellus' excerpts, there is an interesting related passage to be found already in *On Pythagoreanism* IV:

This agrees ... with thinking correctly that the virtues are measured states and means between excess and deficiency, and are not extremes ..., evil opposing evil, and both opposing one good, yet good not at all opposing good, but opposite at the same time to two evils, as cowardice is opposed to audacity ... and both are opposed to courage.... (*In Nic.* 32, 25–33, 7)

Examples follow, taken both from *Eth. Nic.* II 7 and *Eth. Eud.* II 3, illustrating Aristotle's point about the oppositions between vices and between them and virtues (*Eth. Nic.* II 8, 1108 b 11–15) as well as his remark in *Eth. Nic.* II 6, 1106 b 28 ff. on the unity of virtue and the diversity of vice, or, as Iamblichus phrases it, 'the rarity of the perfect, as belonging to something good and not to some manifold evil' (*In Nic.* 33, 15–17).

---

[52] Cf. *Eth. Nic.* 1106 a 16 ff.; 1144 b 1 ff., with 1106 b 16.
[53] Lines 24–7; also Iamblichus, *Ep. ad Sop.*, in Stobaeus, *Anth.* III 9, 5–10.
[54] For the theory of natural virtue in post-Iamblichean Neoplatonism cf. Blumenthal (1984), 480, 482.
[55] Cf. *Eth. Nic.* 1096 b 5–7, 1106 b 29–30; cf. Psellus, *On Phys. Numb.* 76–9, 28–31.

(v) *Particular Virtues*

Psellus' excerpts next concern analogies between certain numbers and specific virtues, namely practical deliberation or wisdom, theoretical wisdom, courage, temperance, and justice (31–52). It is not clear from Psellus' excerpts here whether they derive from a variety of chapters (each devoted perhaps to a particular virtue) or represent a fairly continuous extract from one chapter. It is, however, likely that Iamblichus discussed other virtues besides those retained by Psellus (above, n. 45). The group of virtues mentioned in Psellus is symptomatic of the curious mix of Platonic and Aristotelian ethics that will reappear later. The order in which the virtues are treated corresponds roughly to that used in Plato's *Republic* (428 a ff.), not that in Aristotle, who deals first with moral, and then with intellectual virtues. However, the distinction between practical and theoretical wisdom is Aristotelian, as are the descriptions of practical wisdom as concerned with 'variable matters' (Psellus, 32) and of theoretical wisdom as concerned with 'beings'.[56] The latter is related to the monad and the former to the triad on grounds similar to those given earlier (17–18) for the assimilation of intellect to one and opinion to the triad.

Two forms of courage are distinguished in Psellus' excerpts, 'manly' courage and constancy (37–8). The former comes from Plato (*Laws* 802 e 9, *Symp.* 192 a 4–5). So does the latter, as can be seen from Iamblichus' *Letter to Olympius*, where it is related to courage as defined in the *Republic*.[57] In this *Letter*, however, Aristotelian courage is also present: as Aristotle's courageous man endures pain and danger 'for the sake of the fair', so does Iamblichus' paragon support such things 'for the sake of the good'.[58] The slight difference in formulation points to what one feels must separate the two models of courage: Iamblichus' man appears more indifferent to and unperturbed by the trials of this world than Aristotle's, based as his courage is on unchanging thought fixed on an otherworldly goal. For the two forms of courage, manliness and constancy, Psellus' excerpts give numerical analogues (37–8), the odd (always male in Pythagoreanism, as the even was female) and the foursquare—the latter is Aristotle's comparison (*Eth. Nic.* 1100 b 11–22).

---

[56] τὰ ὄντα (34); compare Aristotle's τιμιώτατα (*Eth. Nic.* 1139 a 5–11, 1141 a 20, 1141 b 3).

[57] Iamblichus in Stobaeus, *Anth.* III 319, 21 ff.; cf. Plato, *Rep.* 442 c 1–3.

[58] Aristotle, *Eth. Nic.* 1117 a 17 ff., 33 ff., b 12–15; cf. Iamblichus in Stobaeus, *Anth.* III 320, 16–21.

The relation between temperance treated as the cause of 'symmetry' in Psellus' excerpts (40) and temperance as described in Plato's *Republic* can again be illustrated from Iamblichus' *Letters*, in which 'symmetry' is regarded as the 'symphony' between the parts of the soul in Plato's definition of temperance.[59] Once temperance is related to symmetry, Iamblichus can find the corresponding number, choosing namely nine, rather than the number three traditional in Pythagorean assimilations, on the mathematical grounds that nine is especially 'generative' of equality.[60]

Psellus' excerpts finally deal with justice. Given the strongly mathematical character of Aristotle's treatment of this virtue, it is hardly surprising to find Iamblichus following him more closely here. Aristotle first describes distributive and rectificatory justice and then introduces (*Eth. Nic.* V 5) Pythagorean 'reciprocal' justice. In his *Letter to Anatolius* Iamblichus presents an Aristotelian theory of distributive justice.[61] Only reciprocal justice is represented however in Psellus' excerpts (46 ff.). Iamblichus replaces Aristotle's brief reference to this as a Pythagorean concept with a Pythagorean definition of reciprocal justice cited by Nicomachus.[62] But Nicomachus' definition is slightly altered: the term ἀπόδοσις at the beginning of the definition becomes ἀνταπόδοσις in Psellus' excerpts (46), under the influence perhaps of Aristotle's references to τὸ ἀντιπεπονθός or ἀνταπόδοσις in Pythagoreanism (*Eth. Nic.* 1133 a 3, 1132 b 21). In relating justice to the number four (or five), however, (48) Iamblichus does little more than follow a well-established Pythagorean tradition.[63]

(vi) *Conclusion*

To judge from Psellus' excerpts, it seems that Iamblichus again followed Aristotle's lead in *On Pythagoreanism* VI. Here it is Aristotle's ethics that provides the lines on which Iamblichus elaborated a

[59] Cf. Iamblichus in Stobaeus, *Anth.* III 257, 11–258, 4; Plato, *Rep.* 431 e 8, 442 c 10–d 1, but also Aristotle, *Eth. Nic.* 1119 b 15–16.

[60] Cf. the references given below, Appendix I, ad loc.

[61] In Stobaeus, *Anth.* III 358, 5–17 (cf. *Eth. Nic.* 1129 b 29–30, 1130 b 30–2, 1131 a 25–7). Cf. Iamblichus, *De myst.* 187, 13–17.

[62] Cf. the references given below, Appendix I, ad loc.

[63] Psellus' text is corrupt here; should 4 at line 48 be corrected to 5? On justice see also Iamblichus, *De an.*, in Stobaeus, *Anth.* I 455, 19–25 (Festugière [1950–4], III 241, with notes) and the references below, ad loc., Appendix I. For later Neoplatonic treatments of the virtues in a more comprehensive context cf. Blumenthal (1984) and the references given there.

'Pythagorean arithmetical ethics'. In view of the small amount of material excerpted by Psellus, it is likely that many topics of Aristotelian ethics were covered by Iamblichus, of which there is no trace in Psellus. Aristotle's influence on the ethics of *On Pythagoreanism* VI has been observed not only in the sequence of topics handled, but also in particular explanations and even in individual expressions. However Iamblichus attempted to change Aristotelian ethics into a 'Pythagorean' theory. This could be done by emphasizing the mathematical aspects of Aristotle's approach—in particular his discussions of moral virtue in general and of the virtue of justice—or by substituting Pythagorean definitions and theories where appropriate—e.g. on the parts or powers of the soul. Plato's ethics was also introduced as was, of course, Pythagorean numerical lore. The theory that emerges is structurally similar to the arithmetical physics of *On Pythagoreanism* V: the first principles, models, and concepts of ethics are found already in the various mathematical properties of numbers. Not only are the basic notions of ethics mathematical in inspiration, but specific virtues are paradigmatically contained in specific numbers. To judge correctly the overall impression given in Psellus' excerpts of a confusion between arithmetic and ethics, it is well to recall the care with which Iamblichus had stressed before in *On Pythagoreanism* (above, p. 48) the distinction between the sciences, as well as the applicability of mathematics outside its proper domain. The same methodological point will be made in Psellus' excerpts from the next book of *On Pythagoreanism*.

5. *ON PYTHAGOREANISM* VII

(i) *General Plan*

In coming to Psellus' excerpts from *On Pythagoreanism* VII, where he finally divulges his source (53 ff.), we reach matters which Iamblichus had presented earlier (above, p. 48) as the subject aimed at by, and transcending mathematics, namely pure beings and the divine. If this subject is not treated in its own right in *On Pythagoreanism* VII, it is at least adumbrated, to the extent that arithmetic foreshadows and leads to the study of being and of the divine. From this point-of-view *On Pythagoreanism* VII represents, in the scheme of the work as a whole, the highest stage in the ascent of the soul of the reader. In approaching the summit of Pythagorean philosophy, it also points to the goal of *On Pythagoreanism* itself, allowing us to view the work as a whole in relation to its finality. Unfortunately, but not surprisingly, it is also here that Psellus' excerpts are most deficient. They are fewer than before and sometimes extremely fragmentary. No general plan is evident. Psellus seems to have cared even less than before about what he was excerpting, and the relevance (and, presumably, danger) of the theological material to Christianity did not escape his notice (cf. 71). But what he does excerpt contains some important clues.

If no general plan is evident in the sequence of Psellus' excerpts, it appears at least that they are taken, as before, from various parts of *On Pythagoreanism* VII. A striking example is the passage at 59–63 which, as it stands, has little to do with the preceding and succeeding sections. A great deal of context must be supplied if some continuity is to be established between it and the other excerpts.

Since Iamblichus followed the general order of Aristotle's physics and ethics in organizing the previous two books of *On Pythagoreanism*, one wonders if something similar might be the case here too, particularly in view of the fact that an Aristotelian work concerning being and the divine was available, the *Metaphysics*.

A direct comparison of Psellus' excerpts with the *Metaphysics* does not at first glance reveal any relation. If, however, we apply a method used above in section 3, comparing Psellus' excerpts with a later Neoplatonic commentary on the *Metaphysics*, we come upon some interesting connections. The debt of Syrianus' *Commentary on the Metaphysics* to Iamblichus' *On Pythagoreanism* will be demonstrated below in Chapter 6. Here I would like to refer briefly to part of Syrianus' attempt to respond in his commentary to Aristotle's onslaught in *Metaphysics MN* on Platonic theories of separately existing Forms, numbers, or 'ideal numbers' (εἰδητικοὶ ἀριθμοί). In *N* 4 Aristotle presents a dilemma: given their metaphysical theories, his opponents are in a position neither to subordinate 'the Good' to 'the One', nor to identify them, since this would produce an absurd plethora of goods. Syrianus, on the contrary, has no difficulty with a plethora of goods (the divine after all is without envy) and therefore maintains against Aristotle the identity of the One with the Good.[64] The passage at 59–63 in Psellus' excerpts, which, as noted above, appears to have nothing in common with the other excerpts, discusses the difference between the Good and the One and compares the

[64] *In met.* 181, 34–185, 27, especially 183, 26–9.

multiplication of the One with the multiplication of the Good. In the case of the latter this multiplication relates to the nature of the Good, which is generative (γόνιμος οὖσα, 60). The connection between these themes and Syrianus' commentary suggests a possible context for Psellus' excerpt: a reaction to a specific argument forming part of Aristotle's rejection of separately existing Forms or numbers in *Metaphysics MN*.[65] This context would disclose in turn the relation between this excerpt and the other excerpts, which have to do with 'ideal' and 'divine' numbers.

If these conjectures about the original context of the excerpt at 59–63 are correct, they would show that at some point in *On Pythagoreanism* VII Iamblichus came to terms, to some extent, with Aristotle's criticisms of Platonic theories of Forms or 'ideal numbers'. If some compromise or adjustment was possible between Aristotle and Pythagoreanism–Platonism in the realms of physics and ethics, it was hardly so when Iamblichus came to the subjects of Aristotle's *Metaphysics*.[66] In order to present a science of separately existing ideal and divine numbers, Iamblichus would have to overcome the arguments in *Metaphysics MN*. However, there is no other trace of this response to Aristotle in Psellus' excerpts,[67] and it may not have been a major preoccupation in *On Pythagoreanism* VII. There is no trace, either, in Psellus' excerpts of a positive theory of 'ideal' or 'intelligible' numbers corresponding to the Forms, which Iamblichus could have presented in conjunction with his response to Aristotle, although earlier references *may* lead one to expect such a theory in *On Pythagoreanism* VII.[68] The excerpts concern almost entirely a sort of number which appears to be different, 'divine' number. The approach used by Iamblichus in treating of this sort of number will emerge as its nature is examined.

[65] It is not clear which, if either, horn of Aristotle's dilemma Iamblichus accepted. The emphasis on multiplication points to Syrianus' position, yet the excerpt speaks of 'difference' (perhaps Psellus' word). Cf. Iamblichus, *De myst.* 261, 9–14 (quoted below, p. 82). Did Iamblichus produce a commentary on Aristotle's *Metaphysics*? Dillon (1973), 22, does not provide sufficient evidence of such a commentary. However Simplicius, *In de an.* 217, 23–8 (referred to by Steel [1978], 124) indicates that Iamblichus discussed at least the σκοπός (goal or intention) of *Met. Λ* (cf. also the scholium on Iamblichus, *Pr.* 22, 1 ff. printed at *Pr.* 127, 16–19).

[66] Cf. Syrianus' general assessment of Aristotle (*In met.* 80, 4–81, 6; discussed below, Ch. 6).

[67] Syrianus cites *On Pythagoreanism* VII while discussing *Met. M*, 8 (*In met.* 140, 2–15), but not in such a way as to imply that Iamblichus was also dealing with the Aristotelian passage.

[68] Cf. above, pp. 60, 62 (but the references are a little vague, and the title of Book VII includes no reference to an 'ideal' [εἰδητικός] arithmetic).

(ii) *Divine Number*

Psellus' theological excerpts begin with a summary and a quotation
(53–8) emphasizing the transcendence of 'divine number' in relation
to other sorts of number, 'hypostatic' (=mathematical?), 'self-moved'
(=psychic),[69] intellectual (νοερός), essential (οὐσιώδης, i.e.: ideal or
intelligible)[70] number. The sorts of numbers listed correspond to
different and ascending degrees of reality. A roughly equivalent list,
this time given in descending order, appears already in *On Pythagoreanism* III, where the Pythagoreans are said to 'fit' mathematicals
(including numbers) to the gods, 'to their being and power, order and
activities, according to an appropriate assimilation—what they
thought especially worthwhile—finding which numbers are related
and similar to which gods'; then to the intellectual (τὸ νοερόν), pure
being, i.e. ideal (εἰδητικόν) number; then to self-moved existence,
defined as self-moved number; then to the heavens and to enmattered
forms, i.e. physical numbers (*Comm.* 63, 23–64, 19). The 'intellectual'
and the 'intelligible' (pure being) are treated as one in this passage,
although they are distinguished in Psellus. But a report in Syrianus
confirms that Iamblichus wished to distinguish them in *On Pythagoreanism* VII:

Since, when they discuss the divine monads, they define differently the intelligible monad (νοητὴν ... μονάδα) from which comes forth the very first
number ..., from the intellectual and demiurgic monad (νοερὰν καὶ
δημιουργικήν) ... concerning which ⟨monads⟩ many of the ancient and more
recent ⟨authorities⟩ have spoken, but most clearly of all the divine Iamblichus
in the seventh book of his Pythagorean treatise.[71]

Thus in *On Pythagoreanism* VII Iamblichus was more precise than in
the earlier books concerning the difference between levels of reality:
above the world of enmattered forms (physical numbers) were to be
found 'hypostatic number' (?), self-moved being (or number), intellectual being (or number), intelligible or pure being or the Forms
(ideal number), and, transcending all, the gods (or divine number).

There is another, more striking difference between the passage in
Book III and Psellus' excerpt at 53–8. The former text calls for an
extrapolation upwards of mathematics, 'according to an appropriate

---

[69] Cf. Iamblichus, *In Tim.* fr. 55, 12–13, and above, p. 62.

[70] Cf. Psellus, *On Phys. Numb.* 4–5.

[71] *In met.* 140, 10–15 (cf. Psellus' excerpts, 73–4). For the intelligible/intellectual distinction in Porphyry as compared to Iamblichus cf. P. Hadot (1968), I 98–101.

assimilation (ἀπεικασία)', towards the divine, whereas the text of
Psellus presents the hierarchy of sorts of number with the purpose of
stressing the transcendence of the divine and thus of denying such
extrapolations (οὔτε ἀναλογίαις ἀπεικάζων, 55). The conflict can
be resolved by reference to Psellus' excerpts at 81–7: assimilation
upwards to the divine unities (ἐνώσεις) of the 'natural sequence' (or
'flow') of numbers is an inferior approach, an analogy. A more accurate approach would consist in starting, not from below, but from the
divine itself; this method depends, it appears, not on analogy, but on
'higher insight'.[72] This difference in approach seems to be followed in
Psellus' excerpts. Having emphasized the transcendence of divine
number (54–8), they discuss divine number on the basis of the inferior
mathematical analogies (64–80), and then refer to the superior, direct
insight into divine number (84–7). What has already been learnt from
Psellus' excerpts (81–7) about the approach by analogy points to an
agenda: relating the numbers of the natural sequence of numbers (i.e.
from the monad to the decad) to the gods. This programme is also
followed in the excerpts relating to mathematical analogy: they discuss
successively the monad (70–5), dyad (75–8), and triad (78–80). Had
Psellus cared to excerpt more, we would in all likelihood find the subsequent numbers of the decad also represented.

I believe that we are now in a position to draw some tentative conclusions about the structure of *On Pythagoreanism* VII. Iamblichus may
have treated in this work of ideal or intelligible number, at least to the
extent that he may have responded in some measure to Aristotle's
attack on theories of separately existing Forms or ideal numbers in
Metaphysics MN. Although Iamblichus clearly believed in the distinct
reality of ideal numbers, he was especially concerned in *On Pythagoreanism* VII with a higher sort of number, 'divine number'. To deal
with this subject he took up again the traditional Pythagorean decadic
order of exposition, such as was used by Nicomachus in his *Theologoumena arithmeticae*, fitting each number, from monad to decad, to
the gods. If we wish to speculate about what works Iamblichus would
have used here, we can say that they certainly did not include
Aristotle's *Metaphysics*, but probably were traditional Pythagorean
works on the decad such as are reflected in Anatolius' piece and used
by Nicomachus' *Theologoumena*. One of these might have been the
Pythagorean *Sacred Discourse* to which Syrianus refers in connection

---

[72] κατὰ κρείττους ἐννοίας (87). Cf. above, p. 47.

with his mention of Iamblichus' *On Pythagoreanism* VII.[73] However, Iamblichus considered the method by mathematical analogy inferior to direct insight into the gods, a subject on which he also touched to some degree.

At the same time a certain amount has been learnt concerning the structure of reality presented in *On Pythagoreanism* VII. A more precise picture of this structure emerges than that found in earlier books of the work. The earlier lack of clarity about whether or not the divine and pure being are distinct is removed:[74] the level of pure being (or the intelligible) is inferior to the level of the gods which is beyond being. So also does a distinction between the intelligible and the intellectual levels, scarcely drawn earlier, clearly emerge in *On Pythagoreanism* VII. This structure of reality is not, however, complete. In what follows I shall attempt to fill it out further, to the extent that Psellus' excerpts permit.

(iii) *The Approach by Analogy*

Most of Psellus' theological excerpts (64–80) relate to this subject. They are not for all that particularly representative or informative. Their defectiveness and the amount of omission will become clearer as they are studied in detail.

The excerpts first suggest that Iamblichus presented a broad analogy between what is highest in numbers (the one, limit, equality) and the divine (64–6). This corresponds to the broad assimilations between numbers and enmattered forms (*On Phys. Numb.* 8–12), and between numbers and virtue (*On Eth. and Theol. Arith.* 24–30) which introduced the more detailed accounts of physical and ethical arithmetic in *On Pythagoreanism* V–VI.

This is followed in Psellus' excerpts by some lines (66–70) having to do with the cause or principle ($\dot{\alpha}\varrho\chi\dot{\eta}$) of divine number. The correspondence between this and the identification of causes and first principles in physical and ethical arithmetic is pointed out. Thus prior to unified divine number is to be found a 'uniform unity' ($\mu o\nu o\varepsilon\iota\delta\dot{\eta}\varsigma$ $\ddot{\varepsilon}\nu\omega\sigma\iota\varsigma$). The language used here implies that despite its unity, divine number (or the divine)[75] presupposes a cause of its unity which, as such, must be prior and superior to it ($\kappa\alpha\tau$ ' $\alpha\dot{\iota}\tau\dot{\iota}\alpha\nu$ $\pi\varrho o\eta\gamma o\upsilon\mu\dot{\varepsilon}\nu\eta$).

---

[73] *In met.* 140, 16–18, and above, p. 20, below, p. 93.

[74] Cf. above, Ch. 2 n. 46.

[75] Cf. also 81–4, where the 'supernatural' beings are described as unities, $\dot{\varepsilon}\nu\dot{\omega}\sigma\varepsilon\iota\varsigma$.

This is a fundamental addition to the structure of reality sketched above: prior to and above the level of the gods (themselves 'above' being) is an ultimate principle of the unity of the gods.

Something very similar can be found in Iamblichus' *On Mysteries*. Here, in one passage, Iamblichus speaks of ascending degrees of unity (ἕνωσις) and being, culminating with the gods:

As for the gods, their order consists in the unity (ἑνώσει) of all; their primary and secondary classes and their many products all came to be in unity. The all in them is the One; the 'beginning, middle, and end' come to be according to the One.[76]

If it is not clear from this passage that the gods are above being and depend themselves on a higher principle for their unity, this can be shown from a later passage of *On Mysteries*:

Before true beings and the universal causes there is one god, the very first, even before the first god and king, remaining unchanging in the singleness of his unity. There is nothing intelligible or otherwise added to him. He is the model of . . . the one father god, the true good, for he is something greater and the first and the source of all. . . . From this One the self-sufficient god shone himself forth . . ., for he ⟨the latter⟩ is cause and god of gods, monad from the One, prior to being and cause of being.[77]

Certain aspects of this text are clarified in a comparison with Psellus' excerpts, notably the expression 'god of gods': this indicates that the first god arising from the ultimate One is the source of the other gods, or, in arithmetical terms, the monad of divine number. On the other hand the text of *On Mysteries* suggests a possible reason why Psellus, in his excerpts, appears to have compared the first of the gods (rather than its source, the ultimate One) with the Christian god.[78] Had Iamblichus used expressions such as those used in *On Mysteries* of the first of the gods, e.g. 'first god and king', a superficial reader could

---

[76] 59, 15–60, 2. The Pythagorean motto is cited also in Psellus, *On Eth. Theol. Arith.* 72.

[77] 261, 9–262, 5 (Festugière [1950–4], IV 23 ff., has noted the Pythagorean character of this text). The same structure, in its basic features, is attributed to Iamblichus by Damascius (using Iamblichus' *Commentary on the 'Chaldaean Oracles'*), *De princ.* I 86, 3 ff. P. Hadot's argument (1968), I 97 n. 1, against the rapprochement of the texts in *De myst.* and in Damascius does not note that the monad named in Damascius is *intelligible*, which makes the principle above it equivalent to the supra-intelligible monad (or 'god of gods') of *De myst.*, and the principle yet above it the same as the ultimate One, cause of the 'god of gods' in *De myst.*

[78] Cf. lines 70–2, discussed immediately below.

have easily taken this to be equivalent to the highest Christian principle.

We have already moved in Psellus' excerpts from the ultimate One, cause of the unity of divine number, to the first of the series of divine numbers, the 'first god'. It is referred to as 'the first', the 'one', a 'henad', and 'triad' (70–1). The latter description shows, unless Psellus' excerpting is seriously misleading here, that Iamblichus is referring to the first of the gods and not to the ultimate One. Describing it as a triad is to indicate, by means of a Pythagorean motto (72, cf. above, n. 76), its dependence on a principle of unity. Is the term 'henad' equivalent to the term 'monad' used in *On Mysteries* of the first god? The structural correspondence between the systems of *On Mysteries* and of Psellus' excerpts suggests that it is, but the excerpts themselves do not yield specific evidence confirming this.[79] If however Iamblichus organized his discourse about the gods on the analogy with the decadic series, one would expect that he would begin by reference to the first of the gods as monad. And Iamblichus, it appears, did refer to a divine monad, for Psellus' excerpts list monads at lower levels—an intelligible monad, a demiurgic monad, an earthly (physical) monad (73–5). Since the treatment of the 'divine' dyad is followed by a similar list of lower levels of dyads (75–8), the list of monads must also have been headed by reference to a divine monad in Iamblichus. But Psellus omits this, which makes his excerpting here particularly obscure and disjointed.

Once the monad in the decadic series was applied by analogy to the gods, more especially (and quite probably) to the first of the gods, source of the other gods, and himself originating from the ultimate One, we would expect that the other numbers in the series, dyad, triad, etc., would have been brought by Iamblichus into relation with the series of the gods. Of this, however, Psellus preserves only a few lines concerning the dyad and triad. The 'divine' dyad is described as 'unlimited power, never failing progression of life, receiving the measure of the first one ($\dot{\upsilon}\pi o\delta o\chi\dot{\eta}\ \tau o\hat{\upsilon}\ \pi\rho\dot{\omega}\tau o\upsilon\ \dot{\epsilon}\nu\dot{o}\varsigma\ \mu\dot{\epsilon}\tau\rho o\upsilon$)' (76–7). The 'first one' is perhaps the first god, or henad (cf. 70–1), a monad also, it seems. The two principles produce the subsequent gods, as monad and dyad, principles of limit and lack of limit, produce the following members of the numerical series. The description of the divine dyad

---

[79] In a reference slightly later (86) to the gods as the 'divine one and ($\kappa\alpha\dot{\iota}$) divine monad and divine dyad . . .,' the first 'and' might possibly indicate a distinction. On the concepts of $\dot{\epsilon}\nu\dot{\alpha}\varsigma$ and $\mu o\nu\dot{\alpha}\varsigma$ cf. Burkert (1972), 231, Staehle (1931), 19.

as 'unlimited power' distinguishes it from the purely negative function of its analogue in the material world, undefined matter. The latter is alluded to in the list of lower dyadic principles next given in the excerpts: intelligible, intellectual, mathematical, and physical dyads (77–8). Psellus omits any reference to a 'divine' triad, as he did in the case of the divine monad, contenting himself with excerpting from the second part of Iamblichus' account, i.e. that concerning the lower triadic levels. Intelligible, intellectual, supra-celestial, celestial, and physical triads are listed (78–80).

(iv) *Conclusion*

I have summarized above what can reasonably be deduced from Psellus' excerpts concerning the general plan of *On Pythagoreanism* VII. It will suffice here to review the main features of the metaphysical theory suggested by the excerpts. The structure of reality in Iamblichus' *On Pythagoreanism* VII turns out to be quite complicated, as compared to the system expressed in earlier volumes of the work. Above the level of the physical world is a series of distinct and ascending orders, psychic/mathematical, intellectual, intelligible (true being), the divine above being, and above all orders an ultimate One, the absolute first principle. As numbers in the mathematical order can be projected downwards paradigmatically, producing physical numbers, so they can be projected upwards as foreshadowing higher orders, producing, in particular, divine numbers. Our excerpts show no trace of a positive theory of intelligible being approached mathematically (i.e. ideal numbers), nor are the relations between psychic, mathematical, and intellectual orders clarified. But this may simply be due to wholesale omissions by Psellus. On the other hand a certain amount is disclosed about the analogy established between numbers and the order of the gods. This order, described mathematically as divine number, is characterized by unity, both of the order itself (ἡνωμένου παντὸς ἀριθμοῦ, 69–70) and of the gods in the order (ἑνώσεις, 83). It thus presupposes a principle of unity transcending it, an ultimate One. The order of the gods is treated as a numerical series which flows out from its first member, the 'first one' (a monad), or rather from the interrelation of the two first members, monad and dyad, acting as principles of limit (or measure) and power limited (or measured). From monad and dyad emerge the first numbers, properly speaking, and so also by analogy do the following members of the order of the gods. Few details concerning this survive, however, in Psellus' excerpts. Psellus does retain traces of Iamblichus' illustrations, for each member of the divine decad, of lower instances corresponding to each of the levels of reality taken in descending sequence. The penetration of monad, dyad, triad through all levels of existence expresses not only the continuity of the structure, but also the extra-mathematical applicability of mathematical concepts. The limitations implicit in the latter idea are brought out in Psellus' last excerpts. Iamblichus is well aware, as we have seen, that his 'arithmetical theology', his numerical analysis of the order of the gods who transcend being, is an extrapolation, an analogy. It is inferior to a direct 'meta'-mathematical insight into the nature of the gods, whatever that may be.

How does Iamblichus' *On Pythagoreanism* VII, as reconstructed from Psellus' excerpts, compare with Nicomachus' *Theologoumena arithmeticae*? More generally, how does the Pythagoreanizing programme expressed in Iamblichus' work compare to that to be found in Nicomachus? Of what importance is this programme in Iamblichus' other philosophical writings? These and other related questions will be taken up in the next chapter.

4
Iamblichus' Work *On Pythagoreanism*: General Conclusions

IN the preceding two chapters the overall intentions and structure of Iamblichus' work *On Pythagoreanism* have been examined as they appear in the first four extant books and in so far as they can be discovered in Psellus' excerpts from Books V–VII. It remains to review briefly the results achieved and to attempt some assessment of the significance of the work as a whole, in relation both to Iamblichus' other works and interests and to the earlier versions of Pythagoreanism sketched above in Chapter 1. The importance of Iamblichus' Pythagoreanizing programme for the later history of Greek philosophy will be the subject of Part II of this book.

But have we reached, even with the help of Psellus' excerpts, an adequate view of the work *On Pythagoreanism* as a whole? There were after all three further books (Books VIII–X) concerning which next to nothing is known. Might they not, were they to resurface some day, alter our general picture of the work? The last three books concerned geometry, music, and astronomy 'according to the Pythagoreans'. In the general scheme of the work they occupied positions comparable to that of Book IV, the Nicomachean introduction to arithmetic. We can therefore expect that they would have been similar in function and character: elementary introductions to the remaining three mathematical sciences, using 'Pythagorean' sources.

But I think we can go further than this. Iamblichus might have composed, for Books VIII–X, new elementary introductions to geometry, music, and astronomy, on occasion citing 'Pythagorean' authorities. It is more likely, however, that he would have reissued 'Pythagorean' introductions to these sciences if such were available, as he did in the case of Nicomachus' *Introduction to Arithmetic* (= Book IV). And certainly such introductions were available to him. But one can only speculate about precisely which ones he would have used. Given his high standing as a Pythagorean in Iamblichus' eyes, Nicomachus would seem the most likely author he would have chosen and there is some evidence that Nicomachus wrote introductions to mathematical sciences other than arithmetic. Nicomachus himself refers to an *Introduction to Geometry* in his *Introduction to Arithmetic* (83, 3 ff.). His brief *Manual of Harmonics* refers to a larger work on harmonics or music which is in all probability one of the major Greek sources of Boethius' *De Musica*. And finally Simplicius refers to a Pythagorean discovery in astronomy reported by Iamblichus 'following Nicomachus'.[1] It is not certain however that Simplicius is inspired, directly or indirectly, by *On Pythagoreanism* X, or that his report means that Nicomachus wrote an *Introduction to Astronomy* which Iamblichus used.

Whatever Pythagorean materials Iamblichus had recourse to in *On Pythagoreanism* VIII–X, I think we can safely say that these volumes were elementary introductions to the three mathematical sciences subordinate to arithmetic. It is thus not likely that they would have significantly altered the system of Pythagorean philosophy or the Pythagorean structure of reality as these are presented in Books I–VII. From the point of view of Iamblichus' reader, the highest stage in his philosophical progress is reached, not in the final books, but in Book VII where a transition is prepared from the realm of mathematical science to the highest levels of Pythagorean philosophy.

1. *ON PYTHAGOREANISM*: A BRIEF REVIEW

Despite the quantity and variety of materials used in *On Pythagoreanism*—Platonic, Pythagorean, Aristotelian texts—a unity of conception and of purpose has been found to organize the whole. The work is a protreptic to 'Pythagorean philosophy', leading the reader from more familiar, 'common' truths up towards the higher 'mysteries' of Pythagoreanism. This movement from the familiar to the transcendent has been observed not only within Book II (the *Protreptic*) but also in the other books. Book I (*On the Pythagorean Life*) already begins the initiation of the reader in providing evidences of the divine origin of Pythagoreanism and in using the actions and speeches of Pythagoras to

---

[1] Simplicius, *In De caelo* 507, 12–14 = Iamblichus, fr. 154 Larsen. Cf. Burkert (1972), 101, Tarán (1974) on Nicomachus' works. The language in Syrianus, *In met.* 103, 6 suggests use by the Neoplatonists of Nicomachean introductions to mathematical sciences other than arithmetic. However for geometry Syrianus and Proclus used Euclid (below, Ch. 8).

introduce the reader, at an elementary level, to Pythagorean philosophy.

The education of the reader continues upwards in Book II. In Book III (*On General Mathematical Science*) the reader at last finds himself in the realm of Pythagorean philosophy properly speaking, which consists of the mathematical sciences and, above them, 'contemplation', the knowledge of true being and of the divine. The initiation to mathematics proceeds step-by-step. The general introduction in Book III leads to specific, more technical introductions to each of the four mathematical sciences (Books IV, VIII–X). From the system of Pythagorean philosophy just alluded to, it will be seen that *On Pythagoreanism* covers only the first, lower half of what Iamblichus considers to be Pythagorean philosophy, namely mathematics. Were it to cover the whole, it would have to deal, after Book X, with true being and (especially) with the divine. However, these higher regions of Pythagoreanism are foreshadowed in Book VII where an analogy is developed between arithmetic and the gods who transcend being.

Within the work a conception of Pythagorean philosophy emerges which is consistent on the whole, although some details, especially those having to do with the structure of reality, are expressed at first somewhat vaguely and appear to receive precise formulation, if at all, only in the later books.[2] But this is a consequence of the order of exposition, i.e. that of a gradual ascent, chosen by Iamblichus for his work.

The figure of Pythagoras is presented at the beginning of the work with the purpose, I have suggested, of recommending Pythagorean philosophy to the reader by providing evidence of its divine origin. Iamblichus collects the legends associated with Pythagoras. But he also indicates his opinion of them: he is concerned with the origin and mission of Pythagoras' *soul*. Pythagoras' soul is in fact one of the souls of the divine company of Plato's *Phaedrus* which parades above the rim of the heavens and contemplates the immaterial Forms, or true being. Pythagoras' soul does not fall from this vision, but is sent down to the material world to impart knowledge to the fallen souls of those who have lost it, thus saving them. This interpretation represents, I have argued, an integration of the Pythagorean legend into Iamblichus' Neoplatonic view of the origin and purpose of soul in the world.

---

[2] Cf. for example the distinction between being and the divine in Books I, III, VII (above, pp. 45, 81). Some vague areas remain unclarified, as far as can be determined (above, p. 45).

Pythagoras seems to have communicated many different sorts of knowledge to mankind, but for Iamblichus the specifically Pythagorean revelation consists in the 'most scientific', unerring forms of knowledge, those having to do with pure, immaterial unchanging realities, namely mathematics and the study of true being and of the divine. The mathematical sciences are inferior to the study of being and the divine, because they deal with inferior objects. Mathematical objects may, through their immateriality and unchangingness, transcend the material world, but they are products, images, of true being. This means, however, that mathematics can train and prepare the soul, as indicated in Plato's *Republic*, for higher wisdom.

Although subordinate, mathematics has a pivotal role. In view of the organization of the material world according to number, mathematics includes in paradigmatic form a theory of physics and of ethics as well as foreshadowing the highest Pythagorean science. These extra-mathematical implications of mathematics are introduced in Book III of *On Pythagoreanism* and became the objects of separate and detailed treatment in Books V–VII. In Book V Iamblichus developed a Pythagorean arithmetical physics, that is, a 'Pythagorean' reformulation of Aristotelian physics, in which Aristotelian criticisms of Pythagorean ideas were met and 'Pythagorean' improvements of Aristotle's theories were introduced. Given the paradigmatic relation between numbers and the forms immanent in, and organizing the material world, the latter were described as 'physical numbers' and were shown, in their instantiation of physical theory, to exhibit the various characteristics of mathematical number. The same 'Pythagoreanizing' of Aristotelian theory, in this case ethics, was attempted in Book VI, the same sorts of associations sought between aspects of ethical behaviour and the mathematical properties of number. When the reader came to Book VII, he moved from these extrapolations of Pythagorean mathematics to lower sciences, upwards to mathematics as anticipating the highest objects of Pythagorean philosophy, the gods. Here Aristotle could scarcely be adapted (Pythagoreanized) for the purpose. A response had to be made to criticisms in the *Metaphysics*, and advantage was taken of the mathematical properties of number in order to foreshadow, by a method of analogy, the series of the gods.

This system of sciences[3] corresponds to a structure of reality which

---

[3] The place of psychology in the system remains obscure. It is parallel in some way to mathematics. But the relation between the two sciences (and their respective objects) is not clearly determined in the available evidence.

is most fully and precisely presented at the highest stage in the 'ascent' of the reader, namely in Book VII. The major aspects of the structure appear to be the following. There is an absolute first principle, an ultimate 'One' above, as presupposed by, the unity of a series of gods. This series possesses unity in itself and in each of its members. On the analogy with a numerical series the divine series originates from its first members, a 'first one' (perhaps also described as a 'monad') and a divine dyad. Acting together as principles of limit and of the power limited, these two generate the following members of the divine order. The order of the gods (or 'divine number', in mathematical analogy) transcends the level of pure being, the intelligible, 'ideal' number, in which monad, dyad, and triad are also found, presumably again in virtue of mathematical analogy. Distinct and inferior to the intelligible is an 'intellectual' level, concerning which little is said in what survives of *On Pythagoreanism*, apart from the idea that here too analogues of monad, dyad, triad are to be found. Below this level comes 'mathematical reality' whose characteristics have served to describe by analogy the higher orders. Proximate in some way to mathematical reality is soul, but the relations between these two orders remain obscure. Below soul and mathematical number is the multiplicity of en-mattered forms ('physical numbers') which organize the material world and where again analogues of monad, dyad, etc. occur.

The structure as a whole represents not only ontological distinctions between types of reality, but also an ontological subordination of these types and a causal derivation going from the higher to the lower, from the ultimate One down eventually to the material world. The details of the derivation of reality are not clear, although the 'flow' of numbers from the first two members of the decad was, it seems, an important model for explaining derivation.

If a brief comparison is made between Iamblichus' 'Pythagorean' structure of reality and the system of hypostases in Plotinus, it will be noted that Iamblichus has introduced new ontological distinctions and levels, namely an order of gods interposed between the ultimate principle and pure being, and an 'intellectual' order distinguished from and inferior to pure being or the intelligible.[4] The evidence does not reveal the reasons for such introductions into the Neoplatonic system of reality. It will also be noted that, in contrast to Plotinus,

---

[4] For Iamblichus as anticipating Proclus' theory of 'henads', cf. below, Ch. 10 n. 25; for the difference between Porphyry and Iamblichus on the intelligible/intellectual distinction cf. above, Ch. 3 n. 71.

Iamblichus makes systematic use of mathematics in the analysis of reality. This gives his more complicated system a strong sense of continuity, a continuity on each level of reality in its articulation in analogy with the numerical progression (or flow) from monad to decad, and between all levels in the pervasiveness of relations imaged in or imaging numerical relations. This mathematization of the structure of reality, which seeks at the same time to preserve the distinctions between physics, ethics, mathematics, and metaphysics, represents a systematic application of the Pythagorean principle that 'all is likened unto number'. It is thus an important consequence of Iamblichus' programme to Pythagoreanize Neoplatonic philosophy.

2. THE RELATION OF *ON PYTHAGOREANISM* TO IAMBLICHUS' OTHER WORKS AND INTERESTS

In order to assess the significance of *On Pythagoreanism* it is necessary first to determine, as far as possible, its place *vis-à-vis* Iamblichus' other philosophical works and the ideas expressed in these works. The problem might be stated in an extreme form by means of the following questions. Is *On Pythagoreanism* without any importance or relevance with respect to Iamblichus' other work? Did he compose it without any regard to what he himself considered philosophically significant? Was it perhaps the work of a beginner (who nevertheless knew a great deal of philosophy and could wrestle with Aristotle), to be put aside when, with maturity, different projects were undertaken?[5]

If these options are implausible, it is none the less not easy to identify the place of *On Pythagoreanism* within Iamblichus' philosophical corpus for the simple reason that much of the corpus is lost. Only quotations from, and reports on, Iamblichus' commentaries on Plato and Aristotle survive. The same is true of other major works, such as the *Commentary on the 'Chaldaean oracles'*. *On Mysteries* is Iamblichus' only work (not counting individual volumes of *On Pythagoreanism*) to be available to us in its entirety. Thus the most that can be attempted is a survey of indications pointing toward the place of *On Pythagoreanism* in Iamblichus' philosophy. However, it turns out that there are a good number of such indications and that they are very

---

[5] Cf. Dillon (1973), 20. Against Dillon's dismissive attitude to *On Pythagoreanism* a more direct approach is required than the occasional rapprochements made by Larsen (1972) in the course of his review of Iamblichus' other works.

strong. They fall into two groups: (i) Iamblichus' own suggestions in *On Pythagoreanism* as to the relation between it and certain of his other works; and (ii) references to Pythagoreanism in Iamblichus' other work.

(i) It has been noted above that *On Pythagoreanism* does not cover the whole range of what Iamblichus represents as Pythagorean philosophy. It deals with the lower Pythagorean sciences, the four mathematical sciences, preparing the way for, and anticipating, the study of true being and of the divine. But it does not deal with these higher regions of Pythagoreanism in their own right. The work as a whole thus indicates what should follow it: a treatise (or treatises) on being and, especially, on the divine. Indeed Iamblichus himself refers the reader, in *On Pythagoreanism* (*Pr.* 120, 15–18), to his work *On God* (*Περὶ θεοῦ*), for a more specific and technical account of the eternal, immaterial, intelligible, unchanging class of the gods. This reference, with its characteristic distinctions between the common (familiar) and the specific, between the elementary and the technical, shows that Iamblichus envisages his work *On God* as a sequel to the mathematical volumes of *On Pythagoreanism*, dealing at a higher level of exposition with a higher subject-matter.

Not much is known about the work *On God*. The subject-matter included the class of intelligible gods: the singular reference of the title should not therefore be taken in a monotheistic sense. The work may perhaps be the same as the treatise *On the Gods* (*Περὶ θεῶν*) cited by Iamblichus in *On Mysteries*, in which he says the reader will find a more accurate treatment of the cosmic and supra-cosmic gods, 'which gods lead up and according to which of their powers, how they set free from fate and through which hieratic ascents, what sort of order the cosmos has and how the most perfect intellectual activity rules over it' (VIII 8, 271, 10–17). Proclus refers to a work *On the Gods* by Iamblichus where he says Iamblichus discussed the gods of the intellectual order, arguing that the major kinds of being of Plato's *Sophist* should be placed at this level and not at that of the intelligible order.[6] *On the Gods* thus seems to have dealt with the divine at a variety of levels, cosmic and supra-cosmic, intellectual, and intelligible. This multi-level approach has been noticed already in the treatment of monad, dyad, and triad in *On Pythagoreanism* VII.

Whether or not *On the Gods* is the work referred to as *On God* in *On*

---

[6] *Theol. Plat.* I 52, 2–13; there is a reference also in Damascius, *De princ.* I 132, 12–13.

Pythagoreanism II, one can conjecture that the latter was inspired at least to some degree by a writing going under the title *Sacred discourse* or *On the Gods* attributed to Pythagoras, since Iamblichus uses it in *On Pythagoreanism*.[7] This work appears to have dealt with numbers, from the monad to the decad, and to have related gods and demons to them, namely as produced by them. Such, roughly, was the structure of Nicomachus' *Theologoumena*, and Nicomachus may have in fact used the Pseudo-Pythagoras.[8] But of the relation (if any) of Iamblichus' *On God* (= *On the Gods*?) to this work, nothing is known. If Iamblichus' *On God* was indeed a 'Pythagorean' theology, i.e. a treatise on the divine based on Pythagorean literature, then it would have completed, on the basis of Pythagorean sources, the coverage of Pythagorean philosophy begun in *On Pythagoreanism*.

Iamblichus also wrote 'theologies' based on Platonic, Egyptian, and Chaldaean sources. His *Commentary on Plato's Parmenides* interpreted the first 'hypothesis' of the *Parmenides* as concerning god and the gods.[9] *On Mysteries* is yet another theology, derived this time from supposedly Egyptian (but also Chaldaean) sources.[10] Finally Iamblichus produced an enormous *Chaldaean Theology* in which the 'Chaldaean Oracles' were interpreted with help of the Pythagoreans and of Plato's *Philebus*.[11]

It thus turns out that if one starts from the system of philosophy presented in *On Pythagoreanism*, one requires as a sequel a work treating of being and especially of the divine. Iamblichus himself refers to such a sequel in *On Pythagoreanism*, namely his (lost) work *On God*. It is possible that this work was a 'Pythagorean' theology. Iamblichus also produced other theologies, based on Platonic, Egyptian, and Chaldaean sources. These too could complete the coverage of Pythagorean philosophy begun in *On Pythagoreanism*, if one assumption is made, namely that Iamblichus saw, and continued to see, a unity between the theologies of the Pythagoreans, of Plato, of the Egyptians, and of the Chaldaeans. In what follows I would like to indicate briefly the extent to which this assumption can be made.

---

[7] *Vit. Pyth.* 81, 20 ff. For this *Sacred Discourse* cf. Thesleff (1965), 164–6.

[8] Cf. Thesleff (1965), 166 (with notes).

[9] *In Parm.* fr. 2; cf. Saffrey and Westerink in Proclus, *Theol. Plat.* I lxxxii–lxxxiii; III xvii ff. For a critique of evidence for a *Platonic Theology* by Iamblichus cf. Saffrey (1987a), 40–1.

[10] Cf. *De myst.* 1, 8–2, 9; 4, 1–4; 5, 8–13; 14, 7–8; 286, 10–11.

[11] Damascius, *De princ.* I 86, 3–87, 4 (discussed above, Ch. 3 n. 77). On *Chaldaean Theology* as a title for Iamblichus' *Commentary on the 'Chaldaean Oracles'*, cf. Larsen (1972) I 58.

In *On Pythagoreanism* Iamblichus uses the Platonic dialogues in such a way as to indicate that he regarded Plato as a Pythagorean. The legend of Pythagoras' apprenticeship under Egyptian priests is repeated:

He spent two and twenty years in Egypt in the temples, doing geometry, astronomy, and being initiated, but not in a superficial or haphazard way, into all the rites of the gods.[12]

Pythagoras is reported as having been educated in mathematics and in theology not only by the Egyptians, but also by the Chaldaeans:

Further they say that his divine philosophy and cult was composite, some things being learnt from the Orphics, some from the Egyptian priests, some from the Chaldaean mages, some from Eleusinian rites. . . .[13]

Iamblichus does not make clear how Pythagoras' 'learning' of the main parts of Pythagorean philosophy (mathematics and theology) from the Egyptians and the Chaldaeans can be reconciled with Pythagoras' role as divine revealer of all sciences to man. Nor can reports he reproduces be regarded as reflecting precisely his own views. However, to judge from *On Pythagoreanism*, it is unlikely that he would have considered Pythagorean theology to be at odds with Egyptian and Chaldaean theology. It is clear at any rate that he identified Platonism with Pythagoreanism.

On Mysteries stresses the dependence of Pythagoras, Plato, and other Greek philosophers on the Egyptian priests.[14] But here Pythagoras appears as a lesser figure than that found in *On Pythagoreanism*. His role as a divine guide to the knowledge which can only be mediated to men through divine help is now assumed by Hermes and by Iamblichus' Egyptian priest Abammon: as the ancient Egyptian priests guided and initiated Pythagoras, so will Abammon enlighten the addressee of the work, Porphyry.[15] Pythagoras and other Greek philosophers are thus disciples *vis-à-vis* the Egyptians, not masters. On the other hand, Chaldaean theology is treated as equal to Egyptian

---

[12] *Vit. Pyth.* 13, 8–11; cf. 89, 7–22.
[13] *Vit. Pyth.* 85, 14–18; cf. *Comm.* 66, 21–67, 2. Iamblichus had Pythagoras' own testimony, so he thought, to the debt to Orphism: cf. Thesleff (1965), 164 = Iamblichus, *Vit. Pyth.* 82, 12–83, 5.
[14] *De myst.* 2, 9–3, 5 (reading ἱερογραμματέων with Parthey; cf. 260, 11). Cf. Proclus, *In Tim.* I 386, 8–12 = Dillon (1973), 140, 312–13.
[15] Cf. *De myst.* 1, 5–3, 5.

theology and indeed as in agreement with it, despite some differences.[16] Even within ancient Egyptian sacred literature there are
divergencies (260, 10–261, 8), but Iamblichus does not consider this a
threat to the integrity of Egyptian theology. An all-too-brief indication
is given of how diversity and unity, not only within Egyptian theology,
but also between Egyptian and Chaldaean theology could be reconciled:

This is true of all of the sciences conveyed to men by the gods. As they
advance in time, they are often mixed in with much that is mortal, losing the
divine character (ἦθος) of the knowledge. (277, 13–18)

This idea, intended to explain the contradictions Porphyry found in
astrology, suggests that the divinely revealed knowledge mediated by
Egyptians, Chaldaeans, their pupils Pythagoras, Plato . . ., acquires
diversity and even impurity in the course of its historical tradition.

It is not certain that this view of the relations between Egyptian,
Chaldaean, Pythagorean, and Platonic philosophy is precisely that
presupposed either by *On Pythagoreanism* or by the *Chaldaean Theology*.
Concerning the latter work, all that can be said on the subject is that
Iamblichus thought it suitable to introduce Pythagorean and Platonic
ideas in his interpretation of the 'Chaldaean Oracles'.

In conclusion, it is safe to say that for the Iamblichus of *On
Mysteries*, a Platonic, Egyptian, or Chaldaean *Theology* could very suitably be read as a sequel to *On Pythagoreanism*. It is likely that such
would have been his view also in his *Chaldaean Theology* and in *On
Pythagoreanism*. In *On Pythagoreanism* itself he refers to a sequel, his
work *On God*, which may indeed have been a 'Pythagorean Theology',
but not for all that very different from what he there understood to be
the theology of Plato, of the Egyptians, and of the Chaldaeans.

(ii) In the preceding pages I have argued that *On Pythagoreanism* is
related to certain of Iamblichus' other works, taking my cue from
indications given in *On Pythagoreanism* itself: a specific reference to a
sequel, the work *On God*; and the system of philosophy presented in
On Pythagoreanism as susceptible of fulfilment also by Iamblichus'
other theological works. In what follows I shall approach the matter
from another angle. The presence of a Pythagoreanizing programme
in what remains of Iamblichus' other works will be brought out, so as
to show that his interest in it extended well beyond the composition of
a work specifically devoted to it. I shall discuss what can be learnt in

---

[16] *De myst.* 5, 8–11 (agreement implied); 249, 3 ff. (differences).

particular about Iamblichus' lost commentaries on Plato and Aristotle. It will soon emerge that a tendency to Pythagoreanize is a very significant feature of these commentaries. I shall confine myself to presenting here some major aspects, rather than all elements, of this large subject.[17] It must also be noted that most of the available evidence has to do with Iamblichus' commentaries on Aristotle's *Categories* and on Plato's *Timaeus*. His other commentaries are, in comparison with these, poorly represented in the reports on Iamblichus to be found in later Neoplatonic authors.

Simplicius makes extensive use of Iamblichus' *Commentary on the Categories* in his own commentary on the Aristotelian text. He also provides a general description of Iamblichus' work: Iamblichus added in various ways to Porphyry's commentary, often including texts taken from a logical work attributed to the Pythagorean Archytas. Not only did Iamblichus believe—incorrectly—the Archytas text to be authentic, but he thought that Aristotle was inspired by the Pythagorean. The harmony of Archytas and Aristotle was to be shown, reflecting the complete indebtedness of Aristotelian to 'Archytas'' logic. Where—and it was seldom—Archytas and Aristotle differed, such differences had to be explained.[18] Simplicius gives an example of this:

It seems, Iamblichus says, that the Aristotelian position has been turned away (perverted, παρατετράφθαι) from Pythagorean teaching. The reason is that the moderns do not have the same view of number and of change as do the ancients, but the former think these are accidents, supervening from outside (ἔξωθεν ἐπείσακτα) whereas the latter see them as essential (οὐσιώδη).[19]

This conception of a perverting among the moderns (Aristotle) of the ancient tradition (Pythagoras) from which they derive their knowledge is similar to the idea found above in *On Mysteries* of a divine revelation of knowledge to man which is gradually corrupted with the progress of time. What it entails here is using 'Pythagorean' logic, the (Pseudo-) Archytas, as a standard or guide for the assessment of Aristotle's

---

[17] Cf. Larsen (1972), chs. V–VI, for a review of the evidence relating to the commentaries of Iamblichus.

[18] Iamblichus, *In cat.* fr. 2 (= Simplicius, *In cat.* 2, 9–25). Iamblichus quotes Archytas in *In cat.* frs. 21, 22, 26, 36, 78, 89, 90, 96, 106, 107, 108, 110, 112. Cf. Larsen (1972), I 233–301. For the date of the (Pseudo-) Archytas and its use of Aristotle's *Categories*, cf. Szlezák (1972), 14–19, who edits the text and indicates that its authenticity was not accepted by all in the fourth century.

[19] Iamblichus, *In cat.* fr. 109.

Categories.[20] Where both texts agree, Aristotle is Pythagorean and right; where Aristotle diverges, he is perverting the ancient tradition. In the case, for example, of the problem of time, this curious retreat to the supposed sources of Aristotle becomes in fact a means of advancing beyond Aristotle in the direction of a theory a good deal more complicated than that found either in Aristotle or in Pseudo-Pythagorean texts.[21]

The reconstruction of Books V and VI of *On Pythagoreanism* suggests that Iamblichus' attitude there to Aristotelian physics and ethics was similar to his view of Aristotelian logic in his *Commentary on the Categories*. He could follow Aristotle's physical and ethical treatises, and yet correct them and substitute Pythagorean materials where appropriate, on the assumption that those treatises were fundamentally Pythagorean in inspiration, if sometimes corrupted or perverted in relation to their source.[22]

Turning to the evidence concerning Iamblichus' commentaries on Plato, we find Pythagoreanism important both in Iamblichus' theories about the Platonic corpus and its exegesis, and in his interpretation of individual dialogues. It is a well-established fact that Iamblichus fixed the canon of Platonic dialogues which became 'for more than two centuries the standard curriculum in the Platonic schools'.[23] This canon consisted of two cycles, the first including ten dialogues dealing successively with ethical, logical, physical, and theological subjects, the second comprising two dialogues, the *Timaeus* and *Parmenides*, which sum up the first ten dialogues and cover respectively physics and theology.[24] This arrangement is hardly arbitrary. Its closest analogue is mathematical: the decad that comprises all numbers, and the first two numbers, the monad and dyad, that pre-contain and produce all other numbers. Porphyry, it might be recalled, had also organized Plotinus' treatises in his edition along numerical lines, dividing them into six sets of nine ('Enneads').

The first dialogue in the first cycle, the *Alcibiades*, was regarded by

---

[20] In Iamblichus' *In cat.* Archytas is set up as a 'guide' (fr. 106, 2 ἡγεμόνα προ-ίσταται), just as Pythagoras is in *On Pythagoreanism* (*Vit. Pyth.* 6, 2–3 ἡγεμόνα ... προστησόμεθα) and Hermes in *On Mysteries* (1, 6–8 ὁ τῶν λόγων ἡγεμών...ὁ...προ-εστηκώς).

[21] Cf. above, p. 68. Much could also be said about Iamblichus' use of specific Pythagorean principles in the interpretation of Aristotle's *Categories*; cf. Iamblichus, *In cat.* frs. 33, 37, 53, 56, 58.

[22] Cf. Syrianus, *In met.* 192, 15–27.

[23] Westerink, in *Anon. Prol. Plat.* xxxvii.

[24] Cf. *Anon. Prol. Plat.* xxxvii–xl; Festugière (1969).

Iamblichus as containing implicitly all that would emerge in the following dialogues, i.e. logic, ethics, physics, and theology. At least, this is Proclus' understanding of why Iamblichus gave the *Alcibiades* first place in the cycle. Proclus says:

And indeed it seems to me that it is for this reason that the divine Iamblichus allotted it the first place among the ten dialogues in which he believes the whole philosophy of Plato to be contained, their entire subsequent development being pre-contained as it were in seminal form in this dialogue.[25]

The metaphor of a seed as 'pre-containing' what will evolve from it is common enough in Neoplatonic philosophy. It should be noted, however, that the subject here is the first member of a series of ten, i.e. a monad, and that the metaphor of the seed appears in Nicomachus and Iamblichus as a way of describing how the monad pre-contains the other numbers of the decad that flow out from it.[26] This provides further evidence of the mathematical conception underlying Iamblichus' canon of Platonic dialogues. For in the first cycle of this canon Iamblichus compared the relation between the first and the following dialogues to the relation between monad and the rest of the decad.

One might also note that in terms of the system of philosophy of *On Pythagoreanism* there is one important gap in the ascending sequence of sciences covered by both cycles of Platonic dialogues, a gap coming between physics and theology. Mathematics, namely, is missing, i.e. the pivotal stage covered in *On Pythagoreanism*.

Some of the exegetical principles Iamblichus applied in interpreting Plato are regarded by him as Pythagorean. One of these consists in explaining the absence of certain matters in a text in terms of the need to introduce various subjects in appropriate contexts, so that, for example, more profound ideas should be presented in higher, more technical treatments. This principle is applied in *On Pythagoreanism*, as we have seen, and is used by Iamblichus in interpreting Plato's *Timaeus*:

... he has allotted deeper investigation of these matters to more suitable occasions; for this was the custom not only of Plato but before Plato of the Pythagoreans, which indeed was something that Aristotle particularly sought, to deal with the problems of philosophy in essays devoted each to a special subject.[27]

---

[25] Iamblichus, *In Alc.* fr. 1 (transl. Dillon, slightly modified).

[26] Cf. Nicomachus, *Intro. arith.* 113, 2–6; Iamblichus, *In Nic.* 11, 11–17; 81, 23–4, and especially 10, 12–13; Hermias, *In Phaedr.* 141, 16–17; Syrianus, *In met.* 3, 22–3.

[27] Iamblichus, *In Tim.* fr. 66 (transl. Dillon). Cf. Dillon's argument for this passage as Iamblichean, (1973), 350–1.

A related Pythagorean principle is applied by Iamblichus as a method of exegesis in interpreting the opening part of Plato's *Timaeus*:

Others ⟨i.e. Iamblichus⟩ consider that it ⟨i.e. the recapitulation of the *Republic*⟩ has been placed before the whole physics as an image of the organization of the universe. For it was the custom of the Pythagoreans to place before scientific teaching the revealing of the subjects under enquiry through similitudes and images, and after this to introduce the secret revelation of the same subjects through symbols . . .[28]

The Pythagorean method of teaching through images and symbols is described in *On Pythagoreanism*.[29]

The recourse to Pythagorean practices as providing exegetical principles was particularly suitable in relation to Plato's *Timaeus*, since it seems that in his *Commentary on the Timaeus* Iamblichus regarded Timaeus' discourse as Pythagorean:

One should put it this way, then, that Timaeus, being a Pythagorean, follows Pythagorean principles (ἀρχαῖς). And these in turn are Orphic principles . . . this Pythagoras himself states.[30]

A rapprochement between Pythagoras and Orpheus has already been found above in *On Pythagoreanism*. Iamblichus' approach to Timaeus' discourse also suggests that in his commentary he made use of Pythagorean mathematical principles in the interpretation of Timaeus' physics, much as he had emphasized mathematical principles in his Pythagoreanizing of Aristotle's physics in *On Pythagoreanism* V. The evidence indeed shows that Iamblichus referred to the relations between the monad and the numbers flowing from it in explaining the relations in the *Timaeus* between the 'Model Living Being (τὸ αὐτοζῷον)' and other living beings (fr. 43), between transcendent soul and other souls (frs. 50, 54), and between the gods (fr. 77). Nor is it unexpected that when he came to Timaeus' account of the constitution of soul through various numbers, Iamblichus drew attention to the special properties (ἰδιώματα) of the numbers concerned, those properties paradigmatic and symbolic of the structure and dynamic of physical and of transcendent reality.[31]

---

[28] Iamblichus, *In Tim.* fr. 5 (transl. Dillon, slightly modified).
[29] Dillon ad loc. refers to *Vit. Pyth.* 37, 4–7; 59, 17–60, 1; cf. also *Pr.* 104, 26 ff.
[30] Iamblichus, *In Tim.* fr. 74 (transl. Dillon); cf. above, n. 13, and Dillon's commentary, (1973), 363–4.
[31] Iamblichus, *In Tim.* fr. 53; cf. also fr. 48. In some brilliant pages Harder (1926), xvi–xvii, argues that Iamblichus used a text (falsely) attributed to the Pythagorean Timaeus

The Pythagoreanizing tendencies of Iamblichus' commentaries on Aristotle and Plato deserve a larger treatment than that provided here.[32] However, the brief review of the subject that I have proposed is adequate, I believe, for the purpose here pursued, namely to show that Iamblichus' interest in Pythagoreanism was not limited merely to composing a work on the subject. In his *Commentary on the Categories* he considered Aristotle's text to be a somewhat corrupt version of Pythagorean theory. (*On Pythagoreanism* V and VI imply a similar attitude to Aristotle's physics and ethics.) Not enough is known of Iamblichus' commentaries on other works of Aristotle to determine if such an approach was adopted there too. In discussing Plato's dialogues Iamblichus resorted to Pythagorean ideas (as he understood them) to explain his canon of Platonic dialogues and to produce exegetical methods to be applied to it. He regarded the *Timaeus* as a physics based on Pythagorean principles. And when his reader moved up the scale of dialogues, reaching the highest level, the theological dialogues (*Philebus* in the first cycle, *Parmenides* in the second cycle)— equivalent to the highest level of Pythagorean philosophy according to *On Pythagoreanism*—there too he would read texts which were, if we follow Iamblichus' interpretation of Plato in *On Pythagoreanism*, Pythagorean in inspiration.

It has been noted above that Iamblichus explicitly connects *On Pythagoreanism* with his work *On God* (*Gods?*). In view of his understanding of the relations between Pythagoreanism, Plato, the Egyptians, and Chaldaeans, *On Pythagoreanism* is also implicitly connected with his works on Platonic, Egyptian, and Chaldaean theology in so far as they constitute appropriate sequels to it. The general position in *On Pythagoreanism* regarding the relations between Pythagoras, Plato, and Aristotle is also found in, and governs, his commentaries on (at least some of) the works of Plato and Aristotle. Both Plato and Aristotle owe their philosophy to Pythagoras. When Aristotle diverges, he corrupts the truth in its tradition among men. This latter idea appears in a larger context in *On Mysteries*, where knowledge is regarded as a divine revelation, mediated by priests, mages, etc., and gradually corrupted with time. From this point of view the Greek philosophical tradition derived from Pythagoras appears as a relatively recent (thus

of Locri in his *Commentary on the Timaeus*, in the way that he used the Pseudo-Archytas in his *Commentary on the Categories*.

[32] Cf. also Iamblichus, *In Philebum* (a 'theological' dialogue) fr. 3, where Iamblichus follows 'Pythagoras' in his exegesis of a passage. Cf. Praechter (1910), 191–3 with 200 n. 2.

corrupted) stage. Could this also be the ultimate point of view presupposed in *On Pythagoreanism*? The same theory of a divine revelation of knowledge to man is found there, the same recourse to the ancients (in Greek philosophy). The connections with Egyptian and Chaldaean teachers are made. But the evidence goes no further. Certainly the historical thesis of *On Mysteries* was not confined to that work. It is found again in what survives of one of Iamblichus' more technical philosophical treatises, *On the Soul*, where the tradition of Greek philosophy and especially its best representatives, Plato and the Pythagoreans, are measured (to their disadvantage) against a more venerable authority, the 'ancients', meaning apparently the Egyptians and Chaldaeans.[33]

3. IAMBLICHEAN PYTHAGOREANISM AND ITS PREDECESSORS

In the final section of this chapter I would like to compare Iamblichus' Pythagoreanizing tendencies with those of his predecessors, notably the philosophers of the second and third centuries AD discussed above in Chapter 1. If Iamblichus' Pythagoreanism is to be assessed correctly, it must be viewed not only within the context of his other work, but also in its relations—of debts and of difference—with its predecessors. Since the fragmentary nature of the evidence concerning most of Iamblichus' work does not permit of asserting without reserve that his understanding of the place of Pythagoras in the history of Greek philosophy and, more broadly, in the tradition of knowledge among men, remained the same in each of his works,[34] it will be prudent to consider separately various aspects of Pythagoreanism appearing in his different works.

The conception in *On Mysteries* (also assumed to some degree in *On the Soul*) of Greek philosophy as a relatively modern, somewhat degraded version of the teachings of ancient Egyptians and Chaldaeans (themselves divinely inspired) appears to have been central to

---

[33] Cf. Iamblichus, *De an.*, in Stobaeus, *Anth.* I 366, 5–11; 384, 27–28 (with Festugière's note, [1950–4], III 236 n. 3); especially 454, 25–458, 21 (with Festugière's notes, 240–8, 263). More and less accurate (and pure) forms of Platonism/Pythagoreanism are distinguished at 364, 6; 382, 11; 454, 27, corresponding sometimes (not always) to earlier and more recent times: cf. 365, 5–366, 11. Cf. Larsen's discussion (1972), I 197 ff., of the *De an.*

[34] However, the frequent connections observed above, not only in sect. 2 of this chapter, but also in Ch. 3, suggest considerable continuity.

many of Porphyry's writings. This was not of course a new idea. As has been pointed out, it was a popular notion since the time of Plato and Aristotle. However, by writing extensively about the Egyptians, Chaldaeans, Persians, as well as about ancient Greek sages, Porphyry gave to this non-philosophical literature an important place in the reading-lists of later Greek philosophy. Plato and Aristotle became subordinate figures, even if, in fact, they provided the system in terms of which the more ancient literature was understood.

If Iamblichus' immediate debt to Porphyry in this respect is evident, his position also seems in some aspects somewhat different. He appears more committed to Porphyry's view than Porphyry himself was. At least, this is the case in regard to Porphyry's *Letter to Anebo* which, although expecting to find the answers to Greek philosophical questions in Egyptian religion, nevertheless formulates philosophical criticisms of certain religious practices. In *On Mysteries*, however, Iamblichus is quite radical in his insistence that all aspects of Egyptian religion must be accepted, though through an interpretation of them, it must be said, that is highly philosophical.

A comparison of Porphyry and Iamblichus on this subject also suggests that Iamblichus was more systematic in the subordination of Greek philosophy to ancient revelation. This subordination expresses itself in the conception of a historical tradition of knowledge among men which is also a gradual corruption of this knowledge. In view of Porphyry's historical erudition one can certainly suppose that such a conception may have been inspired by him. But the emphasis in Iamblichus on a degradation of truth coming with its expression in time reminds one rather of the degradation that had been traced already by Numenius on a smaller scale in his history of Plato's Academy.

If one turns from the universal tradition of knowledge to its expression among the Greeks, one can also observe a more committed and systematic approach in Iamblichus' commentaries on the *Categories* and on the *Timaeus*, as well as in *On Pythagoreanism*, with regard to the relations between Pythagoras, Plato, and Aristotle. Certainly Porphyry tended to Pythagoreanize Platonism and Platonists (Plotinus), and also brought Aristotle into the Neoplatonic curriculum. But in the evidence concerning him there is no equivalent to Iamblichus' rigorous reduction of all in Plato and all that he thought good in Aristotle to Pythagoreanism. Such a reduction was greatly facilitated by the availability of supposedly Pythagorean works that Iamblichus took to prove the dependence of Plato and Aristotle on Pythagoreanism, although in fact they were cribbed from Plato and Aristotle.[35] In this way Pythagoras assumes a dominant role in Greek philosophy such as he does not appear to have in Porphyry. And as the Egyptians and Chaldaeans are original revelatory sources for all mankind, so Pythagoras is for Greek philosophy. Here again, I believe, we must refer to Numenius, to his rigorous reduction of 'true', 'pure' Platonism (as contrasted with its corrupted, i.e. materialized, forms) to Pythagoreanism. However Aristotle, in Numenius, was not, as far as we know, projected backwards on to Pythagoras (and thus integrated) in the way that he is in Iamblichus.

When it comes to the description of what actually constitutes 'Pythagorean philosophy', Iamblichus, in *On Pythagoreanism*, can be said to follow the lead of Nicomachus. He adopts Nicomachus' restriction of Pythagorean philosophy to the most 'scientific' form of knowledge, namely that corresponding to immaterial and unchanging reality. He exploits Nicomachus' notion that each number has specific properties (ἰδιώματα) in developing mathematical paradigms for physics and ethics. Such analogies to physics and ethics are also inspired by Nicomachus, as is the justification for the analogy to physics, namely the idea that the material world is structured according to the properties of numbers. The assimilations that Nicomachus proposed between numbers and deities were also taken up (but with some important changes that will be noted below) by Iamblichus. Indeed it can be said that Nicomachus' *Introduction to Arithmetic* and *Theologoumena arithmeticae* are the most important source of inspiration for *On Pythagoreanism* as a whole.

At the same time, however, there are fundamental differences between Nicomachus and Iamblichus. In general, Iamblichus' view of the system of philosophy and of the structure of reality is much more complicated, reflecting in fact the thought, not of a second century Platonist, but of Porphyry's most important and original pupil. The science of pure immaterial numbers is by no means the highest, as it appears to be in Nicomachus. Above the purely mathematical level are 'intellectual', 'intelligible', and 'divine' orders, all transcended by an ultimate principle, 'the One'. Mathematics thus is returned from the dominant position it seems to have in Nicomachus to an intermediary position such as is assigned to it

---

[35] On Iamblichus' unprecedented activity in resurrecting *Pseudo-Pythagorica* cf. Harder (1926), xv ff.

in Plato's *Republic*.[36] As a consequence Iamblichus is aware of the limits to an 'arithmetical theology': such a theology is based on analogy inferior to a higher, more commensurate grasp of the divine unities that transcend being.

If Iamblichus is closer to Nicomachus in his mathematical physics and ethics, he also shows considerable independence. He separates off into separate volumes the analogies to physics, ethics, and theology, which are treated together in Nicomachus' *Theologoumena*. He develops these analogies far beyond anything in Nicomachus by working them out in relation to Aristotle's physics and ethics. In theology, Iamblichus' approach in *On Pythagoreanism* VII may have come nearer to Nicomachus', yet the metaphysical system guiding this approach was considerably more complicated than that to be found in Nicomachus.

The impression of eclecticism that such comparisons between Iamblichus and his predecessors may convey must be corrected by emphasis on the fact that a comprehensiveness and systematic rigour are found in Iamblichus' conception of the nature of Greek philosophy that are not found in his predecessors. Not only is the reduction, in *On Pythagoreanism* and in some of the commentaries on Plato and Aristotle, of Greek philosophy to Pythagoreanism more comprehensive than it is in Numenius, more radical than it is in Porphyry, but its subordination, in *On Mysteries* and *On The Soul*, to an ancient revelation is more emphatic than in Porphyry. And if Iamblichus is indebted to Nicomachus in his account of what 'Pythagorean' philosophy actually consists of, he nevertheless transformed Nicomachus' Pythagoreanism so that it could express the much more developed system of philosophy and of reality of a successor to Plotinus and to Porphyry. That system was in turn transformed by the fact that it was now seen as 'Pythagorean'. For if mathematics was neither the only nor the dominant science, it nevertheless provided the concepts and theories in terms of which the objects of other sciences could be approached. Mathematical terms and concepts are of course by no means uncommon in the Platonic tradition. But the systematic mathematization which is so striking a feature of later Greek Neoplatonism, the pervasiveness of concepts of monad, dyad, triad, etc., is surely the consequence of Iamblichus' ambitious programme to

---

[36] Cf. *Comm.* 87, 17–88, 2, where Iamblichus insists, against the opinion of 'many of the more recent Pythagoreans', that mathematicals are neither the only nor the highest principles of reality and of science.

Pythagoreanize Platonic philosophy. There had been, of course, earlier attempts by Platonists to revive Pythagoreanism—we have considered the examples of Numenius and Nicomachus—but Iamblichus' attempt was certainly the most elaborate and the most influential.[37] In the following chapters the extent of this influence will be examined in particular in the cases of two later Neoplatonic philosophers, Syrianus and Proclus.

[37] In the Conclusion I shall suggest some hypotheses concerning why Iamblichus sought to revive Pythagoreanism.

PART II

Iamblichean Pythagoreanism in the Athenian School

5

Hierocles

IAMBLICHUS died sometime between 320 and 326, having attracted a large following as master of a flourishing philosophical school in Syria.[1] Of his pupils, only Dexippus and Theodorus of Asine are represented in a significant way in the surviving evidence.[2] Of more importance is the influence Iamblichus would exert after his death on a philosophical school that emerged at Athens in the early 400s, the school of Plutarch of Athens, Syrianus, and Proclus. In Part II of this book I examine in particular the impact Iamblichus' Pythagoreanizing programme may have had on the Athenian school. I hope thus to reach an answer to the question as to the extent to which this programme, in reducing Plato and Aristotle to Pythagoras and in approaching in consequence the philosophical sciences along mathematical lines, gave new direction to the development of later Greek philosophy.

Syrianus had, as I shall show, an intimate knowledge of Iamblichus' work *On Pythagoreanism*: it inspired in particular the conception of true, i.e. 'Pythagorean' philosophy adopted in his *Commentary on Aristotle's Metaphysics*. It will be shown also that Proclus was familiar with *On Pythagoreanism* and used it as a source in his own work. Thus *On Pythagoreanism* constitutes a concrete link between Iamblichus and the first influential members of the Athenian school, a specific text in terms of which the degree of his influence on that school can be assessed in a detailed way.

The analysis will be guided by the two major questions discussed in Part I, namely (i) what is the place of Pythagoras in the history of Greek philosophy? (ii) What is the role of mathematics in philosophy? In looking at the positions taken by Syrianus and Proclus on these issues, I hope to indicate not only the ways in which they are inspired by Iamblichus, but also the ways in which they alter the programme formulated in *On Pythagoreanism*. Iamblichus' treatise will serve thus not only as an historical background for understanding certain ideas in Syrianus and Proclus, but also as a gauge against which the development of their own philosophical positions can be measured.

[1] Cf. Dillon (1973), 6, 11–14.   [2] Cf. P. Hadot (1974); Deuse (1973).

I. THE INTRODUCTION OF IAMBLICHEAN PHILOSOPHY
AT ATHENS IN THE FOURTH CENTURY

Proclus, looking at his intellectual genealogy, saw himself as part of a
succession going back from his teacher at Athens, Syrianus, to
Syrianus' own master Plutarch of Athens (died 431/2) and from
Plutarch back to Iamblichus.[3] If the succession leading from Plutarch
to Proclus is clear enough (indeed as a young man Proclus had joined
Plutarch's school a few years before Plutarch died and was succeeded
by Syrianus), the link between Plutarch and Iamblichus is less evident.
Separated from Iamblichus by more than one generation, Plutarch, we
must suppose, was introduced to Iamblichean philosophy by followers
of Iamblichus. There are indeed good indications that by the end of
the fourth century Iamblichean philosophy had become part of the
intellectual life of Athens. As the evidence for this has already been
carefully presented and discussed,[4] I need do no more than summarize the more important points.

In the middle and late part of the fourth century a certain Priscus,
philosopher and pupil of Aidesius (himself a disciple of Iamblichus),
was resident in Athens. It was to him that the Emperor Julian turned in
order to obtain a copy of Iamblichus' *Commentary on the Chaldaean
Oracles*. This Iamblichean presence in Athens was strengthened
towards the end of the century when another Iamblichus settled there.
Named after the philosopher, he was grandson to Sopatros, Iamblichus' successor in the school in Syria. The relation between
'Iamblichus II' and Iamblichus was not merely one of name and
family. Libanius places 'Iamblichus II' under the tutelage of Pythagoras, Plato, and Aristotle (as well as that of Iamblichus) and he is com-
memorated as having contributed with his wisdom, as well as with his
generosity, to Athens in an inscription of *c.*400.

There was therefore ample opportunity at Athens for Proclus'
philosophical 'grandfather' to come in contact with Iamblichus' ideas.
So little, however, is known about Plutarch that not much more can be
said about his contacts with Iamblichean philosophy than that he had
pupils, namely Hierocles and Syrianus, who adopted this philosophy
and attributed this to his direction.[5] The scarce evidence concerning

---

[3] Cf. Procl. *In Parm.* 1058, 21–2; *Theol. Plat.* IV 70, 12–13, with Saffrey and Westerink's
note 3 (168).   [4] By Saffrey and Westerink, in Proclus, *Theol. Plat.* I xxxv–xlviii.
[5] Cf. Hierocles in Photius, *Bibl.* III 129–30, 173 a; for Syrianus, cf. below, Ch. 6.

Plutarch has even given some scholars the impression that Plutarch broke on certain issues with the Iamblichean tradition. This flies in the face, however, of the professed debts of Plutarch's Iamblichean pupils to their teacher and argues at best for the inadequacy of our information on Plutarch.[6] We are on safer ground, when it comes to the analysis of specific subjects, if we turn to those pupils of Plutarch whose work has in part at least survived.

Among Plutarch's pupils, Hierocles and Syrianus have already been mentioned as well as Proclus, who joined the Athenian school shortly before Plutarch's death. Proclus was certainly younger than Syrianus and probably also Hierocles' junior. But what little is known of Hierocles' life[7]—that he studied with Plutarch, to whom he claimed philosophical allegiance, and taught Platonic philosophy in Alexandria—is not enough to determine if he was Syrianus' senior, contemporary, or junior. For reasons of exposition I shall discuss Hierocles first, moving then to Syrianus, whose work is more immediately relevant to an examination of Proclus. If Hierocles' writings are contemporary with or later than Syrianus' *Commentary on the Metaphysics*, they do not constitute the earliest evidence of the influence of Iamblichean 'Pythagoreanism' on the Athenian school. If, however, they are earlier than Syrianus' *Commentary* they can indeed be claimed as providing the first signs of this influence. These signs may be found in the remarkable theory of the history of philosophy presented in Hierocles' work *On Providence* and in the use made of Pythagoreanism in Hierocles' *Commentary on the* (pseudo-Pythagorean) *Golden Verses*.

2. HIEROCLES ON THE HISTORY OF PHILOSOPHY

The interest of Hierocles' views on the history of philosophy in *On Providence* has recently been emphasized and their Iamblichean origin demonstrated.[8] There are some aspects, however, which may be

[6] Cf. Saffrey and Westerink in Proclus, *Theol. Plat.* I, lxxxiv–lxxxviii; Blumenthal (1975); I. Hadot (1978), 74.
[7] Cf. I. Hadot (1978), 17–20; Aujoulat (1976).
[8] I. Hadot (1978), 67–76, and (1979), who has effectively disproved Praechter's theory that Hierocles represents a 'primitive' Alexandrian (i.e. pre-Plotinian) Christian-type philosophy, a theory recently adopted by Kobusch (1976), on whom cf. Baltes (1978a).

explored further in the light of what has emerged in Part I concerning Iamblichus' treatise *On Pythagoreanism*.

Hierocles' work *On Providence* survives in the form of a two-part *précis* given by the Patriarch Photius in his *Biblioteca* (*cod.* 214, 251). Photius emphasizes in his account Hierocles' desire to show a harmony between the views of Plato and Aristotle on the subjects of providence, fate, and free will. That the impression conveyed by Photius here is unbalanced can be seen from his own indications about the contents of *On Providence* (*cod.* 214, 173 a), according to which the discussion of Aristotle was a subordinate part of a much larger scheme.[9] Only after having presented and defended Plato's views and having shown their harmony with the 'Chaldaean Oracles', Orpheus, Homer, 'and all those others who distinguished themselves before Plato's epiphany (ἐπιφάνεια)', does Hierocles come to a survey of Aristotle's views. Certain thinkers, through contentiousness or ignorance, we are told, attempted to introduce disharmony between the views of Aristotle and Plato, but the harmony was restored by Plotinus' teacher Ammonius Saccas, who purified philosophy and whose lead was followed by a continuous succession of philosophers going from Plotinus through Porphyry and Iamblichus to Hierocles' master, Plutarch of Athens.[10]

If we compare this account with the history of philosophy as understood by Iamblichus, the following differences might be noted. Even if allowance is made for the undue emphasis Photius gives to the theme of the harmony between Plato and Aristotle, it appears that Hierocles' treatment of this theme diverges from that in Iamblichus. Hierocles does not seem to agree with the Iamblichean view that Aristotle was sometimes right (when he was faithful to Pythagorean–Platonic philosophy) and sometimes wrong (when he perverted the truth, primarily as regards transcendent being). Hierocles believes rather that later thinkers falsified Plato's and Aristotle's works so as to bring Aristotle into disagreement with Plato.[11] Hierocles therefore shifts the blame for Aristotle's differences with Plato from Aristotle himself to later thinkers. The theory of falsification (which we have already met above (p. 11) in connection with the protest that some attempted to discredit Pythagoreanism by falsifying 'Pythagorean' writings) implies a more positive view of Aristotle than that taken by Iamblichus. Yet the

---

[9] The point is made by Elter (1910), 180–3, 198.
[10] Photius, *Bibl.* III 125–30, 171 b–173 a, with I. Hadot, loc. cit.
[11] Photius, *Bibl.* VII 191, 461 a.

kind of harmony that Hierocles seeks to promote is not essentially different than that assumed by Iamblichus: if Aristotle is brought into agreement with Plato, it is of course on Platonic terms.[12]

The role given to Plotinus' teacher Ammonius is another novel element in Hierocles' account. Ammonius emerges as having accomplished what had been essentially Numenius' mission: the restoral of unanimity (ὁμοδοξία) to Platonism through the purification of a contentious and degraded tradition.[13] It looks as if a direct rebuttal of Numenius' pretensions is intended; his mission is taken over and, in being attributed to Ammonius, is placed firmly in the tradition going from Plotinus, through Porphyry and Iamblichus, to Plutarch. There is no trace of this to be found in what survives of Iamblichus' work, but his hostility (and debt) to Numenius would certainly have disposed him to take such a position. However, another source has been proposed both for this treatment of Ammonius and for the theme of the harmony between Plato and Aristotle: Porphyry.[14]

Whatever the origin of these novel aspects in Hierocles, it is clear that he (or his immediate source) made them part of a broader conspectus of the history of philosophy that recalls most of all Iamblichus' views.[15] The rigorous reduction of all Greek philosophy to one true philosophy (Platonism) and the perversions thereof is Iamblichean in spirit, as is the insistence on a systematic harmonization of Platonism with ancient Greek and barbarian wisdom (such as the 'Chaldaean Oracles'). Furthermore Hierocles' interpretation of true philosophy as a revelation is also that of Iamblichus: Plato intervenes in human history as an 'epiphany', and Ammonius, the purifier of philosophy, is instructed by the divine (θεοδίδακτος).[16] Is this revelation to be understood, as it is in Iamblichus, as a soteriological mission undertaken by certain superior souls who are interpreted as members of the divine retinue, or 'choir', of Plato's *Phaedrus*? Photius' *précis* is of little help here, although he does give some indications that this was indeed Hierocles' view.[17] However, the *Commentary on the Golden Verses* makes it very clear, as will be seen shortly, that Hierocles' understanding of the revelatory nature of philosophy was Iamblichean.

[12] Cf. also below, pp. 120–4 (on Syrianus' harmonization of Plato and Aristotle).
[13] Cf. also Photius, *Bibl.* VII 191, 461 a: ἀστασίαστον τὴν φιλοσοφίαν παραδέδωκε.
[14] Cf. Dörrie (1955), 343–7; I. Hadot (1978), 75.
[15] Cf. I. Hadot (1978), 67–76.
[16] Photius, *Bibl.* III 126, 172 a; VII 191, 461 a.
[17] Cf. Photius, *Bibl.* III 126, 172 a 3: χορός (cf. *Phaedr.* 250 b c); VII 191, 461 a 33: ἐνθουσιάσας (cf. *Phaedr.* 249 d e).

There is one singular absence in the history of philosophy of Hierocles' *On Providence* as reported by Photius: Pythagoras. One might infer from Photius' silence that Pythagoras was at most of secondary importance to Hierocles. It could also be argued that Pythagoras is the victim of a serious omission in Photius' summary, surviving only in the rushed and generalized allusion in the phrase (quoted above): 'and all those others who distinguished themselves before Plato's epiphany'. Certainly Hierocles' only surviving work, the *Commentary on the Golden Verses*, argues strongly for the importance of Pythagoras, and the evidence of the *Commentary* is weightier than what conjectural inferences may be drawn from the Patriarch's report.

3. PYTHAGOREANISM IN HIEROCLES' *COMMENTARY ON THE GOLDEN VERSES*

The Pythagorean *Golden Verses* are used by Iamblichus in the introductory part of *On Pythagoreanism* (*Protrepticus*, ch. 3). Still available also are Arabic versions of two commentaries on the *Golden Verses*, one attributed to Iamblichus, the other to Proclus. Although there are good reasons for supposing that the Arabic texts derive from Greek Neoplatonic originals, the attributions to Iamblichus and Proclus present some problems. I propose therefore to discuss the Arabic texts in Appendix II below, treating them as providing further indications of Pythagoreanizing tendencies in Neoplatonic philosophy rather than as documents on the basis of which the history of such tendencies may be developed. At any rate the two Arabic texts, like Iamblichus' *On Pythagoreanism*, use the *Golden Verses* as an introductory work, providing the beginner with a primarily ethical initiation to philosophy. The fullest extant version of such a use of the *Golden Verses*, however, is Hierocles' *Commentary*.

Hierocles makes his intentions very clear in the prologue of his *Commentary*. The *Golden Verses*, he claims, contain the general and basic principles of all philosophy: they put the beginner in philosophy on the road to his goal, assimilation to god, through the cultivation of virtue and truth; this they achieve in so far as they provide the rules and starting-points necessary for moving towards the goal (5, 1–6, 2). Such is the work to which Hierocles will put the *Golden Verses* in his *Commentary*. The *Commentary* is thus intended to provide an elementary initiation to philosophy based on Pythagorean principles and aiming beyond itself towards a Pythagorean goal (cf. 7, 17–18), assimilation to god.[18] The *Commentary* is pitched therefore at the same level and has the same purpose as the first two books of Iamblichus' *On Pythagoreanism*. Mixing Pythagorean doctrines with moral platitudes drawn from other sources, the *Commentary* also exhibits the eclectic approach characteristic of Iamblichus' 'Pythagorean' introduction to philosophy. More detailed comparisons will be made between Hierocles and Iamblichus below in the course of reviewing some specific aspects of Hierocles' approach in his *Commentary*.[19]

As compared to the impression that is conveyed by Photius' summary of *On Providence*, the prologue of the *Commentary* shows that Hierocles here sees Pythagoreanism as embracing the basic truths of all philosophy, including by implication that of Plato. The relation between Plato and Pythagoras is made explicit later in the *Commentary* (111, 13–14), where Plato appears as the interpreter in the *Phaedrus* (246 a) of Pythagorean doctrine and where Plato's personage Timaeus (cf. *Tim.* 44 c 1) is described as an 'accurate teacher of Pythagorean doctrines' (6, 1–2; cf. 53, 1). Empedocles is also characterized as a Pythagorean, as he had been by Iamblichus.[20]

If then Platonism (indeed all true philosophy) is for Hierocles, as well as for Iamblichus, to be found already in Pythagoreanism, this philosophy is itself to be seen as divine revelation. Traces of this idea have been noted above as occurring in Photius' summaries. The *Commentary on the Golden Verses* is much more informative on the matter and confirms that Hierocles understood this revelatory aspect of philosophy, as did Iamblichus, in connection with an interpretation of Plato's *Phaedrus*. In ch. 4 of the *Commentary* Hierocles explains the Pythagorean notion of 'demonic' men: these are men excelling in virtue and wisdom who are 'demonic' because of their freedom from subjection to the body. Such men are to be honoured, for they 'rank' (συντεταγμένους, 21, 21) with divine beings and are carried around with the divine choir (τῷ θείῳ χορῷ συμφερόμενος, 22, 1). The connection between this imagery, taken from the *Phaedrus*, and the origins of philosophy emerges in the following lines. These demonic

---

[18] Cf. also I. Hadot (1978), 162–4.

[19] For supplements to the inadequate *apparatus fontium* in Köhler's edition of Hierocles cf. Kobusch (1976), Schwyzer (1978).

[20] 98, 10; cf. Iamblichus, *Vit. Pyth.* 60, 1–6; Burkert (1972), 289 (earlier sources for this idea).

men, of superior and uncorrupted insight, are said to have left us, in
divine-like generosity, commands, exhortations (παραγγέλματα),
prescriptive writings containing the elements of virtue and the principles of truth (22, 3–11). The *Golden Verses* are obviously one of those
writings and are described later (122, 1–5) as an 'educational introduction' (παιδευτικὴ στοιχείωσις) left to us and written by men who
had already 'ascended the divine way'. It does not seem that the *Golden
Verses* are the only source of philosophical wisdom conferred on us for
our benefit by those men of superior insight, those participants in the
vision of the *Phaedrus*. And it is likely that their company includes, not
only Pythagoras, but also Plato.[21]

Hierocles' notion that the *Golden Verses* and other 'Pythagorean'
writings are commands or exhortations (παραγγέλματα), containing
basic rules and starting-points in philosophy (κανόνες, ἀφορμαί)
conferred on men for their edification by superior souls, is an important theme in the first two books of Iamblichus' *On Pythagoreanism*.
Pythagoras is represented in the first book as instructing his followers
with exhortations (παραγγέλματα) concerning friendship (*Vita Pyth*.
123, 27 ff.). Ch. 3 of the following book, the *Protrepticus*, is devoted to
the exegesis of moral aphorisms (γνῶμαι) contained in the *Golden
Verses*, and excerpts from Plato are presented in ch. 5 as Pythagorean
moral exhortations (παρακλήσεις). However there are significant
differences between the exegesis of the *Golden Verses* in Iamblichus'
Protrepticus ch. 3 and that in Hierocles' *Commentary*. Iamblichus'
chapter on the *Golden Verses*[22] is a small portion of a survey that
includes a very wide range of supposedly Pythagorean and admittedly
non-Pythagorean materials. Hence he includes only a selection from
the *Golden Verses*, and interpretation is kept to a bare moralizing
minimum. On the other hand Hierocles' use of the *Golden Verses* as the
text of his *Commentary* is more extensive and his exegesis much more
developed.[23] These differences may help explain why Hierocles does
not seem to have used *Protrepticus* ch. 3 as a source for his exegesis,
despite verbal parallels and similarities in the general tendency of
interpretation.[24] If indeed Hierocles is dependent on a source—and

[21] If 40, 15–17 ('divine men') alludes to the *Phaedo* and/or *Phaedrus*. On 'demonic'
men in Hierocles cf. also Aujoulat (1986), 181–8.

[22] They are also used in *Vit. Pyth*. 81, 3 ff.

[23] At 87, 19–20 Hierocles also cites the *Sacred Discourse* attributed to Pythagoras and,
at 114, 14 ff., the Pythagorean σύμβολα explained by Iamblichus in *Pr*. 123, 3 ff. Cf.
Kobusch (1976), 163–8, for Hierocles' use of other Pythagorean materials.

[24] e.g., compare *Pr*. 11, 14–12, 3 with Hierocles, *Comm*. 94, 2–12.

such is the philosophical system presupposed by Hierocles that it does not pre-date Iamblichus[25]—it was in all likelihood more extensive than *Protrepticus* ch. 3.[26]

Hierocles understands 'Pythagorean' philosophy much as did Nicomachus and Iamblichus, as a (Platonic) flight from material reality and assimilation to god. He also shares their view as to the role of mathematics in this flight: mathematics acts as an intermediary, purifying the soul for the higher vision (116, 20–7). As is appropriate for the level and approach of his work, he does not introduce much in the way of mathematical theory. However when the exegesis of the *Golden Verses* involves explaining the Pythagorean concept of the 'tetractys' (87, 17 ff.), Hierocles embarks on a numerological disquisition on the mathematical and extra-mathematical characteristics (ἰδιώματα) of the tetrad such as can be found in Nicomachus, Anatolius, and other numerological sources.[27] Before doing this, however, Hierocles refers to the *Sacred Discourse* attributed to Pythagoras which he reports as praising the demiurge god as the 'number of numbers' (87, 20–1). A brief interpretation is provided: since the demiurge god made all things,

The number in the form of each thing is dependent on the cause in him, and the first number is there [ἐκεῖ, i.e. in god], for it is from there that number comes here. (87, 21–5)

The passage is too brief to allow us to conclude, for example, that the Iamblichean idea of 'physical number' is implied. But it could well be considered as yielding a brief glimpse into the sort of interpretation Iamblichus might have provided for the *Sacred Discourse*.

Mathematics is not the only intermediary for Hierocles in the ascent to god. 'Hieratic' purifications are required by the 'pneumatic vehicle' of the soul (116, 27–117, 4). The reference, it has been noted, is to the 'Chaldaean Oracles', which are quoted earlier in the same connection.[28] Thus not only does Hierocles appropriate Plato for Pythagoreanism, in this sense 'harmonizing' them (σύμφωνος, 98,

---

[25] Cf. I. Hadot (1978), 71, 93–7, 99–106, 107–110, 112–13.

[26] Jerome (*Ep. adv. Ruf.* 108, ch. 39, 29–31) refers to an otherwise unknown *Commentary on the Golden Verses* by Iamblichus: could this be Hierocles' source? For the relation between Hierocles and the Arabic commentaries on the *Golden Verses*, cf. below, Appendix II.

[27] Cf. Kobusch (1976), 188–91; Aujoulat (1986), 122–38; and especially I. Hadot (1979), who provides extensive references.

[28] I. Hadot (1978), 71; cf. 111, 20 (= *Or. Chald.* 119); 112, 9 (= *Or. Chald.* 120).

20), but Pythagoreanism is also combined with the 'Chaldaean Oracles'. All that is missing for this Iamblichean view of philosophy to be complete is Orpheus, yet he also is present, implicitly, as the alleged revelatory source of the Pythagorean *Sacred Discourse*.[29]

4. CONCLUSION

Hierocles' theories about providence and free will, about the structure of reality and man's relation to it, deserve and have received separate treatment.[30] It has been the purpose of this chapter to show that Hierocles' attitude to the nature and history of philosophy can be related at many points to Iamblichus' views and in particular to his interpretation of Pythagorean philosophy. There appear to be some differences on the subject of Aristotle and (possibly) of Ammonius. There is also the contrast between the absence of Pythagoras in Photius' *précis* of *On Providence* and the centrality of Pythagoreanism for philosophy in the *Commentary on the Golden Verses*. Yet we may here be the victim of Photius' procedures. Detailed doctrinal comparisons between the reports on *On Providence* and the *Commentary* do not suggest that Hierocles held divergent theories in these works.[31] Both works presuppose an Iamblichean mixing of Platonic (or Pythagorean) philosophy with barbarian revelation. For both works philosophy is itself a revelation which, as Photius' report seems to suggest and as the *Commentary* explains, is communicated to man for his benefit by souls less emprisoned by the body and privy to the transcendent vision of Plato's *Phaedrus*. The *Commentary* corresponds in fact in many respects—in intention, level, approach—to the first books of Iamblichus' *On Pythagoreanism*. If the *Commentary*, however, does not depend on *On Pythagoreanism* as its immediate source, it remains that Iamblichean Pythagoreanism provides a context for explaining why a Neoplatonic teacher of the late fourth/early fifth century would choose, as a way of initiating beginners to philosophy, to comment on the Pythagorean *Golden Verses*. And, as noted above, Hierocles' position on the nature and history of philosophy in his *Commentary* represents the essential points of Iamblichus' Pythagoreanizing programme.

---

[29] Cf. above, Ch. 4 n. 13.
[30] Kobusch (1976); I. Hadot (1978); Aujoulat (1986).
[31] Cf. especially I. Hadot (1978), ch. V.

6
Syrianus

ALTHOUGH Hierocles' *Commentary* may be regarded as an example of the influence of Iamblichus' revival of Pythagoreanism on the first members of the Athenian school, it is by no means the only or even the most important evidence of this influence. A more significant and interesting case is provided by the extant works of Syrianus, pupil with Hierocles of Plutarch, successor to Plutarch at Athens in 431/2, and much-admired teacher of Proclus. Three works of Syrianus survive: his *Commentary on Hermogenes* (a textbook on rhetoric), his *Commentary on Aristotle's Metaphysics*, and his lectures on Plato's *Phaedrus* as preserved in Hermias' *Commentary on the Phaedrus*. I shall discuss the second and third of these works. Despite his importance for Proclus, Syrianus has not on the whole received much attention.[1] Certain preliminary but basic problems concerning his work will therefore require clarification, at least to the extent that they have bearing on the 'Pythagoreanism' of Syrianus.

I. THE HISTORY OF PHILOSOPHY IN SYRIANUS

From a philosophical point of view Syrianus' *Commentary on Aristotle's Metaphysics* is doubtless his most promising extant work. Yet the basic intentions and assumptions of the *Commentary* have never been established. Syrianus seems to have so little to say about Aristotle's masterwork, adding so much that seems irrelevant, that his *Commentary* has largely been ignored.[2] As a consequence such a preliminary question as that concerning the incomplete state of the *Commentary* has scarcely been addressed. Yet an answer to this question is required if a better

---

[1] Sheppard has published recently (1980, 1982) detailed and useful studies. However Praechter (1932) remains the best overall survey. Cf. also Saffrey and Westerink, in Proclus, *Theol. Plat.* III xl–li; IV xxix–xxxvii.

[2] Recent exceptions are Sheppard (1982), Verbeke (1981), Madigan (1986); all take Syrianus' *Commentary* seriously. Kremer (1961) has little to say specifically about Syrianus.

understanding of Syrianus' intentions in the *Commentary* is to be reached.

Why does Syrianus' *Commentary*, as we now have it, cover only Books *B*, *Γ*, *M*, and *N* of Aristotle's *Metaphysics*? Do we possess only the remains of what was once a much larger commentary spanning the complete text of the *Metaphysics*? Or did Syrianus choose to comment only on Books *B Γ MN* and, if so, why? The problem has not been examined since it was discussed briefly by Praechter in a footnote in 1903.[3] In what follows the relevant internal and external evidence will be considered.

At the beginning of the extant *Commentary* Syrianus summarizes the contents of *Metaphysics A* and *α*, but not in such a way as to indicate that he himself had commented on these books. Book *A* is mentioned again at 195, 11–13: following the Aristotelian commentator Alexander of Aphrodisias, Syrianus notes that Aristotle's criticism of Plato and the Pythagoreans in Books *MN* occurs already in Book *A*. Syrianus' reference suggests that he did not comment on Book *A*. The bulk of the extant *Commentary* deals with *Metaphysics M* and *N* (treated as one), i.e. with Aristotle's massive polemic with Platonism and Pythagoreanism: Syrianus attempts in his *Commentary* to rebuff Aristotle's criticisms, point by point. In *Metaphysics B* Aristotle formulated a series of puzzles or questions relevant to the science of metaphysics ('first philosophy' or 'theology' as he calls this science). For each puzzle Syrianus' *Commentary* provides the reader with the right (!), i.e. Platonic–Pythagorean, answer (cf. 1, 20–2, 3). Finally Aristotle's unpolemical and general characterization of metaphysics in Book *Γ* appears to have been acceptable to Syrianus, since he contents himself with a paraphrase (expanded at some points), referring the reader to Alexander of Aphrodisias' commentary on the book (cf. 54, 11–15). The surviving books of Syrianus' *Commentary* therefore give the general impression that for some parts of Aristotle's *Metaphysics* Alexander's Aristotelian commentary could serve, but for those parts where the issues were unclear and (especially) where Aristotle attacked Platonism–Pythagoreanism a detailed commentary was required. In other words, for a Platonist, a complete new commentary on Aristotle's *Metaphysics* is not needed: for parts of the work Alexander's commentary suffices.

The general impression given by the surviving books of Syrianus' *Commentary* corresponds exactly to Syrianus' valuation of Aristotle in

[3] Praechter (1903), 260 n. 1.

the important prologue to his commentary on Books *MN* (80, 4 ff.).
Like Iamblichus, Syrianus accepts—indeed admires—Aristotle's
teaching on logic, ethics, and physics (80, 5–7). He is grateful also for all
that Aristotle shows concerning divine unchanging transcendent
realities in the *Metaphysics*. In all this Aristotle is truly a benefactor
(εὐεργέτης) of mankind (80, 10–16). However in attacking Platonism
and Pythagoreanism in some parts of the *Metaphysics* (especially in
Books *MN*), Aristotle is gravely misled and misleading. Such attacks,
Syrianus believes, must be shown to be worthless in order that simpler
pupils may not be led astray and come to despise divine realities and
divine science.[4] Syrianus' attitude to Aristotle therefore calls for the
sort of commentary on the *Metaphysics* that has in fact survived: a partial
commentary including in particular the supplements and correctives
required to turn Aristotle's work into an acceptable treatise on *Platonic*
metaphysics, the science of true and divine beings.[5]

If the internal evidence suggests that Syrianus' *Commentary* need
not have covered all parts of Aristotle's *Metaphysics*, there is some
external evidence that tends to show that the *Commentary* may have
been somewhat more extensive than it is in its present form. Proclus
had a pupil Ammonius who taught in Alexandria and whose lectures
on the *Metaphysics* were recorded by a student, Asclepius.[6] In the
Commentary on the Metaphysics of Asclepius, Syrianus is cited twice.
Neither for the first reference in Asclepius (433, 9–14) nor for the
second (450, 22–5) can satisfactory parallels be found in the extant
books of Syrianus' *Commentary*.[7] In fact this is what one would expect,
since both of Asclepius' references record Syrianus' interpretation of
specific passages of *Metaphysics Z*. Asclepius, one must conclude, seems
to have been acquainted in some way with the particulars of Syrianus'
exegesis of (at least) parts of *Metaphysics Z*. What is more, the first
reference in Asclepius concerns Syrianus' defence of Plato against
Aristotle's criticisms in *Metaphysics Z* 13—precisely the kind of
text that would require Syrianus' intervention.[8] In commenting on

---

[4] 80, 16–29; Saffrey (1987*b*) translates and discusses this passage.
[5] Verbeke (1981) shows the Platonic character of Syrianus' understanding of metaphysics; cf. also O'Meara (1986).
[6] On Ammonius and Asclepius, cf. Tarán (1969), 8; Richard (1950), 192–3; Kremer
(1961).
[7] Praechter refers (loc. cit.) for the first citation to Syrianus, *In met.* 12, 33 ff., for the
second to Syrianus 17, 20 (cf. also 82, 2–11; but 10, 37–11, 1 contradicts Asclepius'
report).
[8] Cf. also Asclepius, *In met.* 418, 15–18: Pythagoreanism defended against Aristotle;
Syrianus is not named, but the defence is very much in his manner. Cf. I. Hadot (1987*b*), 4.

Metaphysics A (ch. 9), Asclepius had already rejected Aristotle's critique of Plato (75, 19 ff.) on essentially the same grounds as those that had been used in another, but similar, context by Syrianus (111, 12 ff., on *Met. M* 4): Aristotle's 'third man' argument illegitimately assumes a similarity (Asclepius) or synonymity (Syrianus) between Forms and sensible objets; Forms of relations are not absurd, as Aristotle suggests, in those cases (such as physiological and cosmic organization) where relations are of the essence (οὐσιώδης) of things. Asclepius (Ammonius) may be dependent here on Syrianus or possibly on an ultimate common source, namely Iamblichus, to whom he refers shortly afterwards.[9] If the relation between the commentaries of Syrianus and Asclepius remains to be determined,[10] it can at least be concluded here that there are indications in Asclepius that Syrianus commented on portions of *Metaphysics Z* and possibly of *A*. But here again Syrianus took the line that is implied in the extant books of his *Commentary*, namely rectification of Aristotle's *Metaphysics* at those points where it diverges from Platonism and Pythagoreanism.

In correcting the aberrations in Aristotle's *Metaphysics* Syrianus believed he was reconciling it with the 'ancient', 'true', and 'best' of philosophies on which Aristotle himself was dependent, the philosophy of Pythagoras (81, 9–11 and 25–31). Aristotle, we are told, owed his book *On Generation and Corruption* to the 'Pythagorean' Ocellus; his physics in general to Plato's Pythagorean, Timaeus; his *Categories* to Archytas.[11] Yet Aristotle sometimes seceded from the ancient philosophy, particularly in the *Metaphysics* (*In met.* 10, 37), introducing disharmony (τὸ διάφωνον) through attempting, it seems, to combine philosophic insight with the received opinions of 'the many' (60, 27–30). Pythagoras had more faithful adherents, 'Pythagoreans' who had received the doctrines of the 'divine' Pythagoras in the 'pure bosom of their thought', Parmenides, Empedocles, and especially Plato.[12] To

---

[9] 77, 9. However, it is not clear that Iamblichus wrote a *Commentary on the Metaphysics*; cf. above, Ch. 3, n. 65.

[10] Cf. Praechter (1903), 260–3 (inconclusive); Asclepius at some points differs from Syrianus: he sometimes accepts Aristotle's distinction between Pythagoreans and Plato and tends to regard Aristotle as attacking certain Platonists rather than Plato himself (cf. Praechter, 259); this must be Ammonius' approach, from whom Asclepius presumably has what he knows about Iamblichus and Syrianus; cf. Madigan (1986).

[11] 175, 8–11; 192, 16–21; cf. *In Hermog.* II 58, 23–5.

[12] *In met.* 26, 21–2; 60, 6–7; 171, 9–15 (Parmenides; cf. Iamblichus, *Vit. Pyth.* 144, 10; Burkert [1972], 280 n. 13: Nicomachus); 11, 35–6; 43, 7–8 (Empedocles; cf. above, p. 115);

these we should add Socrates—Syrianus does not accept Aristotle's distinctions between the ideas of the Pythagoreans, Socrates, and Plato (104, 9–17 and 33–105, 12)—and those who later 'unfolded' the vision of the Pythagoreans, Plotinus, Porphyry, and Iamblichus (26, 21–3). Pythagorean philosophy is linked up in turn with the ancient 'theologians', Orpheus, the 'Chaldaean Oracles', and Homer.[13] Indeed Syrianus wrote a ten-volume work (since lost) on 'the harmony (συμφωνία) of Orpheus, Pythagoras, and Plato with the ⟨Chaldaean⟩ Oracles', and this is presumably the approach taken in the other works (also lost) he devoted to Homer.[14]

In dissenting from Pythagoreanism Aristotle cut himself off from the truth. The difference between Aristotle and the true Pythagoreans is also expressed in Syrianus as a distinction between their 'divine' and his (merely!) 'demonic' nature.[15] Should this distinction be understood in the light of Plato's *Phaedrus* and its depiction of souls joined to a divine vision and souls fallen from this vision? An extraordinary passage in Syrianus' *Commentary on the Metaphysics* points in this direction:

Those divine men ⟨the Pythagoreans, Plato⟩ say that god is 'one' as the cause of unity for all . . . whereas this demonic man ⟨Aristotle⟩, taking the smallest quantity and that which through smallness appears the common measure of homogeneous things, insists that there is no measure, nor 'one', that is not found in a substrate. And it is obvious how from the first cause of beings, or from its cognate monad, the account falls (καταπεσὼν ὁ λόγος) . . . slipping from the incorporeal realm of substances and from the encosmic level, and, brought down to the lowest degree of corporeal things, is thrown upside down,[16] busying itself with the smallest . . . of masses.[17]

Elsewhere in the *Commentary* Syrianus does not fail to link decline and fall in philosophical insight with the myth of the *Phaedrus* (82, 15–20; 83, 7–11; 106, 3–5). But a much fuller treatment of the connection

---

183, 1–3; 190, 35 (Plato; Syrianus rejects Aristotle's claim that Plato and the Pythagoreans disagree: 83, 12–14; 166, 17–18).

[13] 182, 9–28; 14, 35–6 (*Or. Chald.* 108, 2); 89, 16–17 (*Or. Chald.* 8); 126, 24 (cf. *Or. Chald.* 37, 2–8); 192, 31–193, 11.

[14] Cf. Praechter (1926) and especially Sheppard (1980).

[15] *In met.* 6, 6–7; 10, 32; 115, 23–5; cf. Saffrey and Westerink in Proclus, *Theol. Plat.* I 141 n. 5.

[16] ὕπτιος; cf. Plato *Tim.* 43 e and Proclus, *In Tim.* III 343, 18 ff.

[17] 168, 2–14; cf. Vincent (1971), 219–20, and her comments, 220–3.

between the theme of true and degraded philosophy and interpretation of the *Phaedrus* can be found in Syrianus' exegesis of the
Phaedrus as preserved in Hermias' *Commentary* on the dialogue.

2. PHILOSOPHY AS REVELATION IN HERMIAS'
COMMENTARY ON THE PHAEDRUS

It is generally agreed that Hermias' *Commentary on the Phaedrus* consists of notes based on the lectures (that he attended in company with
Proclus) of Syrianus on the *Phaedrus*. Hermias reports, for example, a
puzzle put by 'my confrère Proclus' and 'the Master's' response, and
there are traces elsewhere in the *Commentary* of classroom discussion.[18] It has also been suggested that Hermias added to his notes
material he took from Iamblichus' *Commentary on the Phaedrus*.[19] If this
were the case, we would not be justified in using Hermias *simply* as
evidence for Syrianus' views.

The theory that Hermias supplemented Syrianus' lectures with
Iamblichean material is based on the diversity and sometimes apparently contradictory tendencies of the exegeses that Hermias provides
for particular passages in Plato. However the diversity and apparent
disagreement in exegeses in some instances have to do with the fact
that they represent different *kinds* of interpretation, and are thus quite
compatible in a Neoplatonic view of things.[20] And it is possible that
disagreeing interpretations might have been presented, as alternatives, by Syrianus himself.[21]

A method for testing the theory that Hermias' *Commentary* is a
composite of Iamblichus and Syrianus would consist in examining the
ways in which Hermias cites Iamblichus. Is he cited at first hand, as
additional material, or is he reported as an integral part of a lecture?
Most of Hermias' references to Iamblichus are simple doxographical

---

[18] 92, 6 ff.; 154, 19–23 and 28–30; cf. Praechter (1913), 733; Bielmeier (1930), 31–2;
Saffrey and Westerink in Proclus, *Theol. Plat.* IV xxxi–xxxii.

[19] Bielmeier (1930), 33–5; his position, to which he does not commit himself, has not
generally been accepted; cf. Sheppard (1980), 20 n. 8.

[20] Cf. Praechter (1932), 1744. Thus the interpretations of *Phaedrus* 229 b in Hermias
28, 13 ff. and 29, 11 ff., represent ethical, theological, and anagogical exegeses. For
different kinds of interpretation cf. Hermias, 15, 13 ff.; 54, 19 ff. The exegeses at 39, 10–
23, are perfectly compatible.

[21] Cf. 215, 9 ff.: Iamblichus' interpretation is 'cited', perhaps by Syrianus himself.
There is no contradiction between the exegeses at 145, 2 ff. and 10 ff.: they have to do
with different Platonic texts.

reports that read more like parts of a post-Iamblichean exegesis than as supplements copied directly from Iamblichus.[22] One text is particularly revealing: the opinion of the 'divine' Iamblichus is contrasted with 'our' interpretation which follows more closely Plato and the 'theologians' (136, 17–26): Syrianus, it seems, is speaking, noting Iamblichus' position and taking the liberty of disagreeing. In another passage (150, 24–151, 3), Hermias reports a defence of Iamblichus' position against an objection; the defender of Iamblichus in all likelihood is Syrianus. I conclude therefore that Hermias' way of referring to Iamblichus does not support the idea that *he* inserted Iamblichean materials in Syrianus' lecture notes.[23] It seems rather that in the course of explaining the *Phaedrus* Syrianus took account of Iamblichus' views, defended them when appropriate and even at times disagreed. At any rate the grounds against reading Hermias' *Commentary* as based simply on Syrianus' lectures are inadequate.

But what then of Syrianus' views, as reported by Hermias, on the relation between philosophy, its history, and the *Phaedrus*? The two actors of Plato's dialogue, Socrates and Phaedrus, embody the answer. The *Phaedrus* exemplifies the mission of a superior soul sent down to save fallen souls, to recall them through philosophy to higher realities:

Socrates has been sent down (κατεπέμφθη) to the world of becoming to benefit (ἐπὶ εὐεργεσίᾳ) mankind and the souls of the young. Since souls differ greatly in character and practices, he benefits each in a different way, the young, the sophists . . . turning them to philosophy. (1, 1–5)

Socrates thus provides a protreptic to philosophy tailored to the particular character and needs of the soul to be saved, in this case Phaedrus'. This practice of working on each soul in an appropriate way is connected later (259, 19–23) with the 'Pythagoreans'. But what is of more immediate concern here is the difference between the soul of Socrates and that of Phaedrus that accounts for Socrates' particular soteriological function.

Socrates is referred to as a 'saviour'[24] who seeks to bring back souls who have fallen from the divine company of the gods (τῆς συμπερι-πολήσεως τῶν θεῶν), who have narrowed and particularized themselves in the world of becoming, cutting themselves off from the world

---

[22] Cf. 9, 10 (which Bielmeier, 31, regards as part of an 'Unterrichtseinheit'); 68, 26; 200, 29; note especially the language at 113, 25 and 215, 12 ff.

[23] The quotation at 143, 24, is too brief to prove the contrary.

[24] Cf. 54, 31–3; 33, 2; 64, 30–65, 1; on the idealized portrait of Socrates in general cf. Bielmeier (1930), 62–5.

above (63, 18–23). Socrates is 'sent down'—he has not 'fallen'—and preserves intact his close relation to the divine vision of the gods of the *Phaedrus*.[25] He is in fact the agent and instrument of a god, Eros, who is therefore the primary saviour of souls (8, 8–9; 48, 16–17). It is from Eros that Socrates receives his erotic, i.e. anagogic, power (5, 28–6, 2).

Socrates is such a key figure in this interpretation of the *Phaedrus* that Hermias' *Commentary* is chiefly concerned with him. His relation to other philosophers remains somewhat in the background. However his 'Pythagorean' practice of adapting his instruction to the character of his audience has already been noted. He is also said to share Pythagoras' attitude to writing (210, 21–2; 258, 10) and at one point is interpreted as referring to the Pythagoreans as wiser than he (252, 7). Indeed Socrates, according to Hermias, was in the habit of giving credit for his work to the gods and to those men who are 'companions of the gods' (ὀπαδοὺς θεῶν ἄνδρας):

And indeed he thought it right to call the divine men gods in the *Sophist*, for the wise and divine men are as gods in relation to men. And so he was wont often to credit his works to the divine men, in the *Phaedrus* to Pythagoras, in the *Charmides* to Zalmoxis, a wise man, and the story of Atlantis in the *Timaeus* to the Egyptians.[26]

Socrates is therefore a member—in his own eyes a subordinate member—of a company of 'divine' men, participants with him in the divine vision of the *Phaedrus*, a company including Pythagoras and, we may assume, Plato. As for Aristotle, he is used in Hermias in a way matching in its practice Syrianus' judgement of Aristotle in the *Commentary on the Metaphysics*: Hermias resorts to Aristotle especially when it comes to dealing with problems in logic and physics and when syllogistic formulation for Plato's text is desired.[27] On the movement of the soul there is no disagreement (οὐδὲ διαφωνοῦσιν), it is claimed, between Aristotle and Plato (104, 18–22).

In the *Phaedrus* Socrates approaches philosophy as one of the forms of divinely-inspired madness that have much benefited mankind.

---

[25] Cf. 14, 15–16; 32, 23–6: this causes difficulties later since Plato's Socrates confesses to wrong-doing and has to recant; such deficiencies in Socrates are explained away at 74, 23–33; 76, 15–19.

[26] 253, 18–25 (there is no reference to Pythagoras in the *Phaedrus*, but the connection is already made in Hierocles, *In carm. aur.* 111, 13–14, above, p. 115). This passage shows Syrianus' tendency not to distinguish between the ideas of Socrates and of Plato.

[27] Cf. 105, 7 ff.; 115, 4–6; 217, 26 ff.; 225, 25–6. For Aristotle's debt in logic to Plato, cf. 51, 32–52, 1. There is a reminiscence of *Met. A* 1 in 247, 30–248, 1.

Poetry is another form of such madness (245 a). There is therefore good authority (or pretext) for the frequent recourse in Hermias to the divinely inspired (ἐνθουσιῶντες) poets, Homer and Orpheus, particularly in matters relating to theology.[28] Proof texts for theology are also found in the Chaldaean Oracles,[29] and throughout the *Commentary* emphasis is placed on the agreement between theologians, poets, and philosophers.[30]

In short we may conclude that the understanding in Hermias' *Commentary* of the nature of philosophy, its history and relation to other forms of wisdom, is the same as that found in Syrianus' *Commentary on the Metaphysics*. There are some differences in emphasis, but this has to do with differences in the texts being interpreted. Socrates is the key figure in Hermias. Yet there are indications of the subordination to Pythagoras that is so emphatic in the *Commentary on the Metaphysics*. The positive aspect of Syrianus' evaluation of Aristotle is predominant in Hermias. The negative aspect—Aristotle's errors in metaphysics (theology)—is eclipsed: for theology in the *Phaedrus* higher and more relevant authorities could be used, Plato himself, Orpheus, Homer, whereas Aristotle's *Metaphysics* is the primary theological text with which Syrianus' *Commentary* must contend. Finally the general position of Plotinus, Porphyry, and Iamblichus as the more recent heirs of the Pythagorean tradition is less explicit in Hermias, although of course these philosophers are treated implicitly as members of it.

Yet Hermias' *Commentary* makes one significant contribution to what is known of Syrianus' views on philosophy in the *Commentary on the Metaphysics*: it makes clear the revelatory and soteriological nature of philosophy and the connection of this with interpretation of the *Phaedrus*. True philosophers are divine-like souls who have not cut themselves off from participation in the vision of the heavenly retinue of the *Phaedrus*. To this they owe their superior wisdom. By communicating this divine wisdom to fallen souls they help bring about the return of the latter to their immaterial origins. In this sense

---

[28] Cf. 122, 20-2 (Parmenides is also named); 147, 1-2; 88, 25-33; 138, 16-17; 142, 10-18; 147, 19-22; 148, 21-149, 4; 154, 17-21 and 23-7; 137, 23-138, 10; 147, 22-148, 2 (the blindness of Homer creates exegetical problems however!; cf. 74, 9 ff.; Bielmeier [1930], 65-6).

[29] Cf. 110, 5 (*Or. Chald.* 174); 157, 19 (*Or. Chald.* 23); 184, 21 (*Or. Chald.* 53, 2); 130, 28 (*Or. Chald.* 104, not noted in des Places's edition).

[30] 137, 23-138, 10; 146, 25-147, 6 (a distinction between divine and human poets saves Homer and Orpheus from Plato's criticism); 148, 2-4 and 17-19.

their philosophy is indeed the divinely-inspired beneficial madness that Socrates claims it to be in the *Phaedrus*.

It would be somewhat repetitious to review all of the points on which Syrianus' understanding of the nature, function, and history of philosophy agrees with that of Iamblichus as presented above in Part I. One possible difference—but a difference consistent with the general scheme—is the importance given to Homer in Syrianus. Yet this is hardly a *new* element, either in Syrianus or in Hierocles in whom we have already found it (above, p. 112). If Hierocles' approach to philosophy is also Iamblichean in its general character, Syrianus seems to be closer to Iamblichus than is Hierocles, as regards at least—and this is not unimportant—the evaluation of Aristotle. Even where Syrianus has been found (above, p. 125) to disagree with Iamblichus, it is in a thoroughly Iamblichean manner: fidelity to Plato and the 'theologians' requires his dissent. This case of Syrianus being more Iamblichean than Iamblichus himself will be discussed in more detail below.

One can show without much difficulty how it was possible for Syrianus to come so close to Iamblichus' views. Quite apart from what he may have learnt from Plutarch, he used Iamblichus' commentaries on the *Phaedrus* and on the *Timaeus*.[31] He certainly exploited Iamblichus' *On Pythagoreanism* as a major source-book in his *Commentary on the Metaphysics*. As this fact has not yet been adequately noted,[32] it will require some attention here. It will also provide a starting-point from which Syrianus' metaphysical system may conveniently be approached.

3. MATHEMATICS AND PHILOSOPHY IN SYRIANUS' COMMENTARY ON THE METAPHYSICS

(i) *Syrianus'* Commentary *and Iamblichus'* On Pythagoreanism

Syrianus believes, as we have seen, that Aristotle's *Metaphysics* can be used in Platonic, i.e. 'Pythagorean' philosophy, if certain important

---

[31] Syrianus' references to Iamblichus, in his lectures on the *Phaedrus* (as reported by Hermias), indicate he is using Iamblichus' *Commentary on the Phaedrus*; Proclus' *Commentary on the Timaeus*, which reflects Syrianus' lectures, suggests that Syrianus referred to Iamblichus' *Commentary on the Timaeus* (Iamblichus, *In Tim.* fr. 7).

[32] Although Praechter (1903), 257–8, has pointed it out and collected some of the more important evidence.

adjustments and corrections are supplied. This will entail reading the *Metaphysics* with the help of guidelines (that must be sufficiently differentiated and comprehensive) provided by true 'Pythagorean' philosophy. It is in this spirit that he prefaces his commentary on Books *MN* with a synoptic account of 'Pythagorean' metaphysics (81, 31–83, 31). But where are such guidelines to be found? Whence can such a synoptic account be derived?

It has been shown above (p. 50) that 'Pythagorean' philosophy for Iamblichus consists in the main of two parts, or stages, (1) mathematics (including mathematical transpositions in physics, ethics, and theology), and (2) theology (metaphysics, the divine science or science of the gods).

On the subject of mathematics, Syrianus responds as follows to Aristotle's claim that mathematical objects are mere abstractions from sensible objects:

> But if one familiarizes oneself with the noblest Pythagorean doctrines one will clearly comprehend the being, power, and activity of all mathematical science. ... (101, 26–9)

What follows for more than a page (101, 29–102, 35) is a digest of the chapter headings of Iamblichus' *On Pythagoreanism* III (*Comm.* 3, 7–8, 6) including variants showing that Syrianus is aware of the contents of the corresponding chapters.[33] *On Pythagoreanism* III was therefore in Syrianus' opinion a basic text-book in Pythagorean *general* mathematics.

On Pythagoreanism III was followed by books on each of the four mathematical sciences (Books IV, VIII–X). Corresponding to this Syrianus next suggests on the same page (102, 36–8) that one learn the *individual* demonstrations in the mathematical sciences from the 'leaders' (ἡγεμόνων) in mathematics, and he borrows the language of Plato's *Republic* 527 d 8–e 2 (= Iamblichus *Comm.* 22, 20–3) to express the intellectual regeneration and purification that mathematics can produce. Finally (103, 4–10) he refers, as further reading, to 'the collections of Pythagorean doctrines of Nicomachus and of the divine Iamblichus'. We have seen that Iamblichus (*On Pyth.* III) is the text-book Syrianus uses for 'general' mathematics. Iamblichus (*On Pyth.* IV) is also Syrianus' source for 'Pythagorean' arithmetic.[34] The loss of

---

[33] This is shown by Praechter (loc. cit).

[34] 142, 15–25 = Iamblichus, *In Nic.* 10, 12–24; cf. Syrianus, *In met.* 123, 6–9; 165, 13–14 = Iamblichus, *In Nic.* 6, 20–2; Syrianus, *In met.* 140, 9–10 = Iamblichus, *In Nic.* 11, 8–9.

Iamblichus' accounts of the remaining three mathematical sciences (*On Pyth.* VIII–X) means that detection of their use in Syrianus is not possible. However Syrianus does not in any case have much recourse to those sciences in his *Commentary*.

Syrianus also read and used Iamblichus' 'arithmetical physics' and 'arithmetical theology' (*On Pythagoreanism* V and VII). Indeed it is Syrianus' quotation from *On Pythagoreanism* V at 149, 28–31, that confirms the Iamblichean origin of Psellus' excerpts. What follows (149, 31 ff.) may also be inspired by *On Pythagoreanism* V. At 140, 15 Syrianus refers us to *On Pythagoreanism* VII for the clearest account of the Pythagorean distinction between intelligible and intellectual monads (140, 10–13; compare Iamblichus, *On Pyth.* VII, in Psellus, *On Eth. Theol. arith.* 72–4). There are a number of other passages in Syrianus which recall the arithmetical physics of *On Pythagoreanism* V and a smaller number of places (corresponding to the smaller amount of excerpts in Psellus) which may be compared to the arithmetical ethics and theology of *On Pythagoreanism* VI–VII.[35]

If Iamblichus' *On Pythagoreanism* (in particular Books III, IV, V, VII) was Syrianus' source for Pythagorean mathematics (general mathematics, arithmetic, transpositions of arithmetic), for Pythagorean theology he had recourse to other sources besides the theological foreshadowings of arithmetic set forth in *On Pythagoreanism* VII. In Chapter 4 I have argued that Iamblichus' work *On God* (or *On the Gods*) completed the curriculum of Pythagorean philosophy begun in *On Pythagoreanism* and that it is likely that *On (the) God(s)* included exegesis of the *Sacred Discourse* attributed to Pythagoras. Syrianus cites the *Sacred Discourse* a number of times, once immediately after referring to *On Pythagoreanism* VII (140, 14–18)—thus precisely in the order required by Iamblichus' curriculum—and again at 10, 5; 123, 2 and 175, 4 where it is compared to the 'theologies' of Plato, Orpheus, and Parmenides.[36] These passages show that for Syrianus the *Sacred Discourse* was a source-book for 'Pythagorean theology'. Hierocles also used, as we have seen, the *Sacred Discourse* as a theological source.

From these texts Syrianus derived the interpretation of Pythagorean philosophy in the light of which he read and, when necessary, corrected Aristotle's *Metaphysics*. If, as I have argued in Chapter 3, Iamblichus had in *On Pythagoreanism* VII discussed and responded at

---

[35] Cf. below Appendix I. Compare in particular Syrianus, *In met.* 190, 30–3, with Psellus, *On Phys. Num.* 8–11; Syrianus, 188, 1–4 with Psellus, *On Phys. Num.* 48–9. Syrianus summarizes *On Pyth.* I (*Vit. Pyth.* 64, 16–65, 15) in his *In Herm.* I 22, 3–19.

[36] Cf. also *In met.* 192, 10–13; 106, 14 ff.

least in part to Aristotle's polemic with Platonism–Pythagoreanism in the *Metaphysics*, then he had set the precedent for Syrianus' *Comment-ary*. As Iamblichus had begun the construction in *On Pythagoreanism* VII of a 'Pythagorean' theology or metaphysics, in part through reaction to the *Metaphysics*, so Syrianus, in possession of such a theo-logy, could respond at greater length and in detail to the Aristotelian text.

(ii) *The Tripartite Structure of Reality in Syrianus*

As noted above, Syrianus prefaces his detailed response to Aristotle's attack in *Metaphysics MN* on Platonism–Pythagoreanism with a synopsis of true, 'Pythagorean' metaphysics (81, 31 ff.), i.e. the Pythagorean–Platonic theory of Forms and of numbers, which he takes to be (unjustly) criticized by Aristotle. Syrianus' synopsis does not therefore cover the full extent of the Pythagorean structure of reality. But it does present a fairly systematic framework that can be filled out in more detail and extended by reference to other parts of his *Commentary*.

Pythagorean reality, according to Syrianus, is arranged in three main levels, the intelligible (*νοητή*), the discursive (*διανοητή*), and the sensible (*αἰσθητή*).[37] At each level Forms are to be found that match the particular ontological characteristics of the level (81, 38–82, 2). The intelligible Forms are 'by the gods' (*παρὰ θεοῖς*) and 'com-plete' the ranks of the divine (82, 3 and 12–13)—these vague formula-tions will be clarified later. The discursive Forms imitate the intelligible Forms, assimilating the psychic order to the intelligible (82, 14–15). As contemplated by divine and demonic souls, discursive Forms function as demiurgic principles. But for souls that have fallen, as in the *Phaedrus*, from contemplation and thus from the power of making, they are no more than objects of knowledge.[38] We have access to them in virtue of the fact that the demiurge of Plato's *Timaeus* constructed soul through geometric, arithmetical, and harmonic analogies (82, 20–2). In this way discursive Forms are innate in us and make possible the recollection of Forms in the fallen soul (82, 25). These Forms are 'universals' (*καθόλου λόγοι*), not in Aristotle's sense, as abstracted from sensible objects, but as existing a priori as

---

[37] For this division in Iamblichus, cf. above, p. 44 (Iamblichus' text is very probably the source of inspiration of Syrianus' tripartite division of reality).

[38] 82, 15–20; cf. Praechter (1932), 1746.

part of the being of souls (82, 26–8). However for higher souls, as noted above, they are also demiurgic principles guiding the causes immanent in and organizing nature (82, 28–9). These immanent causes (λόγοι, αἴτια), which are inseparable from sensible bodies, represent the lowest level at which form is found (83, 5–7). To all levels 'the Pythagoreans' applied mathematical terms, not because they were unable to distinguish between levels, but because of the relation of image to model linking each level to the level above it.[39]

In what follows I shall attempt to fill out this general scheme with what can be gleaned from other parts of Syrianus' *Commentary*, beginning with the intermediate, 'discursive' level—where numbers, properly speaking, are found—and then considering how numbers function in paradigmatic extrapolation in physics, as the causes of sensible bodies, and how they anticipate and express the objects of metaphysics, true being and the divine.

(iii) *Number and the Soul*

The relation between the objects of mathematics and soul is, in what remains of Iamblichus' *On Pythagoreanism*, somewhat unclear. This is not the case in Syrianus: intermediate between intelligible and sensible reality, the objects of mathematics are part of the nature of soul (4, 5–11). As we have seen, mathematicals have a double function, as principles guiding the demiurge action of unfallen souls on the world[40] and as innate universals in fallen souls allowing them to regain their lost knowledge. The correspondence between the demiurgic principles of unfallen souls and the innate universals in fallen souls explains how we (the latter) are capable of scientific demonstrations concerning the physical heavens and other material objects: by developing demonstrations applying to physical objects from first principles, or universals, that we possess innately and cognitively (γνωστικῶς), we rehearse the actual constitution of these objects from the same principles functioning 'demiurgically' (δημιουργικῶς).[41] Indeed, Syrianus argues, scientific demonstration, as Aristotle understands it, is not possible if we follow Aristotle in

---

[39] 83, 14–26; Syrianus regards much of Aristotle's criticism as showing only a failure to grasp this point (cf. 180, 17–25; 186, 30–6).

[40] These are subordinates of the demiurge proper of the *Timaeus* (cf. 82, 15–22).

[41] Cf. 88, 24–32; 97, 1–5; 82, 36–83, 1; 27, 30–7; Duhem (1914), II 102–3; also Proclus, *In Tim.* II 236, 23–7.

treating 'universal principles' as abstracted (*a posteriori*) from physical objects. For how could such principles be what is prior scientifically, what is most clear and well known, as Aristotle claims, if they are derivatives of sensible particulars? Aristotle's (anti-Platonic) view in *Metaphysics M* of 'universals', especially mathematical universals, as derived from particulars is inconsistent with his own understanding of the nature of scientific demonstration. Consistency is recovered if such universals are regarded as principles existing prior to the sensible world, functioning cognitively in our souls and demiurgically in the souls that organize the world.[42]

The relation between soul and mathematical objects requires further specification, however. Mathematicals constitute but a portion of the universals in the soul (84, 1–3). What the other universals are is not quite clear in Syrianus, and we must turn to Proclus for further information on this point (below, p. 201). Furthermore, mathematicals appear at several levels in the soul. In producing soul the demiurge gives it number which may be called 'ideal' (εἰδητικός) number— although it is not properly speaking ideal number, i.e. intelligible Form—to distinguish it from the number it produces from itself, mathematical or 'monadic' (μοναδικός) number.[43] Some light is shed on soul's generation from its ideal or essential number of mathematical number at 132, 14–23, and 133, 10–15, where Syrianus represents soul as producing mathematical numbers from two principles that it possesses within itself, a monad and a dyad. Thus we do, after all, 'think up' mathematical number, but not in Aristotle's sense: our souls contain essential numbers, images presumably of intelligible Forms, in particular a monad and dyad that pre-contain all of the formal features of mathematical numbers and from which we generate mathematical numbers. A similar psychic generation takes place for geometrical objects: geometrical figures are produced from essential, indivisible principles in the soul (οὐσιώδεις, ἀμερεῖς λόγοι) when geometry, in its cognitive weakness, projects these in imagination, and thus in extension, so as to grasp them more easily.[44]

There are several important advantages for the Platonist in this distinction between levels of mathematicals in the soul and in the idea

[42] 90, 8–23; cf. 95, 29–96, 6. On the 'universals' in the soul, cf. 4, 37–5, 2; 12, 5–15; 163, 6–8; 91, 20–1; 95, 13–17.

[43] 123, 19–24; cf. 88, 8–9; Praechter (1932), 1759–60; mathematical number is 'monadic' because it is made up of units, monads; cf. Iamblichus as quoted by Simplicius, *In cat.* 138, 10–11 (=fr. 45 Larsen); Merlan (1965), 171–2; Gersh (1978), 139.

[44] 91, 25–92, 5 (cf. Philoponus, *In de an.* 58, 7–13); Praechter (1932), 1752.

that the lower level is a projection of the higher: a place is found for the
creativity of mathematics that reconciles it with a foundation that is
not invented, but 'given', a priori, universal, and necessary; furthermore quantity and extension in mathematicals can be accounted for
without sacrifice of the indivisible, unextended character of their
originals in the soul.[45]

(iv) *'Physical Number'*

The relation between psychic mathematicals, as both causal and
epistemic principles, and the organization of the physical world has
already been noted. To understand physical phenomena we must
relate them back (ἀναφορά) to their paradigmatic mathematical
principles (cf. 98, 16–31; 155, 36–156, 6). Indeed the world is organized
by causes that, as patterned after number, can be described as 'physical numbers'.[46] Syrianus speaks of a science corresponding to this
Iamblichean idea of physical number, 'physical arithmetic' (189, 13;
192, 2–3). The differences between physical numbers and mathematical numbers (in particular monadic numbers produced from essential
numbers in the soul) must be carefully observed, for confusing them is
the source of some of Aristotle's criticisms in the *Metaphysics*.[47] Thus
the dyad that produces mathematical number is not that which produces physical solids (180, 22–5). Yet the connections between physical and mathematical numbers justify Pythagorean analogies between
physics and mathematics; mathematical numbers exemplify, they
bring out formal properties that explain physical phenomena (cf. 143,
9–10; 122, 28–9). Such indeed is the 'physical arithmetic' developed in
Iamblichus' *On Pythagoreanism* V and which Syrianus in part reproduces (above, p. 130). However, Syrianus' treatment of the subject
is limited: he is concerned with it to the extent that it involves distinc-

[45] Cf. Charles (1982), 192 (on Proclus). The theory that mathematicals are projections, imagings forth, of intelligible principles may go back to Iamblichus (cf. *Comm.* 34,
7–12; 43, 21; 44, 9; Steel [1978], 63, 67–8) and appears to have been adopted by Plutarch
of Athens (in Philoponus, *In de an.* 515, 20–9; cf. Beierwaltes [1985], 260, Blumenthal
[1975], 134–6). Its background must be the interpretation of what precisely might be the
medium responsible for the image status of mathematicals in Plato's *Rep.*, and the
identification of the imagination (φαντασία) with this medium. Charles (1971), 251,
refers to Plotinus, IV 3, 30, where imagination acts as a mirror showing forth, articulat-
ing thought. Cf. below, p. 168.

[46] Cf. 122, 25–7; 142, 27 and 32; 188, 5 and 10; 190, 22; Hermias refers briefly to
εἰδοποιοὶ ἀριθμοί (*In Phaedr.* 16, 4–5).

[47] Cf. 122, 25–9; 143, 4–10; 190, 35–7; Proclus, *In Tim.* I 16, 25–17, 4.

tions that serve to dismiss some of Aristotle's assumptions about Pythagorean–Platonic number-theory.

(v) *Number in Metaphysics*

Aristotle's polemic with Platonism–Pythagoreanism in *Metaphysics MN* has to do mainly, of course, with the theory of transcendent immaterial Forms and ideal numbers (εἰδητικοὶ ἀριθμοί). Syrianus consequently has a good deal more to say about this metaphysical level of reality. He understands the relation between Forms and numbers in a 'Pythagorean' way: ideal numbers represent a Pythagorean way of speaking of Forms. Forms themselves are not (mathematical) numbers,[48] but by referring to Forms as numbers the Pythagoreans expressed through mathematical analogy significant ontological (formal and dynamic) features of Forms. Forms can be described as numbers in that as causes they act as measures for their effects, fitting them together and unifying them (103, 15–104, 2; 134, 22–6). The Forms constitute a decad in the sense that they are a comprehensive paradigm for the world, just as the decad contains all numbers (147, 29–148, 9). And just as number is produced from a monad and dyad, so there are two principles producing Forms which, by reason of their analogous function, can be referred to as monad and dyad (cf. 132, 14–20; 134, 22–35; 48, 23–5). However the fact that the realm of Forms is being approached through analogies starting from their images, mathematical numbers, must not be ignored, since mathematical numbers operate with units and quantity, features not relevant to a proper account of Forms (131, 37–132, 2; 186, 30–5). The difference between a mathematical foreshadowing of the formal characteristics of pure Form and a true knowledge of the Forms is found also in the distinction Syrianus makes (as did Iamblichus) between the demonstrative method of mathematics and the higher, direct insight (ἐπιβολή) whereby metaphysics attains its objects (4, 29–5, 2). Yet even when it comes to expressing the relation between metaphysics and the sciences subordinate to it (mathematics and physics), Syrianus cannot avoid mathematical analogy. In reply to Aristotle's puzzle in *Metaphysics B* 1, as to whether metaphysics should study (only) the first causes of substances, or also the principles of all demonstrations, Syrianus defends the latter alternative on the grounds that metaphysics,

[48] Cf. 103, 15 ff.; 186, 30–5; 45, 33–46, 5; for the difference between Forms and universals in the soul cf. 105, 37–106, 5.

like a monad, pre-contains the principles of all the sciences subordinate to it (3, 17–30).

It is clear that Syrianus identifies Aristotelian metaphysics, the
science of being, with 'dialectic', the study of pure intelligible being
(or the Forms) of Plato's *Republic*.[49] Both in turn relate in some way to
the Pythagorean science of the divine which is to be found also in the
theology of Plato's *Parmenides* (cf. 121, 5; 126, 15–16). This theology
deals with the divine characterized as 'divine number' (θεῖος ἀριθμός) in the same way as the Forms are called 'ideal numbers'.[50]
Pythagorean–Platonic theology, it seems, concerns more than the
Forms: higher principles come within its scope. Before such principles are introduced, an important differentiation within the realm of
Forms must first be noted.

In Chapter 3 above a distinction was found in *On Pythagoreanism* VII
between 'intelligibles' (νοητά) and 'intellectuals' (νοερά). It reappears in Syrianus' *Commentary* (cf. 4, 17–18) and expresses itself as a
distinction between 'intelligible' and 'intellectual' numbers (122, 31–
2). Indeed Syrianus refers us to *On Pythagoreanism* for the difference
between intelligible and intellectual monads (140, 11–15). Syrianus
also introduces the distinction in his exegesis of some (Pythagorean?
Orphic?) verses at 106, 15 ff.: Forms come to be 'intelligibly' and
'tetradically' in the 'ideal animal' (τὸ αὐτοζῷον) and then 'intellectually' and 'decadically' in the demiurgic intellect. The language
indicates that this is in fact an interpretation of Plato's *Timaeus* in
which the problem of the relation between demiurge and model is
solved by subordinating the demiurge to the model.[51] Mathematical
expression is given to the subordination: the demiurgic intellect comprises the Forms fully articulated as are the numbers in the decad,
whereas the 'ideal animal' contains the Forms in the way that the
tetrad contains the essential features of numbers; the ideal animal is to
the demiurge as the tetrad is to the decad. Thus mathematical
relations can serve to formulate the structure internal to the realm of
Forms.

The 'intellectual decad' of Forms is subordinate and pre-contained
then in a more unified way in the 'intelligible tetrad' which itself
derives from two more ultimate principles, a monad and dyad. Indeed

---

[49] Cf. 55, 3–32; 58, 13–14; Verbeke (1981); O'Meara (1986), 5–7.
[50] Cf. 124, 24–5; 146, 9; 166, 16–24; 177, 19–27; 179, 23–30.
[51] That this is in fact Syrianus' interpretation of the *Timaeus* is confirmed by Proclus,
In Tim. I 322, 18–323, 22; cf. Gersh (1978), 139–40.

the monad and dyad play a central role in the constitution of reality. The identity and diversity by which they produce Forms are echoed at each succeeding level of being, more and more faintly, down to the organization of nature, each level 'unfolding' from a monad–dyad pair correlative to that level but deriving ultimately from the first and highest pair.[52] This first pair is not to be identified with the first members of the intelligible tetrad, the 'monad itself' and 'dyad itself', but it transcends the tetrad, and therefore pure intelligible being. The supra-intelligible monad, as a unity, itself presupposes a higher principle, the ultimate origin, the One. Although Syrianus' need to invoke theological authorities sometimes blurs rather than sharpens these distinctions between the ultimate One, the supra-intelligible monad and dyad and the intelligible monad and dyad, they emerge with sufficient clarity from the following two passages:

It seems to me that Empedocles supposes 'Friendship' to be nothing other than the One, not the One that is not co-ordinate with anything ⟨i.e. the ultimate One⟩, but that which is co-ordinate with the unlimited dyad, which he refers to as 'Strife', from ⟨both of⟩ which what primarily is and all the intelligibles and the sensible world come to be. (11, 28–31; cf. 43, 11–20)

⟨To Aristotle's argument in *Metaphysics N* 1⟩ one should say that these men ⟨the Pythagoreans⟩ include in the first causes, not such opposites as are non-beings in the sense of being inferior to being, but ... such as are non-beings in the sense of superior to being. For the first principles of beings ⟨or Forms⟩ must transcend being. And yet these men did not begin from opposites ⟨i.e. monad/dyad, limit/unlimited⟩, but they were aware of what transcends the two opposite orders, witness Philolaus ⟨the Pythagorean⟩ who says god produced limit and the unlimited.[53]

Some of the elements of this metaphysical structure can be found in Hermias' *Commentary on the Phaedrus*. Reality, in Hermias, also culminates in an ultimate One (121, 19). He too assumes a distinction between the 'intelligible' and 'intellectual' orders (134, 3–4; 89, 8–15). And he alludes to a supra-intelligible level in the following text:

But if you were to contemplate the beautiful, the wise and the good according to a mode transcending the gods' intellect, you should say that there is a light[54] proceeding from the Good ... Plato says in the *Philebus* that it is not possible

---

[52] Cf. 5, 16–31; 48, 23–31; Praechter (1932), 1756; and especially Sheppard (1982) on the importance of monad and dyad as principles.
[53] 165, 31–166, 1; cf. 112, 35–113, 5 (δυὰς ἀρχηγικὴ/αὐτοδυάς); Sheppard (1982), 2–4.
[54] *Or. Chald.* 49, 1; cf. Proclus, *In Tim.* III 13, 29–14, 4.

for human thought to grasp the Form of the Good with simple insight. Since thus that light proceeds immediately from the Good, it still remains above Form and simplicity. It is thus impossible to grasp it by simple insight (ἐπιβολή). (134, 12–18)

(vi) Syrianus and Iamblichus

If one compares the metaphysical landscape presupposed by Syrianus' Commentary and Hermias with that reconstructed above in Chapter 3 from what remains of Iamblichus' On Pythagoreanism, one will find a large measure of agreement, but also, it appears, some differences. One difference regards the level intervening between the ultimate One and intelligible being (the Forms). In Iamblichus it seems that this level included not only monad and dyad, but also triad and (probably) the following members of a supra-intelligible decad. These 'divine numbers' constitute the most unified order of members who are themselves unities. Yet in Syrianus it appears that only a monad and dyad inhabit this level. This may, however, be a matter of emphasis and context. Hermias refers to the principles that follow the ultimate One as 'the first henads' (121, 19). Syrianus also speaks of 'monads or henads which proceed from the very first cause' (In Met. 183, 24–5) and he makes a distinction, for Forms prior to the demi-urgic (i.e. 'intellectual') Forms, between 'unified' (ἑνιαῖος) and 'essential' (οὐσιώδης) numbers (126, 17)—since the latter constitute the intelligible order, the former must represent the order above it. And if the supra-intelligible level in Syrianus contains 'henadic numbers', it seems reasonable to expect that it extends beyond monad and dyad to the following (properly speaking) numbers of a decad.[55]

Clear disagreement between Iamblichus and Syrianus can be detected however on some specific points. A particularly revealing case is found in Hermias. At issue is the interpretation of the company of twelve gods, led by Zeus, in the Phaedrus (246 e). Some possible exegeses are examined and rejected and then that of Iamblichus is introduced (136, 17–29):

However the divine Iamblichus, noting the name Zeus, relates the passage to the one demiurge of the universe who is spoken of in the Timaeus ⟨i.e. the

---

[55] This allows us to explain the relation between Syrianus' supra-intelligible monad–dyad pair and the doctrine of divine henads attributed to Syrianus by Proclus (In Parm. 1062, 20–34; Theol. Plat. I lxxxvi). The problem posed by this relation is raised by Sheppard (1982).

'intellectual' demiurge). But we, here also admiring the man's insight (ἐπι-βολή), would add only this: that by Zeus is not to be understood simply the one and transcendent demiurge, for this transcendent demiurge does not have a particular place in the 'army' ⟨of the *Phaedrus*⟩, . . . but is present equally in all ranks. . . . This is then our view, following Plato and the theologians: after the demiurgic monad, the one and transcendent Zeus, come three Zeuses . . . each of whom has subordinate to him four further gods.

Zeus is found at three levels: the transcendent demiurge proper on the 'intellectual' level; below him a triad; and below this twelve gods, led by the Zeus of Plato's *Phaedrus*.[56] Of particular interest is the source of Syrianus' disagreement with Iamblichus. The latter had identified the Zeus of the *Phaedrus*, the first member of a series of twelve, with the demiurge of the *Timaeus*. But, for Syrianus, the demiurge is not the first of a series of twelve. He is rather a transcendent intellectual monad, principle (via a triad) of the series of twelve as a whole. In other words precisely because of the sort of mathematical principles that Iamblichus had used for theology—here in particular the distinction between the first (immanent) member of a series and the transcendent principle of the series as a whole—his interpretation of the theology of the *Phaedrus* must be amended.[57] Proclus reports another case of Syrianus being more rigorous in his application of mathematics than Iamblichus,[58] and the general spirit of this disagreement is well expressed by a later member of the Athenian school:

> This is Simplicius' work, Iamblichus bestower of blessings,
> Forgive my defeating you, but it is through your words![59]

It is likely enough that were more to be recovered of Iamblichus' lost works and were a truly comprehensive and detailed treatment by Syrianus of the structure of reality available, other differences could be noted. Useful comparisons could also be made between the hosts of lesser deities and demons in Iamblichus' *On Mysteries* and their counterparts, 'hypercosmic' and 'encosmic'—of which the 'jovial'

---

[56] Cf. also 137, 6–10; 138, 27–139, 1; 142, 10–12; Proclus, *In Tim.* I 310, 3–311, 4 (on Syrianus).

[57] The distinction between immanent and transcendent monad is also applied to theological relationships at 152, 15–19. One might mention here also Syrianus' insistence, against Iamblichus, that the ultimate One is not to be treated as if co-ordinate with the henads in the interpretation of the first hypothesis of the *Parmenides* (cf. Saffrey and Westerink in Proclus, *Theol. Plat.* III xl ff.).

[58] *In Tim.* I 20, 27 ff.

[59] Scholium on Proclus, *In Tim.* I 175, 2 (468, 15–16); cf. Saffrey and Westerink in Proclus, *Theol. Plat.* I cliii; I. Hadot (1987*b*), 30–1.

plethora encountered above is but a dismaying sample!—in Syrianus and Hermias. Enough evidence has, however, been collected, I believe, to conclude that Syrianus' general approach to the structure of reality owes much to Iamblichus, and in particular to *On Pythagoreanism*. Number permeates this structure, not in virtue of the crude identifications of numbers with things that Aristotle finds in the Pythagoreans, but in virtue of the intermediate and pivotal status of mathematical objects: as exemplars of the physical world they express paradigmatically the formal principles immanent in the world; as lower images they foreshadow their origins, the realm of Forms and its own ultimate principles. In distinguishing between many levels or sorts of number—physical, mathematical or psychic, intellectual, intelligible, henadic or divine—Syrianus follows Iamblichus' example and also emphasizes Iamblichus' point that this expresses the transposability of mathematicals to other domains. The result, in Syrianus as in Iamblichus, is a 'physical arithmetic' and a 'theological arithmetic'. If the latter is much more fully represented in Syrianus' *Commentary on the Metaphysics* than in the few remains of Iamblichus' *On Pythagoreanism* VII, its function on the whole is somewhat negative: it acts as a standard against which Aristotle's anti-Pythagoreanism is corrected, rather than as a science presented in its own right. However, enough emerges to indicate that Syrianus, like Iamblichus, finds in mathematics distinctions and relationships that can be used to describe the characteristics of Forms, the structure of the realm of Forms, and its relation to a higher order, that of 'henads', which is also approached in mathematical terms. Syrianus is as aware as is Iamblichus that such a 'theological arithmetic' is based merely on analogy. Besides the evidence given above from Syrianus' *Commentary*, a good example of this methodological caution can be found in Hermias. The subject in question is again the series of twelve gods of the *Phaedrus*:

Some fit, in an arithmetical way, each of the ten gods (subtracting two monads from the twelve) . . . to the ten numbers of the decad . . ., giving the monad to Apollo, the dyad to Hera, . . . But ⟨the text⟩ is not to be understood in a simple arithmetical fashion, but each god organizes and is provident according to his characteristic (ἰδιότης). . . . The characteristic of each is to be learnt from theology. . . . So there are certain characteristics in numbers which imitate the characteristics of the gods and are thus transposed to them. (139, 3–20).

Syrianus rejects the simple identifications of numbers with gods found in traditional Pythagorean decadic works such as that attributed to

Anatolius. If he frequently compares the numbers with the gods[60] it is on the basis of transpositions whose basis and limitations he recognizes. Mathematics can help to lead us to higher things (191, 10–12). It can function as a 'bridge'—Nicomachus' image used by Syrianus in his *Commentary* (*In Met.* 96, 28–30). But its discursive methods and the images it uses are inferior in metaphysics to the direct 'insight' into the Forms and what transcends them such as is revealed by the inspired poets and the divine souls of Pythagorean philosophers.

[60] Cf. e.g. Hermias, 90, 21 ff.; 137, 4–6; 138, 11–13.

7

Proclus: Some Preliminary Issues

'A GREAT haven': so Michael Psellus described the enormous collection of Proclus' works from which he could so often distil his own philosophical writings. Psellus' interest is no doubt responsible in part for the preservation of so much of this collection. But presumably it had imposed itself in such a way as to supplant the works of others long before, in the days of Proclus' disciples and successors at Athens.[1] The thousands of pages of Proclus that have survived represent, however, but a small fraction of the original *corpus*. Yet there is more than enough to provide information on questions that remain unanswered in the scarce remains of the works of Iamblichus and Syrianus. This makes it possible not only to approach Proclus' work from the point of view of Iamblichus' programme to revive Pythagoreanism, but also to fill some gaps in this programme, at least as it was understood and adapted by Proclus. For this reason our discussion of Proclus can be much fuller than is possible in the case of Syrianus. Given, however, our limited purposes in Part II, a selective rather than a comprehensive treatment of Proclus will be appropriate.

Proclus produced his works during a long lifetime of great and regular industriousness. It seems then reasonable to suppose that his ideas might have developed or changed in the course of this long activity. However, few of his works can be assigned to specific periods of his life.[2] His pupil Marinus tells us (*Vita Procli*, ch. 13) that the *Commentary on the Timaeus* was written when Proclus was a young man, still very much under the influence (one could assume) of Syrianus. The work *On Providence* was written when Proclus was no longer young (§45, 5–11). The *Platonic Theology* is certainly later than the *Commentary on the Parmenides*.[3] However an attempt to argue that the *Elements of Physics* is a very early work has not been successful.[4] It has been suggested that the *Elements of Theology* might also be early, in view of

[1] Cf. Saffrey and Westerink, in Proclus, *Theol. Plat.* I clii; Segonds (1985–6), liv ff.
[2] On this question cf. Saffrey and Westerink, in Proclus, *Theol. Plat.* I xxiii–xxiv; Sheppard (1980), 34–8; Segonds (1985–6), xli ff.
[3] Cf. Saffrey and Westerink, loc. cit.
[4] Cf. Dodds, in Proclus, *El. theol.* xviii, 201, 250.

the relative simplicity of its structure of reality as compared with that of the *Platonic Theology*.[5] Yet allowance must be made for the particular pedagogic purposes and restraints characteristic of the *Elements of Theology* (see below, Chapter 9). On the other hand the *Platonic Theology* has been thought to show, in its style, signs of senility,[6] a suggestion that would be difficult to prove. The cross-references in Proclus' works tend to show that he could also revise his works at later stages.[7] It has been convincingly argued on the basis of differences in doctrine that the essays constituting the *Commentary on the Republic* were written at different periods of Proclus' life.[8] However doctrinal comparisons between works or parts of works can in some cases yield only tentative results.[9] In general then one has little choice but to approach Proclus on a systematic rather than chronological basis. However, the precaution can be taken of considering each work individually, in so far as this is possible, so as to allow what doctrinal differences there might be between the works to emerge.

1. THE RIVALRY WITH THE MATHEMATICIAN DOMNINUS OF LARISSA

Proclus' fellow-pupil and colleague Hermias left Athens at some point after his studies with Syrianus and went to Alexandria where he, and more especially his son Ammonius, would train an important group of Neoplatonic philosophers. The relations between the two ex-pupils of Syrianus appear to have been good: Hermias married a relative of Syrianus, and their son Ammonius went to Athens to receive his philosophical education from Proclus before returning to Alexandria to become himself a very influential teacher.

Syrianus had, however, another pupil in the final years of his life, Domninus of Larissa, whose relations with Proclus became far from friendly.[10] Marinus, Proclus' biographer, or rather encomiast (and successor), reports in his *Life of Proclus*:

---

[5] Cf. Dodds, op. cit. xvi–xvii; but cf. Trouillard's comments (1965), 45.
[6] Cf. Dodds, op. cit., xv.   [7] Cf. Dodds, loc. cit.
[8] Sheppard (1980), 15–21, 34–8.   [9] Cf. Blumenthal (1975).
[10] Proclus' reference to 'my colleague Domninus' in *In Tim.* I 109, 30–110, 1 (cf. 122, 18–20; the report of Domninus' views may extend to 123, 10) is not unfriendly and is probably an echo from the period of their common study of Plato's *Timaeus* under Syrianus.

⟨Syrianus⟩ proposed to interpret for him ⟨i.e. Proclus⟩ and for the philosopher and successor, the Syrian Domninus, either the poems of Orpheus or the ⟨'Chaldaean⟩ Oracles', and he asked them to choose. But since they did not agree, each making a different choice, ⟨Domninus⟩ preferring Orpheus and our ⟨Proclus⟩ the 'Oracles', Syrianus, who also had not long to live, was prevented ⟨from realizing his project⟩.[11]

This report is disturbing not only on account of its portrayal of an unseemly disharmony between Syrianus' pupils in the last days of their master's life. More disconcerting is the suggestion that the successor of Syrianus was not the young and brilliant Proclus, but Domninus. However, it is possible that the phrase 'the philosopher and successor' in Marinus is in fact a marginal gloss explaining the word 'him' in the text, a gloss which, as frequently happens, was later incorporated in the body of the text.[12] Since this is the only piece of evidence in favour of Domninus' succession to Syrianus, and since, in one interpretation, it can be set aside, it does not provide a strong enough basis for claiming that Domninus, not Proclus, succeeded Syrianus.[13]

However the disagreement between Proclus and Domninus was clear, and it went further. Proclus wrote a special treatise directed against Domninus, in which he 'purified' Plato's doctrines.[14] Thus Domninus was regarded as a 'heretic' who corrupted the Platonic heritage, which therefore required, as it had in Numenius' time, purification. We are not told of the nature of the corruption for which Domninus was allegedly responsible. Damascius, pupil of Ammonius and of Marinus, allows Domninus mathematical skill but finds him a superficial philosopher.[15] An example of Domninus' inadequacy as a philosopher is given: the oracle of Asclepius at Athens prescribed to Domninus and to Plutarch, Syrianus' teacher, the eating of pork to cure them of an illness. Domninus duly carried out the prescription although it violated the law of his land (so Damascius), whereas Plutarch got the oracle to come up with a prescription more compatible with religious beliefs.[16] The story not only dissociates Domninus

---

[11] *Vita Procli*, ch. 26.
[12] Hultsch (1905), 1522; Saffrey and Westerink, in Proclus, *Theol. Plat.* I, xvii–xix.
[13] Proclus' succession to Syrianus is attested elsewhere in Marinus' *Vita Procli* (chs. 12, 36); cf. Saffrey and Westerink, loc. cit.
[14] Damascius, *Vita Isidori* 191, 2 ff.
[15] Damascius, loc. cit.
[16] *Vita Isidori* 183, 8 ff.; cf. the Arabic *Commentary on the Golden Verses* attributed to Proclus, 11.

from the orthodox tradition running from Plutarch through Syrianus to Proclus, but also points to a heretical trait in Domninus which Iamblichus had found before in Porphyry: a failure to take religious practices seriously and to reconcile them with other sources of divine revelation. It is thus against Iamblichean criteria for the true philosopher that Domninus was found wanting.

Considering the purge which Domninus suffered at the hands of Proclus, it is remarkable that some of his work, albeit little, has survived. It is no doubt due to its pedagogical excellence that Domninus' short *Manual of Introductory Arithmetic* was preserved in company with other mathematical introductions such as Nicomachus' *Introduction to Arithmetic*, Nicomachus' *Manual of Harmonics*, and Euclid's *Elements*.[17] Domninus' manual provides a very clear and simple explanation of the main terms, concepts, and distinctions in the theory of numbers. The concision and orderliness of his exposition is not interrupted by extra-mathematical inferences or learned additions such as appear in Nicomachus' *Introduction* and in Iamblichus' version of Nicomachus (*On Pyth*. IV). Domninus' use of Euclidean ideas in his *Manual* has even provoked a modern admirer to see in his work a rejection of the Nicomachean tradition of arithmetic as perpetuated by Iamblichus and Proclus and a return to the 'mathematically sounder' Euclidean approach to arithmetic.[18] This seems exaggerated: Domninus makes extensive use of Nicomachus in his *Manual* and his chief contribution consists in the clarity and simplicity absolutely essential to a work as short as his.[19] At the end of the *Manual* he promises an *Elements of Arithmetic* (ἀριθμητικὴ στοιχείωσις), probably a more ambitious project in which he intended to explain, among other things, mathematical theories in Plato.[20]

2. PLATO AND PYTHAGORAS

The dispute with Domninus had little effect on Proclus' professional career. Whatever difficulties it might suggest were soon overcome as

[17] Cf. Tannery (1906), 262–3.   [18] Tannery (1884), 107 ff.; (1906), 259 ff.
[19] Cf. Hultsch (1905), 1523–4, with his general estimate of the work, 1525; Domninus is also discussed in some detail by Klein (1968), 32–6; Ebbesen (1981), 251–2.
[20] Domninus, *Manual* 428–9; Ruelle's suggestion (1883), 83, that the other short surviving mathematical piece attributed to Domninus is a chapter from the *Elements of Arithmetic* seems unlikely: it is a self-contained technical solution to a specific mathematical problem (the attribution to Domninus is questioned by Tannery [1885*b*], 137).

Proclus quickly established his position at the head of the Platonic school at Athens. The effect of the conflict on Proclus' intellectual life is less easily gauged since so little is known of Domninus' ideas and of the details of Proclus' argument with him. The reports of Proclus' successors considered above, if they may be taken to reflect the master's view, suggest that Proclus felt it necessary to insist on the proper (Iamblichean) acceptance of religious customs in the face of Domninus' heterodox practice, and on the place and (especially) limits of mathematics in philosophy. The latter point will be discussed in more detail below. It will be appropriate, however, to begin our study of Proclus with some consideration of his views on the nature, function, and history of philosophy.

His views on these topics are in general the same, it would appear, as those of Iamblichus and of Syrianus. One does not have to read far into his major commentaries to find Pythagoreans and Orphics quoted as authorities supporting Plato. Aristotle is given a subordinate place: he is sometimes right, frequently mistaken.[21] It is assumed that true Greek philosophy agrees with, and can be illustrated by, the inspired poetry of Homer and Hesiod and the barbarian revelations of the 'Chaldaean Oracles'.[22]

A text from the opening of the *Platonic Theology* (I, ch. 5, 25, 24–26, 9) may serve to indicate in particular the relation between Pythagoras and Plato:

But we must show that each of these doctrines is in harmony with the first principles of Plato and with the secret revelations of the theologians. For all Greek theology derives from Orphic mystagogy, Pythagoras first (πρῶτον) learning from Aglaophemus the secrets concerning the gods, Plato after him (δευτέρου) receiving the complete science of the gods from Pythagorean and Orphic writings. For in attributing in the *Philebus* the doctrine of the two kinds of principles to the Pythagoreans, he calls them 'dwellers with the gods' (16 c 8) and blessed. Indeed Philolaus the Pythagorean has written many wonderful things about these ⟨first principles⟩.

Plato's theology, or science of the divine, is then Pythagorean in inspiration. Proclus' authority for this, as the reference to Aglaophemus indicates, is the same as that used for the same purpose by Iamblichus and Syrianus, namely the (pseudo-) Pythagorean *Sacred*

---

[21] Below, Ch. 9.
[22] On Proclus' treatment of inspired poetry and its relation to Syrianus' theory, cf. Sheppard (1980), 95 ff., 162–82.

Discourse.[23] The *Sacred Discourse* is also referred to as the authority for the Orphic and Pythagorean source of Greek, i.e. Platonic, theology in the *Commentary on the Timaeus* (III 161, 3–6). In Chapter 9 below evidence will be presented showing that in the *Commentary on the Timaeus* Proclus also regards Plato's physics as 'Pythagorean'. Finally, in providing valuable information on the history of mathematics in his *Commentary on Euclid* Proclus gives Pythagoras a pivotal role: he credits him with the introduction of a philosophical approach to geometry, as compared with the non-philosophical approach that preceded it:[24]

After these ⟨Thales, Mamercus⟩ Pythagoras transformed the understanding ⟨'philosophy'⟩ of geometry so that it could serve to educate the free man, examining its first principles from a basis transcending them and investigating the theorems in an immaterial and intellectual manner.

In other words Pythagoras raised geometry to the role mathematics is given in Plato's *Republic*: to introduce the soul to immaterial reality; to receive its grounding for the true philosopher in more ultimate principles.

Proclus also accepted his teacher's Iamblichean understanding of the history of philosophy as a tradition of the revelation of divine truth by the souls not only of Plato, but also of Plotinus, Porphyry, Iamblichus, and even Syrianus himself.[25] He too considers the souls of true philosophers to be superior to ordinary souls, to be participants in the divine vision of the *Phaedrus* that are sent down to save mankind. Thus his interpretation of the figure and function of Socrates in the *Alcibiades*, in his *Commentary* on that dialogue, is in its essentials the same as Syrianus' treatment of Socrates in the *Phaedrus*. Already the etymology of Socrates' name as Proclus understands it—'saviour of the strength of the soul' (*In Crat.* 8, 18–19)—indicates the nature of his function. There is much more information to be found in Proclus on the theory of superior saving souls, and I shall return to it in more detail in the next section.

In general, then, philosophy for Proclus, as for Iamblichus and Syrianus, is a tradition of divinely revealed truth conveyed to fallen souls for their salvation by a select, i.e. Platonic, succession of superior

---

[23] Cf. Saffrey and Westerink's note ad loc.

[24] *In Eucl.* 65, 15–19; this has been noted by Breton (1969), 25–7.

[25] Cf. *Theol. Plat.* I 5, 6–7, 8; *In Parm.* 618, 1–13; Saffrey (1976), 204–12.

souls. In the texts cited above it appears also that Platonism, in theology, mathematics, and physics, can be reduced to Pythagoreanism.
However this reduction, although occurring in Proclus, is not as
radical as it is in Iamblichus and Syrianus, and does not give a
balanced view of Proclus' general attitude to the relation between
Pythagoras and Plato. As this point is of some consequence in determining Proclus' position with respect to the ideas of Iamblichus and
Syrianus and relates to important modifications in the use he makes of
mathematics in philosophy, it will repay closer attention here.

In reading Proclus, one soon notices that he tends to attribute so
much importance to Plato that Plato emerges from the shadow of
Pythagoras and even dominates him. This may be illustrated from the
very same opening pages of the *Platonic Theology* in which Plato's
dependence on 'Pythagorean' theology is stressed. While indicating
briefly that Platonic philosophy had a long and changing life, Proclus
insists that it was one man, Plato, who revealed the secrets of theology
to men (5, 6–6, 7). The unique place of Plato is stressed again a little
later (13, 8 ff.), where Proclus claims that what distinguishes Plato's
theology from that of the Orphics, Pythagoreans, and Chaldaeans is its
scientific character (20, 4–25). Proclus is thinking here of the science
of dialectic which he takes to be the proper science of theological
objects and which he finds expounded in particular in Plato's
Parmenides. He assumes that such a science is not to be found in the
Pythagoreans, who employ an inferior approach, namely mathematical analogies directed upwards to the divine (loc. cit.). Thus, from a
scientific point-of-view, Plato's dialectic is superior as theology to the
mathematical theology of the Pythagoreans.

A similar tendency to play down the scientific claims of the Pythagoreans can already be found in the early and most Pythagoreanizing of
Proclus' works, the *Commentary on the Timaeus*: there Proclus
characterizes the Pythagorean approach as lofty, inspired, symbolic,
anagogic, *revelatory*, whereas that of Socrates is ethical, *demonstrative*
(ἀποδεικτικόν); in the *Timaeus* Plato combines the revelatory style of
Pythagoreanism with the demonstrative method of Socrates (I 7, 21–8,
4). One will readily agree with Proclus that Plato's dialogues embody
scientific method far more than do such supposedly early Pythagorean
works as the *Sacred Discourse*. But Proclus' recognition of this fact
implies a significant revaluation of the respective importance of
Pythagoras and Plato, and a noteworthy departure from Iamblichus'
position. For Iamblichus, Pythagoras was the first 'scientific' philo-

sopher. Hence Pythagorean literature was to be seen as the standard against which the rest of Greek philosophy, including Plato, was to be read. Plato was made more 'scientific', i.e. more Pythagorean, through a syllogizing of his dialogues. For Proclus, however, Plato had greater claims to being scientific. As a consequence Plato's dialogues receive a primacy and centrality in Proclus' philosophy that go beyond what is allowed for by Iamblichus' position. Specific expressions and consequences of this important shift in perspective will be encountered further on.

This contrast between Proclus and Iamblichus must not, however, be exaggerated. It would be misleading to conclude, for example, that Proclus had doubts about the authenticity and priority of the Pythagorean documents invoked by Iamblichus and Syrianus. Apart from the *Sacred Discourse* and Philolaus (his favourite Pythagorean authority), Proclus makes use of the *Golden Verses*, Timaeus of Locri, the *Hymn to Number*, and other similar (pseudo-) Pythagorean works.[26] Nor can it be inferred that Proclus went so far as to find a doctrinal difference between Plato and Pythagoreanism. Rather, as Iamblichus believed that Pythagoras first gave scientific form to revelations of great (Chaldaean, Egyptian) antiquity, so Proclus included Orphism and Pythagoreanism in the ancient revelations and first found scientific expression of them in Plato.

3. THE THEORY OF SUPERIOR SOULS

Often enough it has been noted that Proclus, following Iamblichus and Syrianus, did not accept Plotinus' contention that part of the human soul remains 'above' in the intelligible world even when the soul descends in its preoccupation with the material world.[27] Hardly any notice has been taken, however, of the fact that certain qualifications need to be introduced into this view of Proclus' position. For him some souls possess a privileged connection with the transcendent

[26] Cf. *In Tim.* I 199, 3–4; 203, 25–7; 316, 18–24; II 8, 9–10; 53, 2–7 (for Timaeus of Locri cf. below, Ch. 9); *In Remp.* II 69, 2–3. Proclus' usual practice, however, is to cite 'the Pythagoreans' in general, rather than specific Pythagorean authorities and works. An exception is Philolaus, who is singled out in particular, it appears, for his closeness to Plato's *Philebus*; cf. *Theol. Plat.* I 26, 4–9; III 30, 19–23 (with Saffrey and Westerink's note, 120 n. 8).
[27] Cf. Dodds's comments (309), in Proclus, *El. theol.*; above, p. 38; Saffrey (1984), 164–6.

world in virtue of which they can in their descent reveal truth and bring about the return of souls that have fallen from their intelligible 'fatherland'. Aspects of this theory have been encountered above in Iamblichus, Hierocles, and Syrianus. It can be found described in some detail in a number of Proclus' surviving works which thus allow of a fuller description and clarification of the theory at least in the version that it assumes in Proclus.

The *Commentary on the Timaeus* discusses at various points the different degrees in the descent of the soul in the world. At the top Proclus places the souls of the gods that do not descend into the world, but govern it from above without being affected or changed in any way in their transcendent independence.[28] These divine souls are 'accompanied' without interruption by lower souls who never descend. Below these come souls who do descend, but remain pure (ἄχραντος), untarnished by vice and affections. And these are followed in turn by souls who not only descend but also become corrupted by the material world.[29] From the first two degrees of this structure it can be seen that it represents a formalization of the divine company of gods and their followers, unfallen and fallen, of the *Phaedrus*.[30] The *Commentary* elsewhere provides more details on the class of descended but pure souls: they accomplish great things in the world (I 111, 14–19); their descent is accompanied by natural portents (113, 4–7)—one thinks of such portents as Iamblichus recounts in *On the Pythagorean Life*; they are called 'heroes' by Plato (II 230, 7–9)—the reference is to *Cratylus* 397 d, as will soon be clear; and, most importantly, they possess in their descent a superior knowledge inspired in them by the gods: the examples of the Sibyl and Heracles are given.[31]

Heracles is named again in the notes taken from Proclus' comments on *Cratylus* 397 d: there he is one of a class of 'heroic souls' who descend into the material world but remain pure (ἄχραντος) and more insightful (νοερώτερος) than other descended souls. Such heroic souls descend so as to benefit (εὐεργεσία) mankind, sharing as they do in the part that 'weighs' man down, but also in the power to lead up and escape from matter (*In Crat.* 68, 17–29). These souls are 'heroes' or

---

[28] On these cf. Dodds, op. cit. 295–6.

[29] III 259, 11–27; cf. I 131, 28–132, 5; II 112, 23–5 (same theory in *In Alc.* §§ 32, 13–34, 10). The systematic triadic arrangement of everything in the *El. theol.* leaves no room for the distinction between the third and fourth degrees in that work (cf. Propositions 185, 202, 204).

[30] Cf. Dodds, op. cit. 296.

[31] III 159, 29–160, 12; cf. also *In Alc.* §§ 132, 10–133, 13; *De prov.* § 19.

'demons', however, by relation (σχέσει), not by nature (φύσει): in their higher status as souls they can be *compared* to heroes and demons which, however, are ontologically different and superior, and correspond, it appears, to the souls that continuously follow the gods of the *Commentary on the Timaeus*.[32]

The theory of superior souls is found also in the essays of the *Commentary on the Republic*, in particular in the sixteenth essay. There, in discussing the figure of Er in Plato's *Republic*, Proclus appears to hesitate as to whether Er possesses a soul superior *in substance* to other human souls or merely superior in kind of life (II 123, 23–124, 12). Proclus prefers, it seems, to assign to Er a superior substance. At any rate, through his superiority, Er was given the power by the gods to receive the vision which he imparts in the *Republic* (123, 14–124, 8). A little later Proclus mentions other souls who have communicated to men divine mysteries, divination, medicine ... (153, 5–154, 5). He does not make clear the ontological rank(s) of such souls, but suggests that soul can be raised to a superior rank by the divine theurgic power in the universe as well as by philosophy (154, 1–12).

Less compatible with the classifications of the *Commentaries* on the *Timaeus* and on the *Cratylus* is the theory presented later in the same essay (331, 10–332, 3) that 'heroic souls', superior in being to human souls, descend into and assume a human existence. If these heroic souls were to correspond to the souls of the heroes proper mentioned in Proclus' other two commentaries, then they ought not to descend. Neither do they correspond to the 'heroic souls' that occur in those works which are superior in relation, but not in being, to other human souls. It seems we must suppose that the psychic hierarchy is more complicated than it at first appears, and includes undescending heroes, descending heroes in human form, descending pure human souls, and descending impure human souls. Or one might infer that Proclus changed his mind in his interpretation of the ontological rank of the heroic communicators of divine truth to man. The latter possibility might account for the difference between the ideas of the sixteenth essay and the fairly standard doctrine of the commentaries on the *Timaeus*, *Cratylus*, and *Alcibiades*. But the fact that the various accounts of the doctrine in these commentaries are not necessarily exhaustive makes it difficult to be certain about this.

---

[32] *In Crat.* 68, 13–19; 77, 14–18; cf. *In Remp.* II 310, 18–21; Dodds, loc. cit. The demons and heroes proper also play a role in elevating man (*In Crat.* 75, 19–76, 4), as exemplified for example in Eros' action on Socrates (above, p. 126).

The distinction in being between (human) 'heroic souls' and heroes or demons proper entails of course a greater distinction between such souls and the gods. Proclus emphasizes the latter distinction in the *Commentary on the Timaeus* in arguing against Plotinus' view (as he understands it) that fallen human souls are identical in nature with those of the gods (III 245, 19–246, 23). It nevertheless remains that in allowing for higher insight and divine inspiration in a *certain* class of descended souls, Proclus preserves at least for part of humanity that access to higher truth that Plotinus' theory was designed to make possible.[33]

4. LEARNING, DISCOVERY, AND REVELATION

Besides providing more details on the ontological character and place of the superior descended souls who communicate insight to man, Proclus also throws light on some problems connected with their saving mission. One of these problems has been raised above in Part I on the subject of Iamblichus' interpretation of the figure of Pythagoras: Pythagoras is said to have 'discovered' many things, but how is this to be related to the impression given that he learnt much from the Egyptians and Chaldaeans and with the claim that he (merely) revealed divinely inspired truths? Another problem may also be raised: can fallen souls, by their own efforts—as appears to be the case in Plotinus—return to true intelligible insight, or do they depend entirely on the intervention of superior souls to make their return possible? Much help with these questions can be found in Proclus' *Commentary on the Alcibiades* which, in so far as it discusses the interaction between Socrates and Alcibiades in the dialogue, is largely devoted to explaining the problems and methods of a philosophical, i.e. soteriological, education.

It is clear from Proclus' commentary, first of all, that learning from another and discovering by oneself are not to be distinguished in such a way as to represent alternatives in the acquisition of knowledge. Rather, both learning and discovery are to be understood as a process of recollection: in learning, the pupil is guided by the teacher so as to

---

[33] One might also mention in this regard Proclus' doctrine of the 'flower' of the soul which, in providing an ontological link with the transcendent, also mitigates his anti-Plotinian position; cf. Grondijs (1960), 37 ff.; Beierwaltes (1963), 261–6; (1985), 174–82.

discover within himself the knowledge that is innate in his soul. More advanced souls also discover the knowledge innate in them, but are capable of this without having so much recourse to a teacher. There are therefore degrees in learning–discovery relating to the degrees to which the souls have fallen: at lower degrees souls require teachers and guides to arouse or provoke in them the discovery which is self-discovery; at higher degrees souls are more capable of such discovery and require less guidance.[34] These ideas might be suitably applied, I believe, as a Procline account of Pythagoras in his role as both scientific discoverer and pupil of barbarian sages: his discovery of the sciences was a self-discovery, a disclosure of the intelligible principles innate in his soul; for this purpose, in his youth at least, some stimulation was provided by his teachers, although one must assume that, in view of the superior status of his soul, his need for this was minimal!

Both Pythagoras and his teachers revealed divinely-inspired truths. However we must be careful again not to set divine inspiration against self-discovery. Proclus introduces divine inspiration as the highest degree in a hierarchy descending through discovery down to learning (§ 242, 4–11). This suggests some continuity between divine inspiration and self-discovery, a continuity also implied in the fact that the principles that are the objects of self-discovery are psychic images of higher divine principles (below, p. 159) and thus are already themselves inspirations deriving from above. These innate principles are cited, in one unfortunately corrupt passage, as the reason why we need (or *don't* need, in another reading of the passage) a guide for learning that transcends our nature.[35] Whatever the true sense of the passage, it is Proclus' general view that we attain higher truths through the guidance and mediation of gods and demons. And the analogy between our reliance on superior guidance for such insights and the function of guides (teachers) in self-discovery again points to some continuity between divine inspiration and discovery. Thus the combination of revelation with discovery in the figure of Pythagoras (or Plato) is no more a contradiction than that of discovery with learning.

The theory of discovery and learning in the *Commentary on the Alcibiades* also points to an answer to the question of the fallen souls' need for guidance and teaching. The degree of indispensability of such guidance must depend namely on the degree to which the soul has fallen. Proclus leaves little doubt that souls at lower levels require

[34] *In Alc.* §§ 225, 4–226, 7; 277, 10–278, 13; 280, 2–281, 14.
[35] *In Alc.* § 235, 15–18; cf. O'Neill (1965), ad loc.

guides and teachers if they are ever to achieve self-discovery. He interprets this action of the teacher on the pupil's soul with the help of Aristotle's account of learning and of change in general. The teacher represents the prior actuality of knowledge, the moving cause actualizing the potential knowledge in the pupil's soul (§ 228, 16–20), or the perfection that brings the imperfect to perfection (§ 235, 10–12). Proclus warns us, however, against certain inferences that this account of teaching might produce. The pupil's soul is not a *tabula rasa*, as in Aristotle, but possesses innately the knowledge that is learned, i.e. discovered, by the pupil (§§ 277, 10–18; 280, 19–281, 7). Furthermore the teacher's action on the pupil is not to be seen as the sole agency responsible for the pupil's self-discovery (§ 281, 10–14):

If, then, one should declare the matter accurately, souls are moved by external agencies, but determine of themselves their scientific replies and so spontaneously demonstrate the truth of Plato's statement that the soul knows everything including itself and requires only an outside stimulus by means of scientific questions. (O'Neill transl.)

The primary agent, then, of the pupil's progress in knowledge is himself. To illustrate this Proclus emphasizes the Socratic idea that it is Socrates' companion who refutes himself, who brings upon himself the discovery of the falsity of his opinions. The situation is quite different from that of

irrational animals . . . 'shepherded with a staff' (*Crit.* 109 b) . . . ⟨and⟩ all those who await healing from outside causes, and wherever the leader leads there the led are led, bereft of the power of ruling and saving themselves; but the human soul, on account of its peculiar characteristic of spontaneity and self-movement (*Phaedr.* 245 c e) is of such a nature as to be active in its own regard, move itself and provide itself with the good. (§ 279, 18–23; O'Neill transl.)

To illustrate the particular kind of action whereby the teacher stimulates the pupil to discover himself, acting on the pupil in such a way as not to override the *primary* agency for which the pupil himself is responsible, Proclus refers to the way the gods and demons work upon us from within, not from without, and in communion with our own natures as self-movers.[36]

These considerations indicate that for Proclus the primary agency for the salvation of fallen souls is to be found in their own selves. In this sense these souls can save themselves. At the same time, however,

---

[36] §§ 281, 15–20; 241, 14–18; cf. *In Parm.* 1031, 11–19; Trouillard (1957), 335.

another agent is required to provoke the souls into self-discovery, a teacher, a guide, a soul of superior insight, a Parmenides, a Socrates, a Plato, a Plotinus, a Syrianus.[37] In this way Socrates' mission of unsettling, pricking, provoking the citizens of Athens had become an expression, some thousand years later, in the same city, of the necessity and role of the succession of 'divine' Platonic philosophers in the world.

[37] Cf. *In Alc.* §§ 73, 1–5; 133, 6–13; *In Parm.* 617, 23–618, 13; 1030, 22–35; *Theol. Plat.* I, ch. 1.; Trouillard (1957), 335–8 (a good discussion of the question of guidance as a whole); Steel (1987), on Parmenides' maieutic role in the *Parmenides* as interpreted by Proclus.

8

Proclus on Mathematics

IN this chapter Proclus' attitude to mathematics will be discussed for the most part as it is expressed in his *Commentary on Euclid*. His recourse in other works to mathematics in relation to physics and metaphysics will be examined in the next two chapters. In these chapters I point also to continuities between Proclus' general account of mathematics in the *Commentary on Euclid* and his use of mathematics in his other works. This presupposes, however, an account of the philosophy of mathematics of the *Commentary on Euclid* in particular as compared to the philosophies of mathematics of Nicomachus and of Iamblichus, the subject of the following pages.

What survives of Proclus' *Commentary on Euclid* may be divided into four parts: the first prologue (on general mathematics); the second prologue (on geometry); the exegesis of the definitions, postulates, and axioms at the head of Euclid's *Elements* I; and commentary on the theorems of Euclid Book I.[1] With the exception of the *Elements of Theology*, no other work of Proclus has been so often translated and studied. In particular the first prologue has attracted much interest and admiration, from Kepler, who inserted large extracts from it in his *Harmonice Mundi*, to Nicolai Hartmann, who used it as an important and relevant mathematical philosophy.[2] As the contents of the first prologue have been summarized often enough,[3] I will not attempt another summary here. There remain, however, some basic issues connected with the first prologue, the resolution of which will require detailed analysis leading, as I hope to show, to some new insights into Proclus' assumptions in the first prologue.

---

[1] Proclus certainly intended to go beyond *Elements* I in his commentary, although he may not have covered the whole; cf. Heiberg (1882), 164–8; Morrow (1970), xxxi. Marinus' introduction to the *Data* can also be read as evidence of the study of Euclid in Proclus' school.

[2] For an example of unbridled enthusiasm for the *Commentary on Euclid* cf. Steck (1945).

[3] Hartmann's account (1909) can be used, allowance being made for his neo-Kantian approach.

I. GENERAL MATHEMATICS

(i) *Iamblichus'* On Pythagoreanism *III and Proclus'* On Euclid *Prol. I*

It has long been known that Proclus' first prologue substantially corresponds to the third book of Iamblichus' On *Pythagoreanism*, On *General Mathematical Science*.[4] The most natural inference from this would seem to be that Proclus used Iamblichus' text extensively in writing his prologue. Proclus after all was Syrianus' prize pupil; he had read with Syrianus Aristotle's *Metaphysics* (Marinus, *Vita Procli*, ch. 13); and it has been shown in Chapter 6 above that Syrianus, in his treatment of the *Metaphysics*, referred the student to Iamblichus' On *Pythagoreanism* as a source-book for true (i.e. Pythagorean) mathematics, summarizing in particular the contents of Book III of Iamblichus' work.

This inference has not, however, been favoured in what little discussion there is of the question. It has been felt rather that Proclus is using, independently of Iamblichus, an older source which Iamblichus also used.[5] It has been claimed, in support of this position, that there are few verbal parallels between the texts of Proclus and of Iamblichus. The fact that this claim is manifestly untrue[6] is not, however, enough to disprove the position it is supposed to support. More decisive appears to be the fact that Proclus' text is better organized, clearer, more consistent than Iamblichus'. The greater clarity, it is assumed, derives from the original source and therefore testifies to the independence of Proclus' text with respect to Iamblichus. The original source has even been identified: Geminus, a mathematician of

---

[4] Cf. Merlan (1960), 8 ff.; Mueller (1987*b*) for detailed comparisons. The correspondences between the chapters in Proclus (the first number in each set) and in Iamblichus (the following number[s]) are: 1: 1–2; 2: 3; 3–4: 5; 5: 8; 7: 11–12; 8: 15–16; 9: 26; 11: 27; and compare 12: 7; 15: 11 and 34. (I use the chapter divisions introduced by Morrow in his translation of Proclus, and his translation much revised.)

[5] Proposed by Festa (without argument) in Iamblichus *Comm.*, IX; intimated by Morrow (1970) in a note, 344–5; and developed by van der Waerden (1980). Under the influence of this idea Mueller (1987*b*) seems disinclined to conclude that Iamblichus is Proclus' source, although he does not seem to have good grounds against such a conclusion.

[6] Compare Procl. 6, 13–15, Iambl. 13, 18–21; Procl. 7, 20–7, Iambl. 18, 26–19, 6; Procl. 8, 25–9, 2, Iambl. 20, 1–5; Procl. 20, 25–21, 4, Iambl. 55, 12–16; Procl. 25, 1, Iambl. 57, 23; Procl. 25, 4–5, Iambl. 57, 24–5; Procl. 25, 23–26, 3, Iambl. 79, 20–4; Procl. 27, 27–8, Iambl. 82, 11–13; Procl. 32, 21–3, Iambl. 7, 10–13; Procl. 34, 20–35, 5, Iambl. 86, 26–87, 5.

the first century AD. Chapters 1–7, 9, 11, and 13 of Proclus' prologue are taken, it is claimed, from Geminus, whose work reappears in a corrupt and confused form in Iamblichus.[7]

The assumption that the greater clarity and organization of Proclus' text argues against his use of Iamblichus' somewhat confused text, and for his proximity to an even earlier original, is admissible if one does not consider Proclus' other works. The implied denial that Proclus himself is the source of the clarity and organization of the chapters of the first prologue of his *Commentary on Euclid* becomes implausible, however, if one reflects, for example, on the skill Proclus demonstrates in organizing the whole tradition of Platonic metaphysics in his *Elements of Theology*. In comparison to this, the task of producing a clearer version of Iamblichus would have been a simple matter. In what follows I would like also to show that the thesis that Proclus' text comes in large part from Geminus, not from Iamblichus, entails anachronism. I shall then show how a chapter in Proclus' prologue (ch. 8) which is not claimed for Geminus—for it quotes Plotinus—represents a revision of the corresponding chapter in Iamblichus, and provides information on Proclus' *modus operandi* in composing his prologue, information that yields an explanation of various differences between Proclus' prologue and its Iamblichean source.

The chapters claimed for Geminus in Proclus' prologue contain matter which cannot be dated without anachronism to the first century AD. For example the terminology of the 'Chaldaean Oracles' (second century AD) assimilated into a Neoplatonic context (first possible with Porphyry, then fully worked out by Iamblichus) can be found in ch. 2 (6, 9) in the reference to intelligible and 'hidden' principles (κρυφίων ἀρχῶν). 'Hidden' is a word derived by the later Neoplatonists from the 'Chaldaean Oracles' and used as a technical term for the highest intelligible causes.[8]

The 'Geminus' chapters in Proclus also contain arguments and theories which constitute elaborations on ideas first found in Iamblichus and (especially) in Syrianus. For example chapter 6 is devoted to arguing against the Aristotelian theory that numbers are mere abstractions from material objects. In the chapter corresponding to

---

[7] Van der Waerden (1980). On Geminus' date, cf. Aujac (1975a), xix–xxiv. For a detailed critique of van der Waerden cf. O'Meara (1988), the major points of which are summarized in the following pages. Cf. also Mueller (1987a).

[8] Cf. *Or. Chald.* 198 (with des Places's references); Syrianus, *In met.* 182, 24; Proclus, *In Crat.* 32, 22 and 28; Saffrey and Westerink's notes in Proclus, *Theol. Plat.* III 145; IV 120–1.

Proclus' preceding chapter (*Comm.* 34, 9–10) Iamblichus briefly rejects the theory of abstraction, but without argument. In his chapter 6 (12, 9 ff.) Proclus assembles arguments against Aristotle: how could mathematicals possess accuracy if they are derived from sensible objects? Where is the indivisibility in mathematicals to be found in sensibles where all is divisible? How could immutable laws be derived from ever-changing sensibles? How could the general be prior in demonstration if it is posterior to sensible particulars? Some of these arguments, expressed in the same interrogative and accumulative form, appear already in Syrianus.[9] This suggests that Proclus, in chapter 6 of his prologue, is strengthening the anti-Aristotelian position of Iamblichus with the help of the anti-Aristotelian arguments that he had learnt from Syrianus. Proclus also rejects in chapter 6 the Aristotelian idea that the soul is a *tabula rasa* (16, 8–10). It is rather 'a tablet that has always been inscribed and is always writing itself and being written on by intellect.' Proclus is assuming a theory of innate ideas (here in particular mathematicals) that derive from intellect and are unfolded by the soul, a theory in which Aristotle's image of the soul as tablet ($\gamma\rho\alpha\mu\mu\alpha\tau\epsilon\hat{\iota}o\nu$, *De an.* 430 a 1) is given a Platonic turn.[10] The origin of this Platonic interpretation of the image of the *De anima* appears to be Iamblichus.[11] In the same chapter finally Proclus explains mathematicals as 'projections' ($\pi\rho o\beta o\lambda\alpha\acute{\iota}$) by the soul of innate intelligible principles.[12] This is again a theory first clearly found in Syrianus and which appears to have its ultimate origin in Iamblichus (above, pp. 133–4).

The place in the history of philosophy of the elaborate Platonic epistemology of the sixth chapter of Proclus' prologue is not then the first century AD. It represents rather a developed stage of the anti-Aristotelian arguments and Platonic theories first found in Syrianus and whose ultimate source of inspiration appears to be Iamblichus. We may conclude in other words that the author of this chapter is Proclus himself. The occasion that provoked it can be found in the

---

[9] Syrianus, *In met.* 95, 29–38; 90, 17–23; cf. above, p. 133. Proclus returns to the polemic against abstraction (applied to geometricals) in *In Eucl.* 49, 12 ff.; 139, 26–140, 18; *In Parm.* 894, 24 ff.; 980, 17 ff.

[10] Cf. also *In Eucl.* 186, 6–7; *In Crat.* 26, 26–7; *In Alc.* §§ 277, 10–18; 280, 19–281, 7.

[11] Cf. Philoponus, *In De an.* 533, 25 ff.; Steel (1978), 148; Segonds (1985–6) II 435; cf. Plotinus V 3, 4, 20–3.

[12] *In Eucl.* 17, 22–18, 4; cf. also 13, 6 ff.; 52, 20 ff.; 78, 20 ff.; 141, 2 ff.; below, pp. 200–1. On the theory of mathematicals as projections in Proclus, cf., for example, Breton (1969), 28–31, 111–22; Charles (1982), 191–201; Beierwaltes (1985), 258 ff.

chapter in Iamblichus corresponding to Proclus' chapter 5: a mention of the Aristotelian theory of abstraction. The technical use of Chaldaean terminology in chapter 2 also shows that this chapter cannot simply be dated to the first century AD, but indicates a date no earlier than Porphyry and very probably later.

The hypothesis that much of Proclus' prologue is not based on Iamblichus' *On Pythagoreanism* III, but is to be assigned to an earlier source from which Iamblichus also was inspired, then (1) involves a number of anachronisms; (2) makes the questionable assumption that Proclus is not himself the source of the greater clarity and order of his prologue; and (3) ignores the evidence of Syrianus' opinion of Iamblichus' book and his recommendation of it to students as a manual of general mathematics.

As the more obvious and likely thesis that Proclus is using Iamblichus has not been examined in any detail, it is desirable to compare the two authors from this viewpoint. Chapter 6 in Proclus comes after a chapter which corresponds to Iamblichus' text, but it does not itself have any equivalent in Iamblichus. The explanation of this has already been found: Proclus is elaborating in chapter 6, in the light of Syrianus' teaching, a defence of Iamblichus' rejection of Aristotelian abstraction in the chapter corresponding to Proclus' fifth chapter. Explanations can also be found from this point-of-view for other additions and omissions in Proclus' prologue as compared to Iamblichus' text.[13] I would like to examine in particular the case of chapter 8, which has not been attributed to Geminus (although it has a corresponding section in Iamblichus, *Comm.* chs. 15–16), since this case will reveal not only Proclus' way of proceeding *vis-à-vis* Iamblichus' text, but also introduce themes of some importance to our larger interests.[14]

In comparing chapter 8 of Proclus' prologue with chapters 15–16 of Iamblichus' *On Pythagoreanism* III, one notices first a difference in the way sources are cited. In Iamblichus, for instance, we find an undeclared allusion to Plotinus I 3, 3, 5–7 (*Comm.* 55, 16–19); in Proclus Plotinus is named and the Plotinian text is more carefully reproduced

---

[13] For example, nothing in Proclus' prologue corresponds to Iamblichus, *Comm.* ch. 4: an explanation of this is suggested by a scholium on Iamblichus' chapter: 'Here the author introduces intelligible matter, as did the Pythagoreans before him, but Proclus does not agree with them' (*Comm.* 100, 11–13). At 8, 7 Proclus refers to 'they ⟨who⟩ call . . .'; who 'they' are is not at all clear from Proclus' text; however, Iamblichus, in the corresponding chapter (ch. 5), is summarizing Pythagorean doctrine.

[14] Cf. Mueller's analysis (1987*b*) of this chapter; he notes many of the facts that I wish to mention.

(21, 20–4). On the supposition then that Proclus is using Iamblichus, we must conclude that Proclus recognized the Plotinian allusion and replaced it with a more faithful quotation. This is not at all unlikely: Proclus, after all, wrote a *Commentary on Plotinus*, a singular honour he reserved otherwise for the ancient philosophers and theologians.[15] The same phenomenon can be observed in relation to the two authors' use of Plato: Proclus quotes explicitly and more fully the texts of Plato implicitly used by Iamblichus[16] and especially quotes texts from Plato which support and illustrate points made in Iamblichus.[17] If then Proclus is indeed using Iamblichus, he is taking advantage of his immense learning to revise the text by naming, quoting more fully, and supplementing Iamblichus' undeclared sources.

A closer comparative examination of the chapters in question in Proclus and Iamblichus strengthens the impression that Proclus is reworking, expanding, and clarifying the Iamblichean chapters. Both authors are concerned with showing the importance of mathematics for theology (metaphysics), physics, politics, ethics, and the productive arts. The Iamblichean text has been summarized above (pp. 48, 50); I shall therefore confine myself here to noting some of the differences in Proclus' version.

(*a*) *Theology*. After his undeclared allusion to Plotinus I 3, 3 Iamblichus concludes his section on this subject thus: 'For all such things provide a major starting point for knowledge of ⟨true⟩ beings and intelligibles' (55, 21–2). Having named and quoted Plotinus more fully, Proclus says:

But that mathematics produces a contribution of the first order to philosophy is clear from these points. But it is necessary to recall the individual ⟨sciences⟩ and show that for theology mathematics prepares intellectual insight. For those truths about the gods that are difficult for imperfect minds to discover and understand, these mathematical theories, through images, show to be trustworthy, evident, and irrefutable.[18] For they show the images in numbers ⟨i.e. arithmetic⟩ of the characters of what transcends being, revealing in discursive objects ⟨i.e. geometry⟩ the powers of intellectual figures. Thus

---

[15] Cf. Westerink (1959). Of course Proclus' quotation of Plotinus is, by modern standards, loose.

[16] Compare Iambl. 55, 8–12, with Procl. 20, 14–26; Iambl. 57, 23–58, 4, with Procl. 25, 3–11.

[17] Compare Iambl. 55, 22–56, 4, with Procl. 22, 17–23, 11; Iambl. 56, 8–13, with Procl. 24, 4–20.

[18] Cf. *In Parm.* 926, 16–29.

Plato explains to us many wonderful doctrines about the gods by means of mathematical forms, and the philosophy of the Pythagoreans conceals its secret theological initiation using such veils. Such also is the entire *Sacred Discourse*, the *Bacchae* of Philolaus, and the whole approach of Pythagoras' exegesis concerning the gods. (21, 25–22, 16)

With this Proclus ends his theological section. What is additional here in Proclus, it is clear, is a recapitulation of the major point concerning the theological relevance of mathematics as expounded by Iamblichus, with the addition of some references. The contrast implied in the latter between Plato's explanations and the secretiveness of Pythagorean initiation will not appear fortuitous if seen in connection with Proclus' distinction, found elsewhere (above, p. 148) between Plato's scientific and the Pythagorean mystical approach.

(*b*) *Physics*. Proclus lists most of the mathematical aspects of physics that occur in Iamblichus. However Iamblichus' 'analogy that travels throughout everything in nature' (55, 25) appears in more correct Platonic form in Proclus as the 'analogy that binds together everything in the world, as Timaeus says somewhere . . .' (22, 19–21). A little later Proclus returns to the *Timaeus* to illustrate further the mathematical structuring of nature (23, 2–11), whereas Iamblichus ends his section with a vague reference to 'noble students of nature who start from first principles' (56, 3–4). Iamblichus' general reference, intended presumably to cover all sorts of ancient Pythagorean cosmology, is narrowed in Proclus so as to refer specifically to Plato's *Timaeus*.

(*c*) *Politics and Ethics*. The chief difference here is the use made of Plato in Proclus (23, 12–24, 20) to illustrate and elaborate on points made more briefly in Iamblichus (56, 4–13).

(*d*) *The Arts*. Proclus' treatment of theoretical arts (24, 23–7) is much shorter than the section on this in Iamblichus (57, 9–22), but it makes Iamblichus' point more clearly and names the art Iamblichus is discussing, rhetoric. As for productive arts Iamblichus says merely (57, 22–3): 'for productive arts ⟨mathematics⟩ has the rank of paradigm', whereas Proclus tells us: 'for productive arts ⟨mathematics⟩ has the rank of paradigm, generating before in itself the principles and measures of what are produced' (24, 27–25, 3). The all-too-brief statement in Iamblichus becomes, with the further words in Proclus, intelligible. Finally, on the subject of the practical arts, Proclus makes explicitly (25, 6–7) the use implicitly made in Iamblichus (57, 26–7) of Plato's *Philebus*.

The differences then between Proclus' chapter 8 and the corresponding part of Iamblichus' book can be accounted for as deriving from a desire on Proclus' part to clarify, explain, and document Iamblichus' text. The reasons for his systematic introduction of passages from Plato will only become fully clear when his views on the relations between Euclid and Plato are examined. But already a distinctive tendency of Proclus that has been noticed elsewhere, namely his inclination to see Plato as more scientific and the Pythagoreans as more mystical, has emerged in our comparisons. This result indicates that the differences in Proclus' text *vis-à-vis* Iamblichus' book are to be taken as expressions of Proclus' own preferences. The study of chapter 6 of Proclus' prologue, in the critique of the Geminus theory above, also shows that this chapter is to be understood as an elaboration of Iamblichus' text in the light of what Proclus had learnt from Syrianus and developed further.

We may conclude then that the supposition that Proclus used Iamblichus directly in composing his prologue yields satisfactory results in the case of the two chapters examined. From this viewpoint the similarities and differences between the texts of Proclus and Iamblichus can be explained. Indeed some of the differences reflect ideas characteristic of Proclus and his teacher Syrianus. The revisions that these differences imply are also compatible with what is otherwise known of Proclus' skill as a philosophical writer. And his use of Iamblichus is made in any case extremely likely through what has been shown concerning Syrianus' use and recommendation of Iamblichus' book. On the other hand the attribution of some chapters in Proclus corresponding to Iamblichus to an earlier source has been shown to be untenable.[19]

These conclusions deserve perhaps some emphasis. They indicate

---

[19] I do not mean to deny that Proclus uses Geminus, merely that the chapters in Proclus corresponding to Iamblichus' work are taken, not from Iamblichus, but from Geminus. It is worth paying attention to the way in which Proclus introduces Geminus in the first prologue: he is named as a proponent of a division of the mathematical sciences *other* than that of the Pythagoreans (38, 1–4), i.e. that of Nicomachus reproduced by Iamblichus (*Comm.* ch. 7) and summarized by Proclus in the preceding pages (35, 19 ff.). The former division is alluded to by Iamblichus (95, 22–4), but Proclus gives it a representative, Geminus. Again Proclus is clarifying and documenting Iamblichus' text. More generally on the liberties taken by Proclus with his sources, cf. Heath (1956), I 33–4.

that Proclus had studied (at least) Book III of Iamblichus' *On Pythag-oreanism* as carefully as Syrianus could have wished, and that Proclus' prologue can justifiably be used as evidence for his attitude to Iam-blichean Pythagoreanism as expressed in *On Pythagoreanism* III.[20] This makes the prologue a privileged source for the study of the evolution of Proclus' ideas in relation to those of Iamblichus.

(ii) *Proclus' Revisions of Iamblichus*

The analysis above has indicated some of the ways in which Proclus altered the Iamblichean original: he documented the Iamblichean material by naming and quoting more accurately and fully from Iamblichus' sources, and clarified Iamblichus by simplifying some passages and expanding others. It can be seen that he accepts the essentials of Iamblichus' position on the importance of mathematics: consequent on the intermediate position of its objects in the structure of reality, mathematics has a pivotal and far-reaching function, for it constitutes a paradigm for physics, ethics, politics, and the arts, and fore-shadows the objects of theology or metaphysics. The latter aspect expresses a function of mathematics that Proclus documents (20, 14 ff.) with the text of Plato's *Republic* that Iamblichus (55, 8 ff.) silently uses, namely the function of leading the soul up to immaterial being. The one important doctrinal difference between Proclus and Iamblichus noted so far concerns the relation between mathematicals and the soul. The somewhat confusing situation in Iamblichus' text is not allowed to persist in Proclus: he firmly places mathematicals in the soul in the way Syrianus had done, that is, they are 'projections' by the soul of intelligible principles innate in it. This clarification is of some importance, for it determines, as I shall show later, the precise way in which mathematics may be used in physics and metaphysics. In what follows I shall supplement these results with comparisons between some other chapters of Proclus' prologue and Iamblichus' text.

The effort observed above to name and quote more accurately and fully the sources Iamblichus incorporated in his text can be found elsewhere in Proclus' prologue. One might note for example his use of

---

[20] In *In Parm.* 758, 37–8 Proclus appears to be using *On Pythagoreanism* IV (*In Nic.* 20, 14–17) rather than Nicomachus *Intro. arith.* 15, 4–10. Proclus' references outside *In Eucl.* to Pythagorean mathematical ideas are often not precise and full enough to enable us to be sure that his source is Iamblichus rather than some other text, for example Nicomachus.

Aristotle to this effect.[21] Especially noteworthy, however, is his use of Plato: he not only supplements Iamblichus' text with quotations from Plato, but also substitutes the original Platonic passage for the (Pseudo-) Pythagorean plagiary cited as an authority by Iamblichus. Thus Iamblichus' 'Archytas' text in *Comm.* 12, 9–13, is replaced in Proclus (3, 14–16) by a reference to the original text of the *Republic*. The same happens elsewhere,[22] most notably at 10, 15 ff., where Iamblichus' authorities, Brontinus and Archytas (*Comm.* 34, 20 ff.), are not reproduced; Proclus refers rather to Plato's *Republic* (the source of Iamblichus' authorities), saying: 'Let us examine after this what the criterion of mathematics might be and let us place before us Plato as guide to this revelation (προστησώμεθα καὶ τῆς τούτου παραδόσεως ἡγεμόνα τὸν Πλάτωνα)' (10, 16–19). The language is Iamblichean.[23] But it also indicates, I believe, how Proclus' substitution of Platonic for 'Pythagorean' texts is to be understood. It is not the case that Proclus suspected that Iamblichus' Pythagorean authorities were forged, copied from Plato. Proclus does not hesitate after all to cite himself in his prologue the *Sacred Discourse* (above, p. 162). Rather he prefers Plato to Archytas, Brontinus, etc., as his guide to mathematics.[24] This preference has to do primarily with the fact that he regards Euclid, as we shall see, as a faithful exponent of Plato, and this in turn makes Plato into the principal authority of his *Commentary on Euclid*. But we may suspect also that the distinction for Proclus between Plato's scientific explanation and Pythagorean revelation (above, p. 162) is responsible at a deeper level for his choice of Plato's dialogues, rather than Iamblichus' Pythagoreans, as appropriate sources for the study of the nature and function of mathematics.

Greater attention to Plato leads, however, to a problem which Proclus discusses in chapter 10 of his prologue, a chapter coming between two chapters corresponding respectively to Iamblichus' *Comm.* chapters 26 and 27. The problem is the following: a major theme in Iamblichus' book (following Nicomachus) is the *scientific* character of mathematics. Yet some members of Proclus' school (29,

---

[21] Compare Proclus, 32, 23–6 and 33, 21–34, 1, with Iamblichus 84, 21–5 (with the scholium ad loc., 103, 22) and 86, 2–6.

[22] Compare also Iamblichus, *Comm.* 44, 10 ff. ('Archytas') with Proclus 45, 15 ff. (Plato's *Meno*); the substitution of Platonic for Pythagorean texts is noticed by Mueller (1987*b*).

[23] Cf. above, Ch. 4 n. 20.

[24] Cf. the opening of Proclus' second prologue: Πλάτωνι συμπορευόμενοι (cf. *Phaedr.* 249 c), 48, 3.

14 ff.) found that Plato after all does not regard mathematics as scientific. In the *Republic* in particular Plato regards mathematics as defective since it does not examine the hypotheses from which it proceeds. Mathematics is therefore subordinate to dialectic, a science that works back to an ultimate unhypothetical first principle upon which all knowledge depends. In defending the scientific character of mathematics Proclus fully recognizes its subordination to dialectic, which he calls 'perfect' and 'true' science (31, 19–23). As receiving its first principles from dialectic, mathematics is science in a secondary way.[25] As if feeling, however, that this might still not be sufficient to save the scientific claims of mathematics, Proclus attempts to defend further these claims. It is not the case that mathematics is ignorant of its first principles, but it receives these principles (as concepts innate in the soul) and demonstrates what follows from them. In this way mathematics elaborates a scientific knowledge of its matter (32, 5–7 and 16–18). Proclus' argument in fact gives to mathematics the characteristics of science as identified by Aristotle. Plato's own approach in the *Republic* is hardly as positive. The distance separating Plato from Proclus' interpretation of Plato can be measured by the fact this interpretation arises from the attempt to reconcile Iamblichus' Nicomachean emphasis on the scientific character of mathematics with Plato's critique of the deficiency of mathematics, a reconciliation based on Aristotle's characterization of science.

2. ARITHMETIC AND (OR?) GEOMETRY

Having introduced 'general mathematics' in Book III of *On Pythagoreanism* Iamblichus presented in the following books arithmetic (a version of Nicomachus prefaced by praise of Nicomachus as a true Pythagorean); the transposition of arithmetic to physics, ethics, and theology; and the three other mathematical sciences, geometry, music, and astronomy. Proclus, however, moves directly from general mathematics in his first prologue to an introduction to geometry in his second prologue (including praise of Euclid as a Platonist) and to the commentary on Euclid's *Elements*. One may consequently wonder if an introduction to arithmetic, perhaps a version of Nicomachus, once came after the first prologue, or if, rather, the undeniable preference

[25] 32, 3–5. Cf. also *De prov.* §§ 50, 28–9; I. Hadot (1984), 123–4 and (on earlier discussions of the problem) 77–9.

for geometry in physics and metaphysics that will be observed in the next two chapters led Proclus to use geometry for the general purposes that arithmetic fulfilled for Iamblichus. Might he also have preferred the Platonic scientific work of Euclid to the Pythagorean Nicomachus?

It is clear first of all from the beginning of Proclus' second prologue (48, 1–8) that the introduction to geometry is intended to follow *directly* on the introduction to general mathematics. This rules out therefore the possibility that an introduction to arithmetic once came between the first and second prologues.[26] On the other hand, it cannot be inferred that Euclid supplanted Nicomachus in Proclus' mind: Proclus knows and quotes Nicomachus;[27] if he did not write a commentary on Nicomachus, at least his pupil Ammonius lectured on Nicomachus in Alexandria;[28] and, most significant of all, Proclus considered himself a reincarnation of Nicomachus.[29] This last fact suggests that Proclus valued Nicomachus no less than did Iamblichus. Finally one might note that Proclus does not show any signs of questioning the primacy of arithmetic (as compared with geometry) in the hierarchy of mathematical sciences.[30] Some explanation of Proclus' preference for geometry must then be found that is compatible with these facts.

I believe that the philosophical background to Proclus' particular interest in geometry (despite the admitted primacy of arithmetic) is to be found in the theory that mathematicals are projections by the soul of innate intelligible principles. It is particularly in geometry, according to Syrianus, that soul projects such innate principles into imagination because in its weakness soul is better able to grasp these principles in the extended form thus given them (above, p. 133). One can infer from this that the inferiority of geometry *vis-à-vis* arithmetic, i.e. its recourse to extension, also makes it more accessible to the

---

[26] Morrow mistranslates the last lines (47, 6–8) of the first prologue, which should read: 'And so, dedicating this book to him, we will circumscribe (περιγράψομεν, i.e. finish, a mathematical pun) the study of mathematical science ⟨in general⟩.' Morrow's speculations ad loc. are consequently unfounded.

[27] Cf. *In Tim.* II 19, 4; 20, 25 ff.; *In Parm.* 619, 10 (in Moerbeke's translation); *Theol. Plat.* II 16, 15; cf. Charles (1982), 201–4 (but I find her structural comparison unconvincing).

[28] Cf. Tarán (1969), 7–10, 14. Ammonius' lectures are incorporated in the commentaries on Nicomachus of his pupils Asclepius and Philoponus.

[29] Marinus, *Vita Procli*, ch. 28.

[30] Proclus, *In Eucl.* 48, 9–15, 59, 15–60, 1; cf. Iamblichus, *Comm.* 14, 23–15, 5; 95, 14–96, 3. On a tradition that assigned primacy to geometry rather than arithmetic (as in Nicomachus and Iamblichus), cf. Burkert (1972), 249.

human soul. In the figures of geometry the soul can better grasp its innate principles because these principles are expressed at a lower, more image-like, level. Proclus also makes this point about geometry (*In Eucl.* 141, 4–12):

Thus soul, exercising her capacity to know, projects on the imagination, as on a mirror, the ideas of the figures; and the imagination, receiving in image-form these reflections of what is within ⟨her⟩, by their means affords the soul an opportunity to turn inward from the images and attend to herself. It is as if a man looking at himself in a mirror and marvelling at the power of nature and at his own appearance should wish to look upon himself directly. . . .

This text not only indicates that the spatial figures of geometry make accessible to soul the road to self-knowledge.[31] It also treats geometry as performing the role assigned to mathematics in general in Plato's *Republic*: to mediate through images between material reality and the Forms. Arithmetic also deals with images, but these are expressed at a higher level; it has no recourse to extension in order to grasp its objects. And its principles possess greater simplicity, unity, than those of geometry.[32] In this way arithmetic stands nearer to metaphysics, whereas geometry finds itself nearer the middle point between metaphysics and the material world, thus more adapted to the capacities and needs of the ascending soul.

There is another feature of geometry that also throws light on its position with respect to arithmetic in Proclus' mind. Plato assigns mathematics in the *Republic* to a faculty of the soul, διάνοια, which Neoplatonists in general took to mean discursive or more specifically demonstrative (syllogistic) thought. Thus for Iamblichus the method characteristic of mathematics is syllogistic. Proclus also characterizes mathematical science as demonstrative in method and attempts to show this in particular in the analysis of Euclid's theorems. Whatever the merits of this enterprise, it was at least easier to apply to Euclid than to Nicomachus, whose arithmetical work is well known for the absence of demonstrations in support of its positions. For Proclus, however,

---

[31] At 62, 11–18, Proclus says: 'In the middle region of knowledge ⟨geometry⟩ unfolds and develops discursive principles (διανοητικοὶ λόγοι); it investigates their variety, exhibiting their existences and properties, their similarities and differences, from which it comprehends within limited bounds the shapes in imagination of figures and refers back to the essential (οὐσιώδη) being of the principles.' Cf. also 52, 20–7; 54, 27–55, 18 (explication into the imagination because of soul's weakness, ἀσθενοῦσα). Cf. Trouillard (1957), 338–40.

[32] 59, 15–20; cf. Breton (1969), 77–8.

this would not have represented a failing in Nicomachus, but would have to do, as I believe we are entitled to infer, with the more intermediate position of geometry, hence its more discursive, demonstrative character as compared with the higher, more insight-like thought of arithmetic.

A fact might finally be mentioned which would have had considerable weight in Proclus' eyes, the significance of which could be understood against the philosophical background just sketched, namely that in treating of the mediatory role of mathematics in the *Republic*, Plato seems to have especially in mind geometry (510 b–511 b).

Enough reasons have been found then that explain Proclus' preference for geometry in such a way as to reconcile it with the ontological and epistemological superiority of arithmetic. Through is greater 'explication' into images of higher hidden principles, through its more discursive demonstrative method, it is, among the mathematical sciences, a privileged mediator between material and immaterial reality. This position does not rule out, of course, the use of the 'images' of arithmetic, but it does represent a shift in fulcrum: the role that Iamblichus gives arithmetic in *On Pythagoreanism* both as an introductory and as a pivotal science—Books V–VII are after all concerned with arithmetic reaching down into physics and ethics and up into metaphysics—is assigned in Proclus rather to geometry. One might also speak of a change from Iamblichus' Pythagoreanizing emphasis on arithmetic to a Platonizing stress on geometry.

We have found then another important point on which Proclus diverged from Iamblichus' Pythagorean programme. The elements for this shift from arithmetic to geometry are indeed to be found already in Iamblichus' subordination of geometry to arithmetic. Even more suggestive is Syrianus' account of geometricals as projections in the imagination by the soul due to its weakness. But there is little sign in Syrianus of the systematic recourse to geometry in philosophy which I think must be regarded as Proclus' own contribution.[33]

---

[33] Marinus tends to see the *Data* as enveloping mathematics (*In Eucl. Data* 254, 5–13): he notes that Euclid has covered 'almost' all of mathematics, geometry, astronomy. Arithmetic is not mentioned specifically (cf. 254, 13–20).

3. GEOMETRY

(i) *The Composition of* On Euclid *Prol. II*

In his second prologue Proclus provides a general introduction to
geometry. The dependence of his first prologue on Iamblichus' *On
Pythagoreanism* III leads to the question whether Proclus, for his
second prologue, might also have used Iamblichus, namely the (lost)
introduction to geometry that constituted *On Pythagoreanism* VIII. The
signs are, however, that this is not the case. In particular, there are
passages in the second prologue that repeat Proclus' revisions of
Iamblichus in the first prologue, applying them now to the case of
geometry.[34] To some extent then Proclus used his first prologue in the
composition of his second prologue. This procedure conforms to what
has been established concerning Proclus' attitude to geometry, for it
assumes that the philosophical functions assigned by Iamblichus to
general mathematics can be instantiated in particular by geometry.
Another aspect of the composition of the second prologue might also
be noted briefly here: the effort to document (the history of geometry
in particular) that already characterizes the first prologue.

(ii) *Euclid as Platonist*

There are a number of good philosophical reasons, as we have seen,
for first studying geometry rather than arithmetic in one's progress
through mathematics to metaphysics. But it remains for Proclus to
explain his choice of Euclid's *Elements* as a manual of geometry, rather
than, for example, the 'Pythagorean' geometry of Iamblichus' *On
Pythagoreanism* VIII. From Proclus' text it appears that Euclid had
been discussed by Syrianus, possibly by Plutarch of Athens, and by
Porphyry.[35] But what did Proclus himself see in Euclid that recommended him as a guide to geometry?

   Proclus claims that Euclid is a Platonist by philosophical confes-
sion (68, 20–1); that the goal of the *Elements* is the construction of the
geometrical figures of Plato's *Timaeus* (68, 21–3; 384, 2–4); and that
Euclid's theorems, starting from hypotheses (given by a higher

---

[34] Compare 62, 4–7, with 22, 6–9, and the references above, n. 9, and below, p. 172.
[35] *In Eucl.* 123, 19–20; 125, 16; 297, 4–5; 315, 15–316, 1; 352, 13–15; cf. Heiberg (1882),
159–62; Mueller (1987*b*).

science, dialectic) and demonstrating what follows them, exhibit the structure of mathematical discourse as described in Plato's *Republic*.[36] Euclid's *Elements* is therefore a manual of Platonic geometry. I believe consequently that Proclus' choice of Euclid is to be understood in relation to his preference for Plato. In particular, his tendency to see Plato as more 'scientific' than the Pythagoreans is connected to his preference of Euclid's manual to a 'Pythagorean' geometry. Evidence in support of this can be found much later in the commentary (426, 6–14) where Proclus contrasts the Pythagoreans who first understood a particular Euclidean theorem with Euclid's demonstration:

> If we listen to those who like to record antiquities, we shall find them attribut-ing this theorem to Pythagoras. . . . For my part, though I admire those who first grasped this theorem, I admire more the author of the *Elements*, not only for the very lucid demonstration by which he secured it, but also because in the sixth book he laid hold of a theorem even more general than this and secured it by irrefutable scientific arguments.

The theme of the scientific, demonstrative, irrefutable character of Euclid's work is prominent in Proclus' praise of Euclid in the second prologue (69, 1–2 and 12–13; 70, 16–18). Such qualities had also been attributed by Iamblichus to Nicomachus in his introduction to Nicomachean arithmetic (*On Pythagoreanism* IV)—with much less justification. At any rate Proclus' choice of Euclid's *Elements* as a manual of geometry, we may conclude, has to do with Euclid's supposed Platonism and the more scientific quality of this Platonic geometry as compared with the geometry of the ancient Pythagoreans.

Proclus of course finds other qualities in Euclid that recommend his *Elements* as a manual. In particular Euclid demonstrates the suit-able pedagogical virtues: clarity, concision, coherence, an absence of superfluity, an appropriate level of generality (73, 15–74, 18). Such virtues had also been found by Iamblichus in Nicomachus.

(iii) *The Method of Geometry*

This subject has already been touched on in the preceding pages. However, there is more to geometrical method than its (Aristotelian) syllogistic derivation of conclusions from first principles and the (Platonic) dependence of such principles on the higher science of

---

[36] Cf. above, p. 166; *In Eucl.* 75, 5–14; Breton (1969), 39 ff., 124.

dialectic. In particular, Proclus, in the second prologue, attributes to geometry not only demonstration but also definition, division, and analysis, the last two elements reflecting a progression away from and a return to first principles (69, 9–19). These four elements of method in Proclus have often been described,[37] and I shall confine myself here to adding a few points.

It might be observed that the four elements of geometrical method are found before in the first prologue, where they are treated as the elements of general mathematics (43, 2–10). Here Proclus is taking his cue from Iamblichus (*Comm.* 65, 1–26; 89, 16–27). From what has been determined above in section (i) we can see that Proclus has taken the four elements of mathematical method he found in Iamblichus and applied them in his second prologue to geometry.

The comparison between the second and first prologues and the Iamblichean source yields another, more important result. Iamblichus discusses definition, division, demonstration, and analysis as features of mathematical method in the context of claiming their independence and superiority *vis-à-vis* comparable features of dialectical, i.e. logical method (*Comm.* 89, 16 ff.). In Proclus' first prologue, however, (42, 9–21) the *dependence* of such features in mathematical method on analogous features of a higher dialectic, namely that of Plato's *Republic* is stressed.[38] The same point is indicated in the application to geometry in the second prologue (69, 13–19). Iamblichus recognizes of course the superiority of Plato's dialectic and finds in it the dividing and unifying features also constitutive of mathematical method, but he does not, at least in *On Pythagoreanism* III, draw the conclusion that the four components of mathematical method are modelled on those of Platonic dialectic.[39] The Nicomachean emphasis on mathematics tends to predominate in Iamblichus' book, and the subordination in terms of method to Platonic dialectic is not worked out clearly. On the other hand Proclus' greater attention to Plato and the *Republic* produces a stronger and clearer position on the subordination of mathematics to Platonic dialectic and leads to his claim in the first

---

[37] Cf. Hartmann (1909); Breton (1969), 123 ff.

[38] In the scholia to Iamblichus' *Comm.* the difference between dialectic as logic and as the supreme science of Plato's *Rep.* is noted (101, 34–102, 2); cf. Proclus, *Theol. Plat.* I 39, 7–21, and already Plotinus I 3, 4–5.

[39] *Comm.* 46, 3–13; cf. Mueller (1987b). In their note (142) to Proclus, *Theol. Plat.* I 40 Saffrey and Westerink refer to Damascius, *In Phileb.* §§ 57 and 59, 3–4, who reports Iamblichus as giving to dialectic a dividing and unifying method. Demonstration, definition, and division are ascribed to dialectic by Syrianus, *In met.* 55, 37–56, 4.

prologue that mathematical method in fact images dialectical method. This is of some consequence, for it implies a clearer view of the precise position of mathematics in philosophy. In particular it calls attention to a science higher than mathematics which prefigures at a superior, more original level, the discursive, demonstrative character of mathematics. The consequences of these clarifications of Iamblichus' position in *On Pythagoreanism* III will emerge when the relations between mathematics and metaphysics are examined below in Chapter 10.

(iv) *The Transposition of Geometry*

Given Proclus' general view of geometry's place in relation to mathematics and to philosophy and the corresponding way in which the second prologue of his *Commentary* echoes the first, it is only to be expected that geometry will be shown in the second prologue (ch. 3) to carry out those functions of extra-mathematical transposition that are attributed (following Iamblichus) in the first prologue to general mathematics. Thus geometry reaches (as did general mathematics in the first prologue) up to true and divine being,

teaching us through images the special properties (ἰδιότητας) of the divine orders and the powers of the intellectual Forms. . . . Here it shows us what figures are appropriate to the gods, which ones belong to primary beings . . . (62, 5–10)

At the intermediate level it unfolds in the imagination discursive principles.[40] Below this level

it examines nature, that is, the species of elementary perceptible bodies and the powers associated with them, and explains how their causes are contained in advance in its own ideas. It contains images of all intelligible kinds and paradigms of sensible ones; but the forms of discursive reason constitute its essence, and through this middle region it ranges upwards and downwards to everything. . . . Always philosophizing about being in the manner of geometry, . . . it has images of all the virtues—intellectual, psychic, and physical—and presents in due order all the forms of political constitution, showing from its own nature the variety of the changes they undergo. (62, 19–63, 5)

The physical, ethical, and metaphysical applications of arithmetic had been worked out by Iamblichus in Books V–VII of *On Pythagoreanism*.

---

[40] 62, 11–18, quoted above, n. 31.

It will be Proclus' concern, however, in the following commentary to bring out these applications in the case of geometry. For there are, he claims, enough explanations of the specifically geometrical, technical aspects of Euclid's *Elements*:

> We are surfeited with those topics and shall touch on them but sparingly. But whatever matters contain more substantial science and contribute to philosophy as a whole, these we shall make it our chief concern to mention, emulating the Pythagoreans whose byword and proverb was 'a figure and a stepping-stone, not a figure, and three obols'. By this they meant that we must cultivate that science of geometry which with each theorem lays the basis for a step upward and draws the soul to the higher world. . . .[41]

Whatever differences then there might be between Proclus and Iamblichus on the preferability of arithmetic or geometry, Pythagorean of Platonic texts, the purpose of Proclus' *Commentary on Euclid* is essentially that of Iamblichus' *On Pythagoreanism*, to use mathematical science as a bridge, as a paradigmatic key to physics and ethics, as a fore-shadowing of and initiation to metaphysics. Proclus even presents the overall purpose of his *Commentary*, as described in the above passage, as 'Pythagorean'.

Proclus carries out the 'Pythagorean' approach to geometry most fully in his commentary on Euclid's definitions. The definitions are regarded as treating of the objects of geometry in their ontological order, i.e. in their real progression from point (def. 1) through line (defs. 2–4) to surface (defs. 5–7) which includes angles (defs. 8–12) and figures in general (defs. 13–14) and in their progression from circular (defs. 15–17) to rectilinear figures (defs. 20–34). For the definitions Proclus provides a mathematical exegesis combined with extrapolations of geometrical concepts on to the objects of lower and higher philosophical sciences,[42] much in the way that Nicomachus had done long before in his *Theologoumena*. However Proclus' text reflects not only his clear and systematic mind but also advances in physics and especially metaphysics since the time of Iamblichus and Syrianus. His

---

[41] 84, 11–20 (cf. 174, 17–21). The Pythagorean saying is quoted in the scholia to Iamblichus, *Comm.* 101, 17–18, and is interpreted by Iamblichus (*Pr.* 125, 1–8) in the same way.

[42] Cf.e.g. 97, 18 ff. (def. 2: Πυθαγορικωτέρων); 128, 26 ff. (def. 9); 131, 21 ff. (defs. 10–12: οἱ Πυθαγορικοί); 137, 8–142, 9 (def. 14: Πυθαγόρειον); 166, 14 ff. (defs. 24–9: οἱ Πυθαγόρειοι); 173, 2 ff. (defs. 30–4: οἱ Πυθαγόρειοι). The vocabulary of transposition found in Iamblichus (above, pp. 48–9) reappears in Proclus: ἔμφασις (22, 7; cf. 138, 24; 173, 10), τελείωσις (cf. 24, 4 and 25), ἀπεικασία (24, 27; cf. 138, 13; 173, 23), δι᾽εἰκόνων (62, 5), κατ᾽αἰτίαν (62, 21), ἀφομοίωσις (cf. 20, 4).

study of the circle (146, 24 ff.; 153, 10 ff.), a fine example of what results, has already been fully and sensitively discussed.[43]

The relations between mathematics (especially geometry) and physics and metaphysics will be examined at greater length in the following two chapters. In preparation for this it may be useful to add a few more remarks about Proclus' transpositions of geometry in his *Commentary on Euclid*. In his 'Pythagorean' demonstration of the importance of geometrical truths for physics Proclus not only refers to the Pythagoreans, but also illustrates his point by quoting from Plato's *Timaeus*. And in applying geometry to metaphysics he makes use of Plato's *Parmenides*. The latter practice is of particular interest, since the *Parmenides* is not seen as a mathematical fore-shadowing of metaphysics, but rather as expounding a higher science whose principles are of normative relevance to mathematics:

Because the line is second ⟨to the point⟩ and owes its existence to the first change from the simple (undivided), the Pythagorean doctrine properly calls it dyadic. But that the point is posterior to the monad and the line to the dyad and the surface to the triad is shown by Parmenides (*Parm.* 137 c) when he denies first plurality, and then wholeness of the One; if plurality comes before wholeness, then number comes before the continuous, the dyad before the line, and the monad before the point.[44]

Thus mathematics is inspired not only in its methods, but also in its doctrines by a higher science, Platonic dialectic, and the objects of that higher science. The paradigmatic role of this dialectic with regard to mathematics is not, however, worked out in any detail in the *Commentary on Euclid*.[45]

4. CONCLUSIONS

The argument showing in the first part of this chapter that Proclus based the first prologue of his *Commentary on Euclid* largely on Iamblichus' *On Pythagoreanism* III not only is significant as yielding evidence of Proclus' familiarity with Iamblichus' Pythagoreanizing programme, but also makes it possible to identify in a specific way the

[43] Beierwaltes (1961), 120 ff.; (1979), 165–239; cf. Gersh (1978), 72–5.
[44] 99, 16–24; cf. 94, 8–18.
[45] Breton attempts this, using the *El. theol.* as a source of dialectical guidelines for mathematics, (1969),93 ff.

points at which Proclus diverged from this programme. Proclus fully accepts the pivotal role of mathematics in philosophy, its paradigmatic function in physics and ethics, its anticipatory and introductory function in metaphysics. But his adoption of Syrianus' view of mathematics as 'projections' by the soul from innate principles results in a clarification in this direction of the unclear relation between soul and mathematicals in the Iamblichean text: this will turn out later to be of some importance for determining the particular way in which mathematical truths can be applied 'downwards' and 'upwards'. In revising, clarifying, and documenting Iamblichus, Proclus largely replaces the Pythagorean authorities in Iamblichus with texts taken from Plato. This appears to relate not only to Proclus' view of Euclid's *Elements* as a manual of Platonic geometry, but also to his tendency to regard Plato as more 'scientific' than the Pythagoreans. The comparison between Proclus and Iamblichus also indicates that Proclus chose geometry to stand for mathematics much in the way that arithmetic does in Iamblichus. This appears to derive from the view that geometry plays more the role of mathematical intermediary than does arithmetic, for its extended figures make innate principles more accessible to the fallen soul and its more pronounced demonstrative character coincides better with the discursive capacity of such a soul. At the same time the concentration on the 'Platonic' background of Euclidean geometry leads to a greater emphasis in Proclus than is to be found in Iamblichus' text on the subordination of mathematics to a higher, 'true' science, Platonic dialectic, which inspires, and can even be used to determine, methods and principles in mathematics.

9
Mathematics and Physics in Proclus

In Book V of *On Pythagoreanism* Iamblichus attempted to show in detail the paradigmatic function of mathematics in understanding the material world; the result was an unusual work on 'arithmetical physics'. According to the reconstruction of the book that I have proposed in Chapter 3, this arithmetical physics consisted in a mathematized revision of Aristotle's *Physics* in which the principles of physical explanation presented in the first part of the *Physics* were shown to be exemplified in the properties of various sorts of number: numbers exhibit the formal, efficient, and material causality at work in the immanent organizing principles of nature, 'physical numbers'. While following the pattern of physical explanation provided by the early books of Aristotle's *Physics* Iamblichus did not ignore Aristotle's criticisms of the Pythagoreans, but attempted to meet such criticisms and improve Aristotelian physics so as to turn it into a true 'Pythagorean' science of nature.

Proclus also wrote works in mathematical physics, the *Elements of Physics* and his *Commentary on the Timaeus*. In this chapter I shall discuss these two works with a view to determining what they show about the function of mathematics in physics. In this way inferences may be made concerning the philosophical standpoint of Proclus' physics *vis-à-vis* Iamblichean Pythagoreanism. At the same time the very bulk of the material in Proclus, as compared to the fragmentary remains of Iamblichus, will permit of a better view of precisely what a later Neoplatonic mathematical physics consists of, at least in the form it takes in Proclus.

I. ARISTOTLE'S PHYSICS GEOMETRICIZED

The geometrical form given to Aristotle's physics in the *Elements of Physics* is so prominent as to seem almost exaggerated. Each of the two books of this short work is headed by a list of definitions in the Euclidean manner. These are followed by a series of propositions with demonstrations and corollaries often using geometrical principles. Euclidean style is adopted even in the language: imperatives, postulations, the QED formula.[1] The imposition of geometrical form is all the more appropriate in that the Aristotelian texts used already incorporate much recourse to geometrical argument. However Proclus shows ingenuity in reworking Aristotle: Aristotle's points are organized into a strict sequence, often clarified and supplemented. In particular strict demonstrative (i.e. syllogistic) form is insisted on in the recasting of Aristotle's arguments in support of his points. Proclus' rewriting of Aristotle here could be compared in its skill to his rewriting of Iamblichus in the first prologue of his *Commentary on Euclid*. However the approach of the first prologue is somewhat different: it is a broad and not too demanding introduction to mathematics, whereas the *Elements of Physics* imposes itself as a demonstration or exercise in scientific rigour. Indeed the purpose Proclus seems to have had in geometricizing Aristotle's physics was to make Aristotle's arguments stronger from the point-of-view of scientific method. Geometry's contribution to physics is then methodological, and this method is essentially that of syllogistic argument.

The tendency to identify syllogistic method with the method of geometry has already been observed in Proclus' *Commentary on Euclid*, as has been a preference for geometry among the mathematical sciences in transpositions into physics and metaphysics. If a comparison in these respects between Iamblichus' arithmetical version of Aristotelian physics and Proclus' geometrical version of the same can serve to indicate how Proclus is inspired by, and yet moves away from the precedent set by Iamblichus, it should also be noted that Proclus' *Elements of Physics* is not to be considered simply as a geometrical substitute for Iamblichus' arithmetical physics. Iamblichus' book covers the principles of physical explanation presented in the *first* part of Aristotle's *Physics*, whereas Proclus' work is based on the second half of the *Physics*, in particular Books VI and VIII supplemented by passages from *De Caelo* I. Proclus deals, not with the question of physical explanation, but with motion and change with particular reference to the inference to the 'unmoved mover' that the analysis of motion produces. Aristotle's argument in *Physics* VIII that motion in the world ultimately presupposes an unmoved cause appears to be Proclus' chief interest in the *Elements of Physics*; the more general

---

[1] Cf. e.g. *El. phys.* 2, 17; 4, 12, 15, 20–1, 25; 10, 15; 12, 4.

propositions he first extracts from *Physics* VI function as the ground-work logically presupposed by this argument. And in reformulating Aristotle's argument Proclus reveals his Platonic point-of-view in stressing at the end the immaterial nature that Aristotle's unmoved mover must have.[2]

The practice of taking definitions, axioms, and demonstrations from Aristotle's physics for purposes which are Platonic in inspiration is not confined to the *Elements of Physics*. It may be found elsewhere in Proclus.[3] However, the value of Aristotle's physics was limited. Like Iamblichus and Syrianus, Proclus considered Aristotle's writings in physics to be defective imitations, produced in a spirit of rivalry, of Platonic physics as revealed in particular in the *Timaeus*.[4] A measure of Aristotle's heretical inclinations is to be found in the criticisms he makes of the *Timaeus*, and Proclus devoted a work (since lost) to responding to these criticisms. The *Timaeus* was then a far better source for true physics. Proclus produced early in his life a vast *Commentary on the Timaeus* of which (about) the first half survives.[5] In the rest of this chapter I shall discuss the conception of Pythagorean mathematical physics that Proclus develops in this *Commentary* in connection with the interpretation of the physics of the *Timaeus*.

2. PLATO'S *TIMAEUS* AS 'PYTHAGOREAN' PHYSICS

At the beginning of his *Commentary* Proclus announces his view that Plato's *Timaeus* is inspired by a work of the Pythagorean Timaeus of Locri:

And indeed the book by the Pythagorean Timaeus *On Nature*, written in a Pythagorean manner, ⟨is that⟩ 'starting from which Plato embarked on writing the *Timaeus*', according to ⟨Timon⟩ the writer of *sylloi*. We have placed this book at the head of our commentary so that we will be able to see what Plato's Timaeus says that agrees ⟨with the Pythagorean⟩, what Plato adds, where there is disagreement. (I 1, 8–16; cf. 7, 18–21)

---

[2] *El. phys.* 58, 20–7 (compare Aristotle, *Phys.* 267 b 19–26). Dodds, in his edition of the *El. theol.* (xviii, 201, 250), has disposed of Ritzenfeld's claim in his edition of the *El. phys.* that the work was written early in Proclus' career while studying Aristotle and before reading Plato and becoming a Platonist.

[3] Cf. *In Tim.* II 93, 30–94, 15 (compare *El. phys.* 30, 10–11; 34, 3); *In Remp.* II 9, 26.

[4] *In Tim.* I 6, 21 ff.; 237, 17 ff.; III 323, 31 ff.; cf. I 7, 15–16; 295, 26–7.

[5] Cf. Festugière (1966–8), V 239–48.

There is some indication in the manuscript tradition that the supposed Pythagorean original was indeed placed before Proclus' *Commentary*.[6] Furthermore it will be noticed that Proclus' project—to comment on his text by measuring it against its Pythagorean source—is the same as that which Iamblichus had adopted before in commenting on Aristotle's *Categories*, when he had measured Aristotle against the putative original, (pseudo-)Archytas. Indeed it is likely enough that Iamblichus had used the same approach in his (lost) *Commentary on the Timaeus*, comparing Plato with Timaeus of Locri, and that Proclus here is following his lead.[7]

There are some differences, however, between the way Proclus uses Timaeus of Locri in his *Commentary on the Timaeus* and Iamblichus' use of (pseudo-)Archytas in his *Commentary on the Categories*. Iamblichus keeps Archytas very much in mind, quotes him frequently, and vigorously compares Aristotle (to his disadvantage) to Archytas. On the other hand Proclus refers to Timaeus of Locri comparatively little in his *Commentary on the Timaeus*, and then in a way that assumes or argues for agreement between Timaeus and Plato.[8] May we therefore conclude that Proclus gradually abandoned or forgot the Iamblichean approach to which he subscribed at the beginning of his work?[9] Could this have to do with the retreat of Pythagoreans in favour of Plato that has already been observed in Proclus?

Appealing as these possibilities may be, I believe that they are open to some serious objections. First of all the range of text spanned by Proclus' references to Timaeus of Locri (see note 8) shows that Proclus did not abandon or forget him. Then it must be stressed that for Iamblichus (and Proclus) Aristotle was something of a deviant requiring active and constant correction, whereas the harmonious relations between a true Pythagorean and Plato would scarcely call for such critical vigilance. Thus the difference in exegetical practice resulting from the different relationships between Archytas and Aristotle and between Timaeus of Locri and Plato might suffice to account for the less prominent role of Timaeus of Locri in Proclus' *Commentary* as compared to that of Archytas in Iamblichus' *Commentary on the Categories*. Thirdly, although Proclus does indeed distinguish

---

[6] Cf. Marg (1972), 2.

[7] So Harder (1926), xvi–xvii; cf. above, pp. 96, 99. Marg concedes that his doubts on this are a little exaggerated, (1972), 92.

[8] *In Tim.* II 79, 4–11; 101, 9–14; 188, 9–190, 11; III 138, 3–11.

[9] Cf. Harder, loc. cit.; Marg (1972), 91–2.

between a Pythagorean revelatory approach and the Socratic demonstrative method, he also subordinates the figure of Socrates to that of Timaeus in analogy to the subordination of lower to higher beings (I 354, 5–16), and the figure of Timaeus in Plato's dialogue he characterizes as a Pythagorean whose discourse functions and is to be interpreted according to Pythagorean principles.[10] Finally, Proclus indicates that he regards Plato's *Timaeus* as a Pythagorean work (I 15, 23–5), exemplifying a Pythagorean approach to physics (204, 3–5). Indeed Plato alone, as compared to other physicists (one thinks of Aristotle), followed Pythagorean methods and doctrines.[11]

I believe consequently that the *Commentary on the Timaeus* shows a tendency to Pythagoreanize in the manner of Iamblichus and Syrianus, a tendency less pronounced in Proclus' other works. A telling sign of this can be found in the fact that the *Commentary* makes use of a good number of specific 'Pythagorean' authorities and texts, whereas the usual practice in Proclus' other works is to refer on occasion and in a vague way to 'the Pythagoreans' (above, ch. 7 n. 26). The reason for the particular Pythagorean emphasis of the *Commentary on the Timaeus* can be surmised: we know that it was one of Proclus' first major works, completed probably shortly after Syrianus' death, and it is a fair guess that it reflects in some respects, especially in its earlier parts, the influence of Syrianus.[12]

3. THE GEOMETRICAL METHOD OF PLATO'S PHYSICS

It remains to determine the extent to which Proclus' programmatic claims for the Pythagorean character of Plato's *Timaeus* affect the actual interpretation of physics to be found in his *Commentary*. To what extent, in particular, does Proclus develop the *Timaeus* into a work of mathematical physics? In what sense does Proclus show the physics of Plato's dialogue to be mathematical? Plato himself brings in so much mathematics that it might at first appear impossible for a commentator not to find mathematical physics in the dialogue. Yet Plato's text presents more than enough ambiguities and difficulties to

[10] *In Tim.* I 129, 31–2; 223, 5–6; III 168, 7–9; cf. *In Parm.* 723, 19–20; *Theol. Plat.* IV 88, 2 ff.

[11] *In Tim.* I 1, 25–6; 2, 29–3, 4; 33, 7–11; 262, 10–11; 267, 1–2.

[12] Thus, for example, the ontological subordination of the figures of the dialogue appears to be Syrianus' idea (Proclus, *In Tim.* I 20, 27 ff.: Timaeus as the 'monad' of the group). Cf. Sheppard (1980), 34–8.

leave open for the interpreter a wide range of possible approaches and options.

In the first section of this chapter the chief contribution of mathematics to physical argument in the *Elements of Physics* was found to be methodological: Aristotle's text was given the strict demonstrative form Proclus assumed to be characteristic of geometric method. In his *Commentary on the Timaeus* Proclus describes the method of Plato's *Timaeus* also as 'geometrical', which is to say rigorously syllogistic in form. However, Timaeus' discourse is preceded in the dialogue by Critias' recounting of the myth of Atlantis. This follows, according to Proclus, the Pythagorean practice of fore-shadowing with images the scientific account that begins with Timaeus' discourse.[13] Timaeus then proposes five hypotheses or axioms, from which he derives physical conclusions of which the first three are: that the world is constituted; by a demiurge; who made use of an eternal paradigm. In the following commentary Proclus frequently emphasizes the geometric method that he believes characterizes Timaeus' speech. As this motif in Proclus' *Commentary* has been fully examined elsewhere,[14] it will be sufficient merely to note that the assimilation of scientific (demonstrative) to geometric method is characteristic of Proclus not only here and in the *Elements of Physics* but also, as we will see, in his metaphysical (theological) works, and that this assimilation is related to the attitude to geometry expressed in his *Commentary on Euclid*.

4. IS PHYSICS A SCIENCE?

Mathematics in the form of geometry lends much more to physics than merely its syllogistic method. It also helps to resolve for Proclus a major problem posed by the physics of Plato's *Timaeus*, namely that concerning the questionable scientific status of physics. The problem is introduced by Timaeus towards the beginning of his discourse (*Tim.* 29 b c):

And in speaking of the copy ⟨i.e. the world⟩ and the original ⟨i.e. the Forms⟩ we may assume that words are akin to the matter which they describe; when they relate to the lasting and permanent and intelligible, they ought to be last-

---

[13] *In Tim.* I 4, 8–9, with 30, 2–10; 33, 1–11.
[14] By Festugière (1966–8), II 7–9, also (1963), 565–7; to Festugière's evidence one could add *In Tim.* I 265, 3 ff.; 283, 15–19; 332, 6–9; 345, 3–4; II 7, 19–20; 114, 14–15.

ing and unalterable, and, as far as their nature allows, irrefutable and immovable—nothing less. But when they express only the copy or likeness and not the eternal things themselves, they need only be likely and analogous to the real words. As being is to becoming, so is truth to belief. (Transl. Jowett)

This passage casts a shadow over the cosmology that follows, for it suggests that true and abiding, i.e. scientific, statements can be made only of the Forms and that all that can be claimed for what is said about the physical world is likelihood, not truth. In this sense then there can be no science of nature, strictly speaking, nor can Timaeus' account be taken to be such a science. The interpreter of Plato seems faced with a choice between ignoring or glossing over this passage, so as to be able to regard the cosmology of the *Timaeus* as scientific;[15] abandoning the hope of finding physical science in the *Timaeus*; or determining the way in which an account of nature, in being 'likely', attains a certain degree of truth and to this extent approaches, without being, science.

Proclus resolves the problem along the lines of the third option, using a key provided by the structure of geometrical demonstrations. Such demonstrations rest on axioms and hypotheses, which can thus be regarded as the principles or 'causes' from which conclusions in geometry result or are derived. In physics the world and its contents are the results ('conclusions') to be explained, to be related back, that is, to their constitutive first principles. But for a Platonist such principles (both of the world and of scientific discourse) must be transcendent, immaterial, and unchanging. Platonic physics must then begin and be derived from meta-physical causes. But this also means that it is based on immaterial unchanging truths and in this way is related to science. Thus discourse about the world can be true to the extent that it refers to transcendent principles. And it is the relation between axioms/hypotheses and conclusions in geometry that serves to bring out the scientific basis of physics.[16]

An example will help to illustrate and specify further the extent of the scientific claims of physics. Propositions held to be universally true occur in astronomy. They are true in this way, however, only to the extent that they express the universal mathematical laws to which the heavens are subject. In so far as they apply to particular heavenly

---

[15] In the strong Greek sense of science of course. To the extent that modern physics regards its claims as probable, it seems to be no more ambitious than Timaeus' discourse.

[16] Cf. I 337, 29–338, 5, with 346, 29–347, 2; 348, 23–7.

bodies they are liable to be inaccurate. Thus if the astronomical law that 'the celestial circles bisect each other' is universally true, this has to do with the *geometrical* principles at issue, for in the case of particular celestial bodies there can be no point of bisection in the geometrical sense required by the law: a physical point of bisection is divisible, therefore defective, as compared to the indivisibility of the geometrical point.[17] The deficiency of such laws when applied to physical bodies relates not only, however, to the difference in ontological character between these bodies and the immaterial principles from which the laws derive. It is also due to the fact that we know of physical objects through sense perception, which limits our scope—our access to the heavens, for example—and makes us prey to all sorts of perceptual error.[18] In fact the scientific aspect of physics and (yet) its failure to attain anything more than probability reflect its hybrid character: in introducing mathematical laws it starts from a basis inspired by universal and unerring principles; but the formulation of these laws by, and in relation to, physical bodies diminishes their universality and accuracy, given the 'errant' nature of these bodies and the fallibility of our perceptual access to them.

The 'mixed' character of physics[19] is found by Proclus also in the fact that much of Timaeus' discourse is concerned, not with the world, but with its transcendent 'divine' causes: the demiurge, the Forms, the lesser gods, soul. In this sense the *Timaeus* can be regarded as a 'theology': not a theology, or science of the divine *per se* such as Proclus finds in the *Parmenides*, but a discourse on the divine as producing the world:

Thus Socrates shows that he wishes the physics to be Pythagorean, one that begins from the divine cause, and not one such as he rejected in the *Phaedo*, which blinds the eye of the soul, holding as responsible causes winds and ether according to Anaxagoras. For true physics must be attached to theology, as nature depends upon the gods.[20]

The reference to Pythagoreanism reminds us that Iamblichus, according to Proclus, emphasized the theological aspects of the *Timaeus*.[21]

[17] *In Tim.* I 349, 6–350, 1; 346, 29–347, 2; cf. *In Parm.* 796, 26–39. For this in Plato cf. Allen (1970), 163–4.

[18] I 351, 2–352, 27; 346, 12–347, 2; cf. II 51, 6–27; Blumenthal (1982), 9–10.

[19] Cf. also I 410, 11–19; III 356, 17–22.

[20] I 204, 3–10; cf. also I 8, 4–13; 84, 22–85, 4; 217, 25–8; III 152, 7 ff.; 168, 7–20.

[21] Cf. Iamblichus, *In Tim.* frs. 25, 54. Compare Iamblichus *Comm.* 56, 3–4 (quoted above, p. 162).

But it is not clear how much of Proclus' explanation of the semi-scientific status of physics he owed to Iamblichus.

These ideas also explain for Proclus the superiority of the physics of Plato to that of Aristotle. Aristotle concerns himself mainly with immanent causes, matter and form in nature, and pays less attention than does Plato to the transcendent efficient, paradigmatic, and final causes (I 2, 15–3, 20). It follows that to the extent that he neglects the divine presupposites of nature Aristotle diminishes that which gives physics what scientific value it can have (cf. I 295, 26–7).

5. THE APPLICATION OF MATHEMATICAL TRUTHS IN PHYSICS

It can be seen from the preceding section that the contribution of mathematics to physics is not confined to the area of method. Geometry provides a scientific form of demonstration to physics. But physics also introduces specific mathematical principles and laws in its explanations. What might be called the substantive (as compared to the methodological) contribution of mathematics to physics is no less important for Proclus than it is for Iamblichus. A particularly striking aspect of Proclus' *Commentary on the Timaeus* is the somewhat complicated, oblique way in which mathematical truths are sometimes applied to physics. They are not simply read into nature, but are transformed in various ways in the course of being applied. In order to reach a better understanding of this procedure it will be useful to examine once more the place of mathematical objects in the scheme of reality, in particular *vis-à-vis* natural objects. For it is a reasonable assumption that the ontological relations between these different sorts of objects imply certain conditions governing the application of the one sort to the other.

The nature of mathematical objects as projections of principles innate in the soul has been discussed above in Chapter 8 in connection with the *Commentary on Euclid*. However, the place of this nature in the structure of reality, as determined by Proclus in the *Commentary on the Timaeus*, remains to be identified. We might begin with the simplified three-level system—sensible/mathematical/intelligible objects—that Iamblichus attributes (*Comm.* 10, 7–11, 15) to the 'Pythagoreans'. The same 'Pythagorean' system reappears in Syrianus (above, p. 131) and in Proclus' *Commentary on the Timaeus*, at I 8, 13–27, and again at II 23, 9–25:

After the mathematical grasp of these words (*Tim.* 31 c–32 a) we must turn to a physical interpretation. For we must not digress by remaining in mathematics (for the dialogue is about physics), nor must we neglect mathematics, seeking out only the perceptible, but we must join the two and always weave together mathematicals and physicals, just as the realities themselves are woven together and are homogeneous and of the same parent[22] according to the derivation from Intellect. And indeed if in general the Pythagoreans place mathematical reality between intelligibles and sensibles, as more unfolded than intelligibles and as more universal than sensibles, why then must we think only of physics, neglecting mathematicals? For how is the sensible ⟨world⟩ organized? According to what principles? From what principles did it come if not mathematical ones? Such principles then obtain first in souls, having descended from Intellect, and then are found in bodies having come from souls.

Proclus indicates at various points in his *Commentary* that certain distinctions must be introduced in the three-level scheme. (i) Firstly, for the *human* soul as knower, we must distinguish between the objects of its mathematical thought and the mathematical principles constituting its essence: although the monadic quantitative numbers of arithmetic are images of the essential psychic numbers, the former are not to be confused with the latter.[23] In the *Timaeus* Plato introduces geometrical and harmonic elements in the constitution of the soul: Proclus indicates that these also are not to be interpreted according to ordinary mathematical usage (as the objects studied in mathematics), but are to be understood in a higher sense (II 245, 23–246, 4). Indeed all four of the mathematical sciences are pre-contained essentially at a higher level in the constituents of soul (II 238, 10–239, 16). (ii) A distinction must also be made between psychic essential number, the mathematical unfolding or discursive image of this, and the empirical or 'opinative' number produced in the perceptual observations of astronomy.[24] Both mathematical and opinative number are generated from psychic number, but opinative number is derived *indirectly*, through perception of enmattered images ('physical numbers') of

---

[22] A Plotinian image (cf. IV 3, 6, 10–15) that recalls also Archytas as quoted by Iamblichus (*Comm.* 31, 4–7 = *In Nic.* 9, 1–5).

[23] Cf. *In Tim.* II 164, 17–165, 12; 166, 4–12; 193, 17–27; 212, 5–9. Cf. above, p. 133 (Syrianus).

[24] Cf. *In Tim.* I 255, 7–26; III 85, 23–31; 89, 7–13.

psychic number. (iii) Other distinctions need to be made in connection with *divine* soul as organizer of the world. Proclus makes use of the Iamblichean notion of 'physical numbers' as immanent formative causes, and distinguishes them (as images) from the mathematical principles according to which soul organizes the world.[25] The latter must be closely related or identical to the psychic mathematicals with which the demiurge composes soul's nature. In this work the demiurge imitates the Forms, which in consequence can also be referred to as 'number'.[26] The subject of 'ideal' and 'divine' number will be examined in the next chapter and need not delay us here.

This scheme of different sorts and levels of numbers, which is essentially the same as that proposed by Syrianus, may be used to determine the conditions under which mathematics is applicable in physics roughly as follows. To be used in physics, the objects with which the mathematician deals must, on the one hand, be purified of the features produced through their being projected from the soul's nature. These features include quantity in arithmeticals and extension in geometricals. By removing such additions in mathematicals we can approach nearer to the principles innate in the soul which, as divine demiurgic principles, guide her in her organization of the world. Allowance must be made, on the other hand, for the fact that the principles of the soul are not expressed perfectly in the world: the materiality of the world diminishes the universality and accuracy of such principles as reflected in the world. These two requirements show that an indirect and qualified, rather than a direct and simple application of mathematics to physics is appropriate. Our reliance on perception for matching mathematical principles with their physical analogues introduces a further limiting factor. The results of 'opinative' mathematics, such as astronomical calculation based on observation, must, it appears, be far inferior to those of 'projected' mathematics since they do not derive from discursive articulation of the psychic principles governing the world, but depend on perception mediating particularized and fleeting instantiations of such principles. Such qualifications and conditions for the application in physics of mathematics can plausibly be inferred, I believe, from Proclus'

[25] Cf. *In Tim.* II 25, 1–3; 39, 18–19; 161, 7–12; 164, 21–8; 166, 4–12; 193, 17–27; cf. *In Parm.* 869, 3.
[26] *In Tim.* II 194, 4–17; cf. I 41, 25–42, 2; II 161, 3–32; III 19, 14–26; 32, 26; *Hypo. astron.* 2, 1–5.

scheme of reality. Whether he does in fact observe them may be determined at least in the following examples of the use of mathematics in
his *Commentary*.

(i) In the first case Proclus is commenting (II 20, 19–28, 7) on the
passage of the *Timaeus* concerning the proportion (ἀναλογία) that
the demiurge uses to link and unify the elements of the world:

Wherefore also God in the beginning of creation made the body of the
universe to consist of fire and earth. But two things cannot be rightly put
together without a third; there must be some bond of union between them.
And the fairest bond is that which makes the most complete fusion of itself
and the things which it combines, and proportion is best adapted to effect
such a union. For whenever in any three numbers, whether cube or square,
there is a mean, which is to the last term what the first term is to it, and again
when the mean is to the first term as the last term to the mean—then the mean
becoming first and last, and the first and last both becoming means, they will
all of them of necessity come to be the same, and having become the same with
one another will be all one. (*Tim.* 31 c–32 a, transl. Jowett)

As in other similar instances, Proclus discusses first the mathematical
aspects of this passage and then turns, in a clearly marked transition,
to consider the passage with reference to its physical doctrine.

(a) The *mathematical* question the passage poses for him concerns
the kind of proportion—arithmetic, geometric or harmonic—to which
Plato is referring. Proclus agrees with Nicomachus (*Intro. arith.* 129,
14–20) that Plato is thinking of geometric proportion. For Plato speaks
of the *same* relation (λόγος) between extreme and middle terms (in
geometric proportion the proportion is the same, e.g. double in 1 : 2 =
2 : 4), not of an equal quantitative difference between the terms (as in
an arithmetic proportion such as 1 : 2 = 2 : 3), nor of the same frac-
tions of the extremes (as in a harmonic proportion such as 3 : 4 = 4 : 6,
where the middle term exceeds and is exceeded by a third of the
extremes).[27] Proclus then brings out the property or feature characteristic of geometric proportion, namely the *identity* (ταυτότης) of relation that the middle term produces in regard to the extremes, binding
them together and communicating to each the same relation. This
identity he regards as superior to the 'equality' characteristic of arithmetical proportions and to the 'similarity' he attributes to harmonic
proportions, and he describes it as leading up to and depending on
unity (ἕνωσις).

---

[27] Cf. Nicomachus, *Intro. arith.* 126, 12–128, 19.

Proclus then moves (b) to the *physical* interpretation of the Platonic passage (II 23, 9). He stresses that the mathematical theory must not be confused with the physics of the passage, for the transition is 'to another *genus*',[28] but that the mathematical theory can throw light on the physics. What then in physics is the proportion binding the elements of the world? For Proclus it is the cosmic life that penetrates the world giving it the unified life of a living animal. There are other principles of unification—the demiurgic causes 'above' this life and the particular forms and qualities of the elements 'below'—but Proclus takes Plato to be referring to an immanent (rather than transcendent) and causative (rather than caused) 'physical proportion', the life-principle of the universe. The living texture and rhythm of the universe reflect the work of this physical analogue of geometric proportion: it gives physical substances 'rational and homologous'[29] relationships to each other, i.e. the same proportional relations link them as terms in a series; it produces the development out of unity and return to its cause, the multiplying and reuniting of the life of the world, a pattern that recalls the progressive and regressive aspects of geometric proportion: the subsequent terms of a geometric series are produced by the same proportion; the middle term 'brings back' the third to first term. The participation of the elements in each other in the world also has its analogue in geometric proportion, in which extreme terms can function as means (e.g. $2 : 4 = 1 : 2$). Proclus finally attributes identity to the cosmic life, a feature corresponding to the property he found to be characteristic of geometric proportion.

Proclus does not propose then a direct mathematical reading of the physics of Plato's passage. For him Plato is not simply thinking of a mathematical proportion linking the elements of the universe. Rather, a *physical* cause must be found that possesses a nature and function analogous to what is characteristic of geometric proportion. The parallel between this physical cause (the cosmic life-principle) and geometric proportion is developed in such a way as to avoid mathematizing the specific physical character (or categorial domain) of this cause and its effects. The geometric proportion of the mathematician is not the binding power of the universe, but it illustrates in its own field features which also are found in its 'sister' (above, p. 186) in the natural realm. The parallel between geometric proportion and the cosmic life-principle depends, we can assume, on the fact that they

---

[28] II 23, 30–2; this is Aristotle's caveat, *An. post.* I 7, 75 a 38.
[29] On these mathematical terms cf. Festugière ad loc. (III 52 n. 2); cf. *In Tim.* I 17, 4–6.

represent projections of the same original psychic principle, the one in the discursive thought and imagination of the geometer, the other in the material world. Proclus does not tell us what geometric proportion purified of its projected (discursive, extended) aspect might turn out to be, but one can imagine that it would coincide essentially with the cosmic life-principle. He does, however, allow for the distortions that the material world can produce in the action of this life-principle: sensible objects, as divisible and 'other', attain identity and unity only in that, through the action of the life-principle, they reach an 'affinity to identity and, through it, to unity' (27, 10–13).

(ii) The second case of mathematical physics I propose to examine comes a little later (II 28, 14–42, 2), in commentary on the next lines of the *Timaeus*:

If the universal frame had been created a surface only and having no depth, a single mean would have sufficed to bind together itself and the other terms, but now, as the world must be solid, and solid bodies are always compacted not by one mean but by two, God placed water and air in the mean between fire and earth. (*Tim.* 32 a b, transl. Jowett)

In explaining this passage Proclus first argues, very much as Aristotle does, that change takes place between contraries and that there must therefore be two contrary elements of the world, fire and earth (II 28, 14–30, 8). He then tries to show why two intermediate elements are needed to link the extremes. The demonstration of the Platonic postulate is provided first in mathematical and then in physical terms.

(a) The mathematical demonstration begins with numbers, for they are what is 'originative' ($\dot{\alpha}\varrho\chi o \varepsilon\iota\delta\acute{\varepsilon}\varsigma$) and 'self-existent' ($\alpha\dot{\upsilon}\tau o\varphi\upsilon\acute{\varepsilon}\varsigma$) as compared to 'geometrical necessity' (30, 13–15); i.e. the objects of arithmetic, hence its demonstrations, are higher than those of geometry, thus nearer the source in psychic nature.[30] Proclus then argues that 'solid' numbers (cubes), as distinct from 'plane' numbers (squares), require two middle terms in a proportion: e.g. in the series 8, 12, 18, 27, the cubes that are the extremes 8 (2^3) and 27 (3^3) are linked by 12 ($2^2 \times 3$) and 18 ($3^2 \times 2$), whereas only one middle term *may* suffice to link two plane numbers, as in the series 9 (3^2), 12 (3×4), 16 (4^2). The fundamental feature of the middle terms linking two solid numbers (cubes) is the fact that each middle term is made up of two 'sides' of one extreme and one side of the other (thus $2^2 \times 3 = 12$, $3^2 \times 2 = 18$).

---

[30] Cf. also 34, 4–27, where it is claimed that what Plato says is truer in arithmetic than in geometry.

(b) The same principles hold for Proclus in physics: physical planes may be linked together by one middle term, whereas physical solids require two middle terms. Thus two elements, water and air, are needed to connect fire and earth. On the subject of physical planes Proclus cites the view of Iamblichus—whom he praises as alone having gone beyond the mathematical problem to consider the physical one—that they are the powers and forms of solids. As for solids, in this case the elements, the extremes (fire and earth) must each contain three powers or qualities in order to yield the one different and two common qualities needed by the two middle terms, as demonstrated in the case of cubic numbers (39, 19–27). This produces the physical series:

Fire (fineness, sharpness, mobility)
Air (fineness, bluntness, mobility)
Water (thickness, bluntness, mobility)
Earth (thickness, bluntness, immobility).

In this series the properties of the 'middle' elements link the extremes much as the 'sides' of the middle terms link cubic numbers: each middle element is composed of two qualities of one extreme and one quality of the other. The same principle of mediation governs physical and arithmetical solids.

It appears then that the physical elements are linked to each other according to a structure of double mediation echoing that which links two solid numbers. This represents but an instance of the general principle that 'physicals are images of mathematicals' (39, 18–19). However, Proclus does not regard his demonstration of why two middle elements are required as merely an application of mathematical theory in physics. His argument is based rather on analysis of the physical nature of the elements themselves, an analysis which shows up the three aspects that each element must have if it is to function with the other elements in the constitution of physical bodies. And it is with physical, not mathematical, arguments that Proclus rejects theories according to which fewer than four elements might be required or which would find in each element fewer than three powers or qualities required to link together the elements.[31] If then the same structure of double mediation occurs both in mathematics (for solid numbers) and in physics (for the elements), this is supposed to result,

---

[31] Cf. 28, 20–30, 4; 37, 14–41, 9.

I would suggest, not from direct application of mathematics to physics, but rather from the fact that mathematics articulates in a clearer and more accurate way a principle which governs and is expressed also in a more imperfect way in the physical structure of the world.

In this second case of Proclus' use of mathematics in relation to physics, the approach seems to be as indirect and oblique as that observed in the first case. Proclus does not simply settle issues in physics by reference to mathematics. However, mathematics shows up more clearly principles that also obtain in physics and that can be formulated on the basis of physical analysis. In both cases I believe we can conclude that Proclus' approach to mathematics in connection with physical theory is consonant with what one would expect given the places assigned to mathematical and physical principles within the structure of reality. Proclus' laudatory reference to Iamblichus' attention (in his lost *Commentary on the Timaeus*) to the physical dimension raises the question as to the extent of Proclus' debt, in his way of using mathematics, to Iamblichus. Certainly Iamblichus was as clear about the need to avoid confusing mathematics with physics, as about the paradigmatic value of mathematics in physics. And it appears to be the case that Proclus here (37, 14 ff.) is following in general Iamblichus' physical approach as described at 36, 20–37, 14, even if he is expanding, clarifying, and perhaps altering some of the details of this approach.

(iii) The third case that I wish to mention concerns Proclus' use of 'opinative' mathematics in physics. As we might expect, calculations based on sense-perception have little value for him. Thus, when astronomical calculations lead to a theory of the precession of the equinoxes that conflicts with Plato's system, Proclus does not believe such calculations are a match for the divine authority of Plato and the Chaldaeans. Even the observations made by the Chaldaeans suffice, Proclus believes, to discredit the theory.[32]

6. CONCLUDING COMMENT

The results of the above study of Proclus' treatment of physics show both his debt to Iamblichus and his originality. His preference for

[32] III 124, 19–125, 4; cf. III 62, 6–63, 24 (Festugière ad loc. also refers to *In Remp.* II 220, 4 ff.). On this subject cf. Segond's full study (1987).

geometry among the mathematical sciences expresses itself in his geometricizing of Aristotle's physics and in his identification of the scientific method of Plato's *Timaeus* as 'geometrical' (i.e. syllogistic). However he shares Iamblichus' views on the relative value of Aristotle's and Plato's physics and, in his *Commentary on the Timaeus*, treats Plato's physics as essentially 'Pythagorean' in inspiration, a Iamblichean approach due perhaps to Syrianus' influence on the young Proclus. In interpreting the 'Pythagorean' physics of Plato's *Timaeus*, Proclus makes considerable use of mathematics as a source of paradigms for physics. However, he distinguishes between the domains of physics and mathematics and does not simply impose mathematical solutions to problems in physics. His use of mathematics is rather oblique, reflecting, I believe, the fact that mathematical principles are not for him the direct model of the universe, but are quantitative discursive projections by the human soul of higher principles which, on the divine level, guide the making of the world. In a Pythagorean physics such as that suggested in Nicomachus' works, a more direct application of mathematics to physics is assumed, and this is also the impression given by the fragments of Iamblichus' *On Pythagoreanism* V. However, Iamblichus is clear about the need to avoid confusing mathematics with physics, and Proclus praises him for having paid attention, in his interpretation of the *Timaeus*, not only to the mathematical, but also to the physical dimension.

A final comment might be ventured on Iamblichus' and Proclus' Pythagorean mathematical physics as seen from a modern standpoint. Their 'realism' with respect to the existence of mathematical objects is certainly a plausible position and is combined in an interesting way with another plausible approach in which such objects are explained as constructions ('projections') for which the mathematician is responsible.[33] What would create greater difficulty today would be the overall metaphysical view according to which these constructions are (indirectly) models of the universe, in so far as the universe is the work of divine soul using principles from which derive the projections of the mathematician. On the other hand, this overall metaphysical view certainly gives some account of the mathematical background of physics. However, the sense in which physics is mathematical is no doubt very different from what is the case in modern mathematical physics. One obvious difference consists in the kind of

[33] Cf. Annas (1976), 151.

mathematics used by Iamblichus and Proclus. This mathematics is dominated by Nicomachus' arithmetic which, apart from its mathematical limitations, tends to treat numbers as if they each possessed particular qualities or properties of a rather metaphysical character. This attitude to arithmetic, as a sort of disguised metaphysics, also affects Proclus' view of Euclidean geometry, since here also geometrical figures are assigned individual metaphysical properties. When then it comes to physics, which in Iamblichus and Proclus takes the form of an Aristotelian natural philosophy revised so as to conform to Neoplatonic metaphysics, a correspondence can be established between it and mathematics for the simple reason that both reflect the same metaphysical assumptions. This is surely very different from the mathematical symbolization and analysis of abstract quantitative relations that might be regarded as characteristic of modern mathematical physics.[34]

[34] Cf. Sambursky (1965), 3; Brunschvicq (1929), 60.

Mathematics and Metaphysics in Proclus

In the preceding chapter I have argued that Proclus' conception of the relations between mathematics and physics, as expressed in his *Commentary on the Timaeus*, can be regarded as representing quite closely Iamblichus' Pythagoreanizing programme with regard to physics. In this programme Iamblichus also pointed to the use of mathematics in other sciences, in ethics and psychology for example, and materials relating to such a mathematical ethics and mathematical psychology can also be found in Proclus.[1] However, mathematics, for Iamblichus, was of most importance as a preparation for and anticipation of the highest level of science, that of the study of pure intelligible being and of the gods. Proclus, as has been seen, uses the same approach in his *Commentary on Euclid*, and in other works, in particular in the *Elements of Theology*, the *Commentary on the Parmenides*, and the *Platonic Theology*, both discusses mathematical transpositions upwards to the divine and develops in detail an account of the science of the divine, dialectic or theology.

According to the reconstruction proposed above in chapter 3 of *On Pythagoreanism* VII, Iamblichus may possibly have reacted to Aristotle's attacks on the Platonic theory of intelligible Forms and numbers, anticipating the fuller response given by Syrianus in his *Commentary on the Metaphysics*. It seems at any rate that Iamblichus in his book suggested analogies between the properties and flow of numbers from the monad to the triad (and possibly to the decad) and the gods, i.e. an ultimate principle, the One, and an order of unities intervening between it and the level of intelligible being, the same principles being traced in their lower forms on the intellectual, psychic, and physical levels. At the same time Iamblichus stressed the limitations of such theological transpositions of mathematics, their inferiority as compared to a higher approach to the divine. This higher

---

[1] Cf. *In Tim.* II 193,7–27; 195, 11–24; 212, 3–9; 237, 11–240, 2; 245, 23–246, 9; III 337, 17–24; *In Remp.* I 212, 23 ff.; II 47, 23 ff.; 136, 19 ff.; 169, 4 ff.

approach was presented, it seems, not in *On Pythagoreanism* itself, but in other primarily theological works such as that *On God* which may have made use of (pseudo-)Pythagorean authorities.

In the following pages I shall examine some of the ways in which Proclus adopted and developed Iamblichus' Pythagoreanizing approach to the highest levels of philosophy. In particular I would like to bring out the distinctions Proclus makes between the science of the divine proper and the theological transpositions of mathematics, distinctions which will entail a brief account of Proclus' conception of the science of the divine. Although insisting, I believe, even more than did Iamblichus on the subordination of theological mathematics to the science of the divine, Proclus betrays in certain areas of his account of this science the influence of Iamblichean theological mathematics, as will be shown towards the end of the chapter.

I. THE *ELEMENTS OF THEOLOGY*: A GEOMETRICAL METAPHYSICS?

If the prologues of Proclus' *Commentary on Euclid* were to be well known and highly valued by mathematicians, historians, and philosophers of mathematics, his *Elements of Theology* was to have, in other circles, no less great a success. Already in the Middle Ages it was translated into a number of languages, Georgian, Arabic, Hebrew, Armenian, and Latin,[2] and the Latin translation of an abbreviated and modified Arabic version, the *De causis*, became a basic textbook of metaphysics in Western Medieval philosophy. The *Elements of Theology* remains the first book of Proclus to be read by philosophers and historians of philosophy. This success is due in part no doubt to the pedagogic qualities of the work, a (relative) clarity and simplicity of exposition which takes a form that is also intellectually appealing and impressive: the work consists of a series of propositions, each proposition being accompanied by one or more demonstrations, the premises constituting the demonstrations sometimes deriving as conclusions from earlier arguments, the whole appearing in this way as a systematic and rigorous deduction of a series of abstract metaphysical truths. The impression of scientific rigour is reinforced by the Euclidean character of some of the arguments and language.[3] It is not then

---

[2] Cf. Dodds's edn., xxix–xxx; Boese (1985).
[3] Cf. e.g. 6, 30; the scholium on 58, 11; Lowry (1980), 37.

without reason that Proclus' work has been seen as a metaphysical system demonstrated *more geometrico*, in the manner of Spinoza, the first such attempt in the history of Western philosophy.[4]

But in what sense is the metaphysics of the *Elements of Theology* geometrical? Is geometrical demonstrative method applied to metaphysics in the way that Proclus applies it to physics in the *Elements of Physics*? If one compares the two works one soon notices some important differences. Firstly, the *Elements of Physics*, as indicated in Chapter 9, does not deal with physics in general, but is concerned with motion and change as pointing to the existence of an immaterial principle of motion. On the other hand, the *Elements of Theology* covers the whole range of the science of the divine ('theology'), going from the highest principle of all reality, the One, down through the lower levels of the divine to the lowest, the level of soul.[5] Secondly, the *Elements of Physics* is much nearer to Euclid in form than is the *Elements of Theology*, in that its demonstrations are preceded by definitions, whereas the *Elements of Theology* simply presents a succession of propositions which function as the *conclusions* of the demonstrations supporting them.[6]

This last point is sufficient to show that the *Elements of Theology* is not a geometricized metaphysics in the way that the *Elements of Physics* is a geometricized physics; Proclus does not simply apply Euclidean demonstrative method to metaphysical doctrine. How then account for the undeniable geometrical aspects of the *Elements of Theology*? Our study of the *Commentary on Euclid* in Chapter 8 has led to conclusions that are relevant here. One of these conclusions was that Proclus tends to see geometry as exemplifying particularly well scientific reasoning on the discursive level. Hence geometrical method is assimilated by him to what we would call logical rigour. In whatever context this rigour is applied we will find in consequence a tendency in Proclus to allude to geometrical procedures and terms. Although closely associating geometrical with scientific method, Proclus also insists, in his revision of Iamblichus in his *Commentary on Euclid*, that geometry

---

[4] Cf. the references given by Hathaway (1982), 123–4.

[5] On soul as the lowest level of the divine, cf. *Theol. Plat.* I 114, 23–116, 3; Plotinus V 1, 7, 47–9. Dodds points out in his edn. of the *El theol.* (X, 187) that the word 'theology' in the title is to be understood in its Aristotelian sense (=metaphysics, first philosophy, science of the divine), which Proclus and Syrianus (cf. above, pp. 120–1) identify with the highest Platonic science, dialectic.

[6] On the fact that the *El. theol.* is not simply a geometricized metaphysics, cf. also Lowry (1980), 37; Hathaway (1982); Lohr (1986), 59–60.

derives its method from a higher science, Platonic dialectic: the parts of this method (definition, division, analysis, and demonstration) are already found in dialectic. In his theological works Proclus also brings out these four constituents of dialectical method.[7] This method can appear geometrical to the extent that it is the source of and is imaged in geometrical method. If then the *Elements of Theology* appears in certain respects to be somewhat geometrical and in other respects not, this may be because the work is not a geometrical theology or metaphysics at all, but something quite different: a treatise of theology or dialectic, whose method is proper to it, while recalling to some degree the derivative but more familiar and accessible procedures of geometry.

To show more fully that the *Elements of Theology* is an example of theology or dialectic proper it will be necessary to examine what Proclus conceives theology or dialectic to be. For this purpose we will need to refer to Proclus' other theological works. For if the *Elements of Theology*, as an introductory manual, possesses a certain clarity, it is by no means self-explanatory. Like other manuals it distils and orders the results of a long and complicated development of thought whose assumptions and turning-points can disappear under the surface of didactic exposition. These assumptions in Proclus' way of conceiving theology or dialectic can be detected more easily in his two major theological works, his *Commentary on the Parmenides* and his *Platonic Theology*.

2. THE SCIENCE OF DIALECTIC

Towards the beginning of his *Platonic Theology* (I 17, 18–20, 25) Proclus presents four different ways of communicating knowledge of the divine: the inspired approach exemplified in Plato's *Phaedrus* and characteristic of the 'Chaldaean Oracles'; the symbolic approach to be found in Plato's myths and in Orpheus; the use of images, in particular mathematical images, to express the divine that is practised by Pythagoras and Pythagoreans as well as by Plato; and finally the one truly scientific approach, which is to be found only in Plato, in dialectical exposition of the divine in the *Sophist* and particularly in the *Parmenides*:

---

[7] Cf. *Theol. Plat.* I 40, 5–13 (with Saffrey and Westerink's notes); *In Tim.* I 276, 10–14.

The scientific ⟨mode of exposition⟩ is peculiar to Plato's philosophy. For he alone, as I believe, among those known to us, undertook to distinguish and order appropriately the ordered progression of the divine kinds, the differences between them, the common characteristics of all levels and those proper to each. (20, 19–25)

This fourfold division can be found elsewhere in Proclus.[8] It expresses very clearly the difference between mathematical imagings of the divine and the science proper of the divine. If this distinction is one that Iamblichus himself had made in *On Pythagoreanism* VII, it takes a form in Proclus that represents, as we have seen in Chapter 7, a new departure: Proclus finds *in Plato alone* the science of the divine, properly speaking. The subordination of theologizing mathematics to theology or dialectic thus becomes also a subordination of Pythagoreanism to the philosophy of Plato. And this subordination of Pythagoreanism to Plato in turn makes more evident the limitations of theologizing mathematics and the superiority and distinctiveness of Platonic dialectic.

But what then is the science of the divine? Proclus, as noted above and in connection with the *Commentary on Euclid*, regards Plato's *Parmenides* as an exposition of this science and devotes his very long *Commentary on the Parmenides* to showing this. If his *Commentary* cannot be regarded as a reliable guide to reading Plato's dialogue, it is a rich source of information concerning Proclus' own conception of Platonic dialectic and is testimony of the lengths to which he had to go in order to make Plato's text correspond to this conception. It will suffice then, in order to sketch briefly Proclus' views on the science of the divine, to note some aspects of his interpretation of the *Parmenides*.[9]

In connection with explaining the roles of Socrates and of Parmenides in the Platonic dialogue, Proclus describes the ideal attributes of the student (Socrates) and teacher (Parmenides) of dialectic.[10] The student must, among other things, have an adequate intellectual preparation, in particular in logic, physics, and mathematics, for these sciences prepare the mind for contemplation of the divine by making the divine more accessible to it through images.

---

[8] Cf. *In Parm.* 646, 21–647, 16 (on the Pythagorean use of mathematical images as contrasted with dialectic cf. also 623, 29–34; 924, 4–9); *Theol. Plat.* I 9, 20–7; *In Remp.* I 84, 26–85, 1; *In Tim.* I 129, 31–130, 8.

[9] The following does not attempt to give a complete account of Proclus' concept of dialectic; cf. Beierwaltes (1979), 246 ff.

[10] On Parmenides as teacher ('leader') of Socrates, cf. Steel (1987).

Thus, in a passage that could also come from the *Commentary on Euclid*, Proclus suggests that

if he ⟨the student⟩ wonders how the many could be in the One, and all in the indivisible, let him think of the monad and how it is shown that all forms of odd and even are ⟨pre-contained⟩ in it, the circle and sphere, and the other forms of numbers.[11]

The teacher, who leads the student of dialectic, on the other hand,

will not wish to reveal the divine truth with many words, but to reveal many things with few, speaking in unison with thought. Nor will he start from the familiar, but will consider matters from on high, from the most unified principles, since he is removed from what is at hand, and is near to the divine. (927, 38–928, 9)

To these attributes of the teacher of dialectic we should add that of scientific rigour, the strict syllogistic exposition of the subject that Proclus finds in the *Parmenides* and that he sometimes conceives as 'geometrical' in character,[12] that is, as suggested above, as exemplifying scientific method.

Plato's figure Parmenides exhibits in the dialogue these attributes of the ideal 'guide' to dialectic: simplicity, purity, scientific rigour, presenting the subject by starting from 'on high', from 'the most unified principles', and demonstrating all else on the basis of such principles. These principles correspond to the hypotheses that Parmenides proposes to Socrates. They are hypothetical in two senses: as representing the beginnings of the ascent through hypotheses to an 'unhypothetical' first principle that is described as the first phase of dialectic in Plato's *Republic*;[13] and as corresponding to what functions as hypotheses, that is 'common notions' or axioms, in geometry.[14] We may say then that just as geometrical demonstrations proper have as starting-points certain evident truths, so, on a higher level, do dialectical demonstrations start from certain fundamental metaphysical truths such as are expressed in the hypotheses of the *Parmenides*. And indeed just as the first principles of geometry are a priori concepts given in psychic nature which the geometer 'projects'

[11] *In Parm.* 926, 16–29 and ff.; cf. above, p. 161.

[12] Cf. *In Parm.* 645, 9–27; 727,8–10; 1132, 20–6; 1140, 19–22; 1195, 26–30; 1206, 1–3.

[13] Cf. *In Parm.* 622, 21–623, 28; 1033, 20–1034, 30 (where Proclus says he is following Syrianus); Beierwaltes (1979), 253–74.

[14] Cf. *In Parm.* 930, 6–9; 1034, 1–2; 1092, 19–34; 1099, 39–1100, 10; Beierwaltes (1979), 261 ff.

or 'unrolls' in his demonstrations, so the dialectician takes his beginning from certain primary a priori metaphysical concepts which he then articulates in his demonstrations.[15]

The idea that there are certain metaphysical concepts given in psychic nature and transcending mathematical concepts can be found already in Syrianus.[16] In Proclus—if only because of the large amount of his work that survives—the meaning and importance of this idea is clearer. In particular Proclus associates (i) the (Stoic) notion that there are certain truths universally held by mankind, such as the existence and providence of the divine, with (ii) the (Aristotelian) notion that certain principles are known, not by demonstration, but by a sort of intellectual insight (νοῦς), and with (iii) the geometrical concept of certain truths as evident, axioms.[17] Associating these notions, Proclus thus finds at the highest level of human reflection a number of concepts, of metaphysical content, intuitively known as given in the nature of soul, and functioning as the starting-points of the demonstrations of the dialectician.[18]

In demonstrating fundamental metaphysical insights the dialectician does not attempt to prove them. Rather he 'unfolds' or explicates them, showing what they presuppose and what they entail. This procedure corresponds in fact to the structure of syllogistic argument, whereby the conclusion shows what is implied by the premises. In the treatment of his first hypothesis the dialectician begins with a truth that is not, according to what Plato suggests in the *Republic*, the very first metaphysical truth which all other metaphysical truths presuppose.[19] The dialectician must therefore work back from his starting-point to such an ultimate truth and then, again following the procedure prescribed by the *Republic*, work down from this truth, showing how all other truths derive from the first. In doing this the dialectician unfolds a series of concepts that corresponds to and speaks of the unfolding of the structure of reality from its ultimate source in the One.[20]

---

[15] Cf. 1151, 38–1152, 5; the first hypothesis of the *Parmenides* is described as a νόημα in *Theol. Plat.* II 66, 1–8 (quoted below).

[16] Cf. O'Meara (1986), 12.

[17] Cf. the wealth of references collected by Saffrey and Westerink in their note in *Theol. Plat.* I 159–61; Trouillard (1972), 51–67.

[18] Cf. *In Parm.* 980, 8–982, 30; 1125, 13–22.

[19] Cf. the references given in n. 13 above.

[20] Cf. *Theol. Plat.* III 82, 23–83, 2; the text quoted below, p. 202; *In Parm.* 1032, 15–29.

The very first metaphysical truth from which the dialectician derives his science of the divine is, in Proclus' opinion, the first hypothesis of the *Parmenides*:

What then is the very first concept (νόημα) of the science proceeding from intellect and revealing herself? What other shall we mention but the simplest and most knowable of all her concepts? For this concept is most akin to the contemplation of intellect. What is it then? Parmenides says (137 c): 'The One, if it is one, may not be many.' For the many must participate in the One. But the One does not participate in the One but is the One itself.[21]

From this truth Parmenides demonstrates, according to Proclus, the derivation, in order and according to strict syllogistic procedure, of subsequent metaphysical truths, expressing thereby in scientific form the derivation of all levels of the divine from an ultimate principle. Proclus summarizes the procedure thus:

For the first conclusions are made evident immediately from the smallest number and the most simple and most knowable ⟨of concepts⟩, common concepts so-to-speak; and the conclusions subsequent to these ⟨are demonstrated⟩ through more numerous and complex ⟨concepts⟩; and the last are the most composite. For Parmenides always uses the first conclusions for demonstrations of the subsequent and offers, as an intellectual paradigm of the order in geometry and in the other mathematical sciences, this chain of conclusions fitted to each other. If then discourse brings an image of the things it interprets (*Tim.* 29 b), and as are the demonstrative unfoldings ⟨explications⟩ so must what are demonstrated be in order, it is necessary, I believe, that the first conclusions demonstrated from the simplest premises must be absolutely primary and joined closely to the One, those that are multiplied continuously and depend on complex demonstrations being products at a greater distance, in 'alienation', one might say, 'from the One'.[22]

I have suggested elsewhere (1986) that Proclus' conception of dialectic represents a theory of metaphysics whose originality and coherence has hitherto been scarcely noticed, a result no doubt of the fact that it regards itself as no more than an exegesis, and an improbable one at that, of Plato. In view of the lack of evidence concerning Syrianus it is difficult to determine the extent of Proclus' debt here to Syrianus, although we may suppose that a certain amount derives

---

[21] *Theol. Plat.* II 66, 1–9.
[22] *Theol. Plat.* I 45, 20–46, 9; Saffrey and Westerink indicate that at the end Proclus is quoting Plotinus, VI 6, 1.

from Syrianus.[23] Even less is known of how Iamblichus conceived dialectic or the science of the divine. But one can reasonably suppose that Iamblichus did not, as does Proclus, discount the scientific claims of Pythagorean theory, reserving for Plato alone the title of true dialectician. This probably means that Proclus did not find in Iamblichus' accounts of Pythagorean theology an approach corresponding to his conception of dialectic. In other words there is some likelihood that in clarifying and systematizing the distinction between theologizing mathematics and theology or dialectic proper, Proclus came to conceive of the latter science in a way that no longer corresponded to Iamblichus' treatment of the subject.

Be that as it may, it might be noted that in his attempt to formulate the nature of dialectic as a science independent of, superior to, and paradigmatic for mathematics, Proclus is largely guided by his understanding of the structure of mathematical science, in particular geometry. Thus dialectic, like geometry, 'projects' or 'unfolds' innate a priori concepts, demonstrating them by means of rigorous syllogistic arguments. The concepts are of course of a higher order, nearer the intelligible principles of soul and of a broader application than the concepts explicated by the geometer. But it remains that mathematics, and in particular geometry, provides Proclus with the model (he would say the image) of scientific discourse whereby the distinctiveness and superiority of dialectic *vis-à-vis* other sciences can be determined. The same phenomenon will be observed in the following section with respect, not to form, but to the content of dialectic. In general one might say that in imposing limits on Iamblichus' Pythagoreanizing of Platonic philosophy, in subordinating Pythagorean mathematics and theologizing mathematics to Platonic dialectic, Proclus adopted for this a principle, namely the image-status of mathematics that he found in Iamblichus' Pythagoreanizing programme itself.

We may conclude finally that Proclus' description of Platonic dialectic in his *Commentary on the Parmenides* and in his *Platonic Theology* corresponds in many respects to the structure of the *Elements of Theology*. The chain of syllogisms described in the passage quoted immediately above is a distinctive feature of the *Elements of Theology*. The propositions that precede and are supported by the syllogisms can be regarded as the metaphysical concepts which the dialectician

[23] Cf. above nn. 13, 16.

seeks to unfold. Indeed the fourth proposition, 'All that is unified is other than the One itself', turns out to be what Proclus considers as the very first metaphysical concept, the first hypothesis of the *Parmenides* ('The One, if it is one, may not be many') if, applying the first proposition, we describe all multitude as unified. The first three propositions and their demonstrations prepare the way and lead up to the first metaphysical truth, after which Proclus proceeds to unfold truths concerning divine causes in general and concerning each level of the divine treated in particular and in descending order. Thus the *Elements of Theology* shows the motion upwards and downwards that Plato attributes to dialectic in the *Republic*. However it is especially in the *Parmenides* that Proclus finds dialectical exposition, and the correspondence between the fourth proposition of the *Elements of Theology* and the first hypothesis of the *Parmenides* suggests that the major source of inspiration of Proclus' work is the *Parmenides*, as he interpreted that dialogue.[24] Thus another striking originality of the *Elements of Theology*, besides its rigorous syllogistic form—namely the fact that, contrary to Proclus' normal practice, no authorities are cited—can be clarified, if the work is seen as an exposé of dialectic: an authority is in fact present in the work, namely Plato, for the work unfolds the science of the divine that Plato alone communicated to mankind.

3. MATHEMATICAL THEOLOGY AND DIALECTIC

In the preceding section I have attempted to indicate how Proclus, emphasizing a point already made by Iamblichus, drew a clear distinction between theologizing mathematics and theology or dialectic proper, and how, in order to bring out the distinctiveness and superiority of the latter science, he gave it a form derived from his own understanding of the structure of geometry. In this section I shall suggest that a similar situation arises with regard to the *content* of theology: in his account of this content, i.e. the divine, Proclus seeks to proceed independently of theologizing mathematics, but this account can nevertheless be seen to be inspired to a considerable degree by theologizing mathematics.

A first example of this may be found in the presentation of the gods that Proclus calls 'henads' in the *Elements of Theology*. Having dealt

---

[24] Dodds indicates in his edition (e.g., 188, 189, 190) connections with the *Parmenides*; such parallels could be multiplied.

with the supreme principle, the One, and its relations to its products in the first part of the *Elements of Theology*, Proclus turns in propositions 113–65 to the gods that are subordinate to the One and that transcend the level of intelligible being, the henads. Iamblichus had also treated of an order of gods corresponding to these henads in *On Pythagoreanism* VII,[25] and what remains of this treatment in Psellus' excerpts shows some similarities with Proclus' approach. In both Iamblichus and Proclus this order of gods is considered as unified both in itself and in each of its members.[26] Both treat first of the general properties of the order as a whole before discussing specific properties. For both each god is distinct, forms part of a serial ordering, and is reflected in its effects in corresponding features found on the successive lower levels of reality.[27]

Yet one notices also in Proclus' account of the henads aspects that differentiate it from the theologizing arithmetic of *On Pythagoreanism* VII. It appears first that in referring to the henads as 'divine number' Proclus gives to the term 'number' a broad, non-mathematical sense, i.e. that of group or class.[28] Furthermore, in discussing the specific properties of the henads, Proclus does not take in turn each of the distinct members of the order as does Iamblichus when he deals with the monad, dyad, triad of the order. Rather each property is presented without reference to particular henads. Finally the properties that are named by Proclus—the 'paternal', the 'generative', the 'perfective', the 'protective', etc. (props. 151 ff.)—are not especially mathematical in character. It is true that their analogues can be found in mathematical objects: Proclus elsewhere relates the 'paternal' to the monad and the 'generative' to the dyad,[29] whereas the triad is traditionally regarded as perfective. But it is surely significant that Proclus, in introducing these different properties of the henads, does not attribute them to particular members of a numerical series, as does Iamblichus. It is as if Proclus wishes to avoid an identification of each of the henads with each number in a decadic series.[30] In this we may regard Proclus

[25] Saffrey and Westerink argue, in *Theol. Plat.* III ix–lxxvii, against there having been a theory of henads in Iamblichus, on the basis of a study of later reports in Proclus and Damascius and *before the first-hand evidence provided by Psellus' excerpts could be considered*.

[26] Proclus, *El. theol.* props. 113–14; cf. above, p. 84.

[27] Proclus, props. 133, 135; 126, 136; 129, 131, 145; cf. above, pp. 83–4.

[28] Dodds's translation of ἀριθμός (a possible exception may be 104, 9–10); Merlan argues against this (1965), I believe unconvincingly.

[29] Cf. *Theol. Plat.* I 122, 3–10.

[30] Merlan (1965), 175–6, argues that Proclus thought of the henads as constituting a decad, but the evidence is not that clear.

as applying with rigour the distinction he finds between theologizing mathematics and theology proper. In consequence however Proclus' treatment of the henads in the *Elements* is somewhat general and vague. If the henads are not to be seen simply as the monad, dyad, triad of a decad, it is not clear what individually they are supposed to be.

If Proclus' account of the henads in the *Elements of Theology* seeks to establish itself independently of the account of the same matter yielded by theologizing mathematics, it must be admitted, however, that the source of inspiration of much of what Proclus says of the henads is mathematics and theologizing mathematics. I have indicated above the broad similarities of treatment between the section on henads in the *Elements* and *On Pythagoreanism* VII. To these one might add Proclus' frequent recourse to mathematical principles and laws. For example the law of mean terms serves to link not only the members of the order of henads but also almost everything else in Proclus' theological universe.[31] The principles of 'limit' and the 'unlimited', principles that occur in Plato's *Philebus* and that Syrianus and Proclus identify with the Pythagorean monad and dyad,[32] are responsible for the constitution of the order of henads. Indeed the concept of the monad and its relation to the series it generates is of great importance to the ordering of reality as Proclus conceives it in the *Elements*.[33] One might reasonably say then that despite his effort to separate (Platonic) dialectic or theology from (Pythagorean) theologizing mathematics, Proclus in effect produces a theological account that cannot but strike us, in certain respects, as heavily indebted to mathematics.

The same can be observed, I believe, in Proclus' other theological works, his *Commentary on the Parmenides* and his *Platonic Theology*. In the *Commentary on the Parmenides*, for example, Proclus treats of the henads in the same very general way that characterizes the account in the *Elements of Theology*: the henads are described collectively in terms of a number of metaphysical properties.[34] In his interpretation of the *Parmenides* Proclus indicates that mathematical terms occurring in Plato's (theological) text are to be understood, not in a mathematical, but in a higher sense.[35] And when he analyses the orders of the gods in terms of the relations between monad and dyad, he notes that he is

---

[31] Prop. 132; cf. prop. 148; Dodds, in his edn., xxii.
[32] Cf. above, p. 146; Sheppard (1982); Beierwaltes (1972), 179 ff.
[33] Cf. e.g. props. 21–2 (with Dodds's comment, 208), 204 (178, 28–31).
[34] Cf. *In Parm.* 1048, 14–1049, 3.
[35] *In Parm.* 1129, 22–6; 1204, 19–41.

using a mathematical image.[36] And yet the use of mathematical relationships to describe meta-mathematical realities is such that it is not clear sometimes how such realities could otherwise be presented.[37]

In the *Platonic Theology* Proclus also treats of the gods in a fashion that is in part inspired by mathematics while at the same time separating itself from theologizing mathematics. On the subject of the henads he claims that:

There must be an order among the henads such as we see among numbers, some being nearer the ⟨first⟩ principle, others being further away, some being simpler, others more composite, greater in quantity, but lesser in power. And we have rightly recalled the numbers. For if we must contemplate the order of the very first monads among themselves and the production of beings, using numbers as images, it is necessary that in these monads those that are nearer the One be shared in by those that are simpler in being, those that are further being shared in by those that are more composite. (III 17, 18–18, 3)

If emphasis is placed here on the function of numbers as images of higher realities, in other contexts it looks as if mathematical principles *are* what governs the orders of the gods: the monad and its relation to a number series, the interplay between monad and dyad in the production of the decad are the structural principles that constitute Proclus' world of gods.[38]

Of course Proclus made use of other sources in his theology such as the general metaphysical truths he found stated in the hypotheses of Plato's *Parmenides* as well as in the utterances of the 'Chaldaean Oracles'. However, we might plausibly claim, given the examples cited, that his 'Platonic' theology, although asserting its independence of and superiority to 'Pythagorean' theologizing mathematics, is still marked by this theologizing mathematics. The somewhat ambivalent character of his theology—both mathematical and not mathematical in form and content—is testimony to its origins as, in part at least, a critical reaction to the theologizing mathematics of Iamblichus' Pythagoreanizing programme.

---

[36] *In Parm.* 662, 4–12.
[37] Cf. e.g. *In Parm.* 703, 12–704, 10; 706, 27–33.
[38] Cf. e.g. *Theol. Plat.* II 38, 3–8; 71, 5–8; III 8, 1–9, 11; 30, 19–34, 19.

4. CONCLUDING COMMENT

In the first chapters devoted to Proclus above I have suggested that Proclus, far from simply adopting Iamblichus' Pythagoreanizing programme, changed that programme in various significant ways. He altered the relations between the figures of Pythagoras and Plato in such a way that Plato and his dialogues took over the pre-eminence given by Iamblichus to Pythagoras and Pythagorean works. For Proclus Plato was the first scientific philosopher and it is only in Plato's writings that the scientific exposition of truth is to be found. This shift in focus is accompanied by a shift in the attitude taken to mathematics in its relations to the other parts of philosophy. While acknowledging the mediatory and pivotal role of mathematics, Proclus insisted on the limitations of mathematics, in particular as regards a distinct and higher science, Platonic dialectic. In reducing Pythagorean theology to the status of theologizing mathematics and in claiming to find in Plato alone the science of the divine, Proclus was able to distinguish much more clearly than could Iamblichus between these two approaches to the divine.

In presenting the latter point in this chapter I have not tried to survey the full breadth of Proclus' metaphysics. I have sought rather to give some indications of how Proclus attempted to separate Pythagoreanizing theologizing mathematics from Platonic dialectic. For this purpose Proclus had to elaborate an interpretation of what precisely Platonic dialectic is: Plato himself gives only some obscure hints, in particular in the *Republic*. Elaborating an approach inspired, it appears, in some respects by his teacher Syrianus, Proclus conceived of dialectic very much after the pattern of the structure of geometry as he understood it: dialectic is a demonstrative science, explicating certain a priori metaphysical truths given in the soul. These truths are more profound and general than geometrical axioms, concerning as they do the first principles of all reality, the gods. This characterization of dialectic, if effective in permitting of a sharp discrimination between the science of the divine and theologizing mathematics, is nevertheless based on an assimilation of mathematical method to scientific method in general. And although in his theology Proclus attempts to describe the gods independently of mathematical assimilations, he often introduces what are in effect mathematical concepts and laws. Theology thus establishes itself in Proclus in large part in relation to mathematics and theologizing mathematics. The *Elements of Theology* may be regarded as a worthy expression of the originality and vigour Proclus brought to bear on the effort to go beyond the Pythagoreanizing theology of Iamblichus in the direction of the formulation of a truly Platonic metaphysics. And it is precisely this Iamblichean background that provides a means of grasping and measuring the extent of Proclus' achievement.

Conclusion

THE themes examined in this book, in their integration into Neo-platonic philosophy by Iamblichus and in their adoption and revision by Syrianus and Proclus, continued to have considerable influence on subsequent thinkers. Proclus' successor at Athens, Marinus, appears to have been a better mathematician than philosopher. At any rate he shared the high regard for mathematics that has been found already in Iamblichus, for we are told:

Some wonder why, if we learn ($\mu\alpha\nu\theta\acute{\alpha}\nuο\mu\varepsilon\nu$) everything, the immaterial, the material, and what is between them, not all are called mathematics ($\mu\alpha\theta\acute{\eta}$-$\mu\alpha\tau\alpha$), but only the intermediate . . . and we say there are two reasons for this, one that mathematics possesses the solidity of demonstration, for we learn it accurately, but we conjecture rather than learn the others, for which reason the philosopher Marinus said 'Would that all were mathematics!'[1]

The place and function of Pythagoras in the history of philosophy and the role of mathematics in philosophy would thus merit investigation in their development in the thought of Marinus and in his successors. It seems, for example, that Damascius, later head of the school, claimed to make a return, in opposition to Proclus, to Iamblichean philosophy.[2] The fortune of Iamblichus' Pythagoreanizing programme could also be examined in regard to the Alexandrian school. One might note here, for example, that Proclus' pupil Ammonius, in his more favourable attitude to Aristotle, took more seriously the Aristotelian idea of numbers as abstractions and attempted to combine this with the idea of numbers as projections of higher a priori concepts.

Worth considering also would be the impact Iamblichus' Pythagoreanizing programme would have, in the form given it in the Athenian and Alexandrian schools, on later periods. One might mention as an example Boethius' short theological work known as the *De hebdomadibus* which would provide, in its geometrical form, a

---

[1] Elias, *In Porph. Is.* 28, 24–9.
[2] Cf. Westerink (1971).

model for scientific discourse to Western Medieval theologians.[3]
Later the Latin translation of Proclus' *Elements of Theology* would
become a paradigm of metaphysics for Bertold of Moosburg; the short
altered Arabic version of the *Elements* in Latin, the *De causis*, had
already served and would continue to serve as the basic textbook,
along with Aristotle's *Metaphysics*, for Medieval metaphysics. When
Proclus' *Commentary on the Parmenides* became available in Latin to
Nicholas of Cusa, he would use it extensively in the development of
his profound theories of the philosophical importance of mathematics
with regard, in particular, to the divine.[4] One might mention furthermore the great interest taken by mathematicians in the Renaissance in
Iamblichus' philosophy of mathematics as reformulated in Proclus'
prologues to Euclid, an interest expressed in the idea of a *mathesis
universalis* that can be traced up to Descartes and beyond.[5]

It is not the purpose of this book, however, to examine the later
history of Neoplatonic Pythagoreanism, as a thesis about the origins
and history of wisdom and a theory about the relations between
mathematics and the philosophical sciences.[6] I have been concerned
rather with its beginnings in Iamblichus' philosophy and its reception
by the first major philosophers of the Athenian school, with the aim of
throwing some light on this obscure but important phase in the history
of late Greek philosophy. The results might be summarized as follows.

A tendency to Pythagoreanize is common in the history of Platonism and is represented in different forms and to different degrees
among Iamblichus' immediate philosophical predecessors, Numenius, Nicomachus of Gerasa, Anatolius, and Porphyry. However,
Iamblichus' programme to Pythagoreanize Platonic philosophy was
more systematic and far-reaching. This project is expressed in a
number of Iamblichus' commentaries on Plato and Aristotle and is the
subject of a ten-volume work by Iamblichus, *On Pythagoreanism*. In
this work, in so far as it can be analysed on the basis of the extant (first
four) books and of Psellus' excerpts from Books V–VII, various
materials—texts from Plato, Aristotle, (pseudo-)Pythagorean literature—were assembled so as to initiate the reader, step-by-step, to
'Pythagorean' philosophy. At first the reader is presented with a

---

[3] Cf. Schrimpf (1966), Evans (1980), Lohr (1986).
[4] Cf., for example, Imbach (1978), Schultze (1978), Beierwaltes (1975), 368–84.
[5] Cf. Crapulli (1969), and Klein (1968), who discusses Proclus' work on Euclid in
connection with Descartes.
[6] Valuable materials concerning this are collected in Mahnke (1937).

portrait of Pythagoras that expresses Iamblichus' interpretation of him as an uncorrupted soul sent down to communicate wisdom to souls that have fallen away from insight. This interpretation of Pythagoras reflects Iamblichus' Neoplatonic theory of the various relations of soul to, and functions in, the material world. Pythagoras' revelation stands, in Iamblichus' view, for all that is true in the history of Greek philosophy: Plato and later true Platonists are Pythagoreans, as is Aristotle, to the extent that he remains faithful to Pythagoreanism/ Platonism. Pythagorean philosophy, for Iamblichus, is distinguished especially by its concern with immaterial realities, objects which give it its scientific, i.e. demonstrative, character. One branch of this philosophy consists in mathematics, which has the special character of acting as a mediating knowledge, as Iamblichus shows in the case of arithmetic: arithmetic not only functions as a scientific paradigm for inquiries that are scarcely scientific, concerned as they are with material reality, physics, ethics, politics, poetics, but also prepares the mind and anticipates the intuitive truths of the highest level of Pythagorean philosophy, the science of the divine, theology. This highest level of Pythagoreanism was treated, not in *On Pythagoreanism*, but in a sequel no longer extant, *On God*. In developing the paradigmatic function of arithmetic in physics and ethics, Iamblichus adopted much of Aristotle's work on these subjects, modifying and elaborating it so that it would reflect better what Iamblichus regarded as its essentially Pythagorean inspiration. (In his *Commentary on the Categories*, Iamblichus also adopted and Pythagoreanized Aristotelian logic.) As for the relations between arithmetic and the science of the divine, Iamblichus distinguished between Pythagorean use of mathematics to image the divine and a higher approach to the divine. Little is known, however, of this higher approach in Iamblichus; mathematical imaging seems to have taken the form of matching the numbers of the decad and their properties to the divine at its highest levels and at lower levels in a hierarchy of reality of considerable complexity. The extent of Iamblichus' Pythagoreanizing programme can be seen in the fact that he established a canon of Platonic dialogues and an exegetical approach that are reflections of this programme. In Pythagoreanizing Neoplatonic philosophy Iamblichus in effect developed it further, one significant result being the mathematization of all areas of philosophy that is so striking a feature of later Greek philosophy.

In the second half of this book the impact of Iamblichus' Pythagoreanizing programme on his successors was examined in regard to some influential members of the Platonic School at Athens. Use of Pythagorean literature in the philosophical curriculum can be observed in the case of Hierocles and elsewhere (see Appendix II). Syrianus knew Iamblichus' *On Pythagoreanism* and recommended it to his students. He shares Iamblichus' views on the nature and history of philosophy as the revelation of wisdom by the pure soul of Pythagoras, whose inspiration was followed especially by Plato and the Platonists and to some degree Aristotle. He finds thus in Aristotle's *Metaphysics* some truth concerning higher immaterial realities, but must correct Aristotle in terms of a theory of the nature of Pythagoreanism, the major source of which is Iamblichus. Syrianus' pupil Proclus shows similar tendencies, particularly in his early *Commentary on the Timaeus*, where he takes Plato's dialogue as expressing Pythagorean cosmology. However, Proclus also reacted critically to the Pythagoreanizing programme. He found the first *scientific* expression of truth, not (as Iamblichus had) among the ancient Pythagoreans, but in Plato's dialogues. In consequence Plato supplants Pythagoras as the central authority in Proclus' writings. Furthermore, although fully accepting the pivotal role played by mathematics in the philosophical sciences, Proclus modifies this role in various ways. Geometry, rather than arithmetic, is chosen as the pre-eminently mediatory mathematical science, on account of its discursive, demonstrative method. Proclus thus assimilates geometric to scientific method and gives to his philosophical work in physics and metaphysics a marked geometrical aspect. He also insists on the subordination of mathematics to the science of the divine, dialectic or theology, in such a way as to make clear the inadequacy of Pythagorean mathematical imagings of the divine. This requires, however, a definite concept of the science of the divine as supposedly communicated in Plato's writings, a concept that is largely inspired, both in regard to the method and contents of dialectic, by Proclus' view of the structure and contents of mathematics. The originality of these important features of Proclus' philosophy cannot, I believe, be adequately appreciated if no reference is made to their background as a reaction to Iamblichus' Pythagoreanizing programme.

In conclusion I would like to address a question that can scarcely be ignored: Why did Iamblichus seek to Pythagoreanize Platonic philosophy? Why did he attempt to reformulate this philosophy as the revelation of truth to the ancient Greeks by a divine soul? This question takes on greater importance if we suppose that it concerns not just the internal history of Greek philosophy but also the broader intellectual patterns of the period. Ought Iamblichus' project to be seen in the light of the political success and the increasing theoretical sophistication of another revealed truth, Christianity? Is Iamblichus' figure of Pythagoras the pagan response and counterpart to Christ?

Certainly the pagan philosophers of late Antiquity were very aware of the threat that Christianity represented for them. Already in the second century Celsus had attacked the pretensions of Christians that their religion was the ancient wisdom that had inspired Greek philosophers. Porphyry, who attacked under Plotinus' direction various gnostic sects, wrote a critique of Christianity that was all the more dangerous than Celsus's in that it was based on a superior philological, historical, and philosophical competence. Perhaps in Plotinus and certainly later in Proclus there are veiled references to Christianity.[7] However, it would be difficult to show, on the basis of the extant remains of *On Pythagoreanism*, that Iamblichus had Christianity specifically in mind as a target against which his Pythagoreanizing programme was to be directed. At most one could point to structural parallels between his figure of Pythagoras (his divine authority, attributes, mission, words and deeds among men) and Christ.

There is, however, another hypothesis that I would like to suggest, one that is perhaps less attractive, but that can appeal to some evidence. In speaking of the relations between Iamblichus and his teacher Porphyry above (p. 25) I have recalled the fact that many of Iamblichus' works were rebuttals of specific writings of Porphyry. Iamblichus seems to have been concerned to an unusual degree with establishing himself by attacking and out-trumping his former teacher. Now one of Porphyry's major philosophical works was his *Life* and edition of Plotinus. Indeed the industry Porphyry displayed in publishing Plotinus' work, summarizing it for beginners (in the *Sentences*) and commenting extensively on it (the commentaries are no longer extant) suggests that the promotion of Plotinian philosophy was one of Porphyry's major interests. The *Life* and edition of Plotinus were not, as indicated above in the Introduction, a work merely of erudition, but were designed to invite, introduce, and lead the reader up to the highest truths in a systematic way through the portrayal of Plotinus as ideal philosopher and the reordering of Plotinus' treatises in an anagogic series. But this is also the purpose and structure of Iamblichus' work *On Pythagoreanism*: it too invites the

[7] Cf. Saffrey (1975).

reader to philosophy through the figure of Pythagoras and leads him up through the successive stages of Pythagorean philosophy, the final stage being reached, not in the work itself, but in a Pythagorean theology. We may then suppose that here, as in other instances, Iamblichus reacted to and sought to outdo the work of his master. Porphyry's system of Plotinian philosophy would be supplanted by a doctrine of far greater antiquity and authority, a doctrine that would include the texts of Plato and Plotinus as subordinate, the doctrine of Pythagoras. If this was indeed the intention of Iamblichus' Pythagoreanizing programme, we must allow that it had some success. For it played a considerable role, along with Porphyry's edition of Plotinus, in the history of later Greek philosophy. And Iamblichus' successors could of course come to consider his Pythagorean theology as a revelation of much greater antiquity and purity than that of the Christians.

APPENDIX I

The Excerpts from Iamblichus'
On Pythagoreanism V–VII in Psellus:
Text, Translation, and Notes

THE text of Psellus' works *On Physical Number* and *On Ethical and Theological Arithmetic* which I published in 1981 is reprinted here.[1] Information concerning manuscripts, principles of the edition, and other textual matters may be found in O'Meara (1981) and in the discussion of the manuscript tradition of Nos. 4–6 in Psellus, *Philosophica minora* II. I have inserted, *very* tentatively, vertical lines where I would suggest the joints between Psellus' excerpts might occur (for grounds in favour of this I refer the reader to Chapter 3 above and to the note on *On Physical Number*, line 27, below). Given the nature of Psellus' texts, the English translation makes no pretence at elegance. For translation of Greek mathematical terms I have followed the 'Glossary' in D'Ooge *et al.* (1926), 291 ff., where references to explanations of these terms may be found. Finally I have appended references linking Psellus' excerpts to similar passages in Neopythagorean and Neoplatonic literature (similarities in vocabulary and phrasing in Iamblichus' extant works are also noted). This is not intended, however, to replace the analysis proposed above in Chapter 3.

---

[1] By kind permission of Johns Hopkins University Press. I have made one minor change, at *On Eth. Theol. Arith.* 48, where, rather than indicating as before a lacuna after δικαιοσύνη, I would suggest correcting τέτταρα to πέντε (as required by the context), but hesitate in view of the persistent indecision in Neopythagorean texts (cf. the references given ad loc.) as to whether justice is to be identified with the numbers four or five.

Περὶ τοῦ φυσικοῦ ἀριθμοῦ

Ἐθαύμασας εἰρηκότος μου κατὰ τὴν χθὲς συνουσίαν ὅτι
ἔστι φυσικὸς ἀριθμὸς ἄλλος ὢν παρὰ τὸν μαθηματικόν. εἰ δέ γε
τὴν ποικιλίαν ᾔδεις τοῦ ἀριθμοῦ, ἀπήτησας ἄν με καὶ τὸν νοητὸν
5 καὶ οὐσιώδη καὶ εἰδητικόν. ἔστι γὰρ ὡς ἀληθῶς ὁ μὲν τοιοῦτος
ἀριθμὸς ἀνωτάτω τε ὢν καὶ πρώτιστος, ὁ δὲ μαθηματικὸς ἐν κοινοῖς
ἐπινοήμασι θεωρούμενος, ὁ δὲ φυσικὸς περὶ τῶν τελευταίων καὶ
τῶν γινομένων καὶ περὶ τοῖς σώμασι διαιρουμένων. οἱ γὰρ ἐγ-
κεκραμένοι λόγοι τοῖς σώμασι φυσικοί εἰσιν ἀριθμοὶ ἔν τε τοῖς
10 ζῴοις ἅμα καὶ τοῖς φυτοῖς· ἕκαστον γὰρ τούτων χρόνοις ὡρισμένοις
καὶ γεννᾶται καὶ αὔξεται καὶ φθίνει. | καὶ χρὴ τόν γε φιλόσοφον
τοῖς φυσικοῖς αἰτίοις προσαρμόττειν τοὺς οἰκείους ἀριθμούς. |

Καὶ ἐπειδὴ τὸ εἶδος ἐν τῇ φύσει πρῶτόν ἐστιν αἴτιον καὶ
ἀρχηγικώτατον (κατ᾽ αὐτὸ γὰρ τὸ εἶναι πᾶσιν ὑπάρχει), καὶ ἀριθμοὶ
15 οὖν ὅσοι τὸ εἶναι παρέχουσι τῇ φύσει καί εἰσιν οὐσιώδεις, τοῖς
εἴδεσίν εἰσιν ὁμοφυεῖς. φυσικοὶ οὖν ἀριθμοὶ κατὰ τὸ εἶδος οἱ
περιττοὶ πάντες, οἱ ἰδίως καλούμενοι τέλειοι, οἱ σύμμετροι οἷον
οἱ πολλαπλάσιοι καὶ ἐπιμόριοι, οἱ τεταγμένοι ὥσπερ οἱ τετράγωνοι
καὶ κύβοι. τὸ κάλλος τὸ ἐν τοῖς ἀριθμοῖς, ὃ ἐν τῇ συμμετρίᾳ
20 αὐτῶν διαφαίνεται· τὸ αὔταρκες, ὃ ἀπὸ τῶν τελείων ἀριθμῶν ἐστι
κατάδηλον· τὸ γόνιμον, ὃ ἐν τῷ ἑπτὰ καὶ ἐννέα θεωρεῖται· ἡ
δύναμις, ἥτις κατὰ τὴν τετρακτὺν μάλιστα ὁρᾶται· τὸ ἀρχηγικόν,
ὃ ἐπὶ τοῦ ἑνὸς θεωρεῖται· καὶ τὸ ταὐτὸν καὶ τὸ ἀμιγὲς καὶ τὸ
παραδειγματικόν, ὃ ἐπὶ τῶν πρώτων ἀριθμῶν ἐμφαίνεται· καὶ τὸ
25 ἴσον, ὃ ἐπὶ τοῦ τετραγώνου θεωρήσειεν ἄν τις· ταῦτα γὰρ πάντα
τῷ κατὰ τὸ εἶδος φυσικῷ προσήκει αἰτίῳ. |

Ἐπεὶ δὲ καὶ ἡ ὕλη ἐν τῇ φύσει αἰτίαν οὐ σμικρὰν παρέχεται, καὶ
ταύτην ἐν τοῖς φυσικοῖς ἀριθμοῖς ἀνευρήσομεν, τἀναντία λαμβάνοντες
πάντα τῶν προειρημένων ἀριθμῶν οὓς περὶ τῶν εἰδῶν εἰρήκαμεν. εἰσὶν
30 οὖν τῇ ὕλῃ προσήκοντες ἀριθμοὶ οἱ ἄρτιοι, οἱ ἀτελεῖς, οἱ ἑτεροποιοί,
οἱ ἀνόμοιοι, καὶ οἱ ἄλλοι πάντες ὅσοι τὴν ἐναντίωσιν ἔχουσι πρὸς
τοὺς εἰδικοὺς ἀριθμούς. |

Ἔστι δὲ καὶ ποιητικὸν αἴτιον ἐν τοῖς ἀριθμοῖς τοῖς φυσικοῖς,
καὶ γνοίη τις ἂν τοῦτο ἀπὸ τῶν γονίμων ἀριθμῶν τῶν ἐν τῇ ζῳογονίᾳ
35 δεικνυμένων. | καὶ ἡ κατὰ τὴν ἑτερότητα δὲ καὶ ἀνισότητα κινητικὴ
ἀρχὴ ἐν τοῖς ἀριθμοῖς ποιητικήν τινα αἰτίαν ἐνδείκνυται. | μάλιστα

2 cf. Plato, *Tim.* 25 e 2–3   3–8 cf. Iambl. *Comm.* 64, 2–19; 92, 27–93, 2; *In Nic.* 3,
10–16; Syrian. *In met.* 122, 13–15; 135, 9–10   5 cf. Iambl. *Comm.* 64, 2; Bertier *et al.*
(1980), 170–1   6 cf. Iambl. *Comm.* 15, 6–7   6–7 cf. Iambl. *In Nic.* 4, 4–8
7 cf. Iambl. *Comm.* 18, 15   7–11 cf. Syrian. *In met.* 25, 26–7; 190, 30–5   11–12 cf.
Iambl. *Vit. Pyth.* 118, 16; *Comm.* 61, 19–20; Syrian. *In met.* 188, 2–3   14–15 cf.
Nicom. in Phot. *Bibl.* III 41 (143 a 10); Iambl. *In Nic.* 77, 25–78, 1   15–16 cf. Iambl.
Comm. 63, 29   19–20 cf. Iambl. *In Nic.* 34, 23–4   21 cf. anon. *Theol. arith.* 61,

On Physical Number

You were surprised when, at our meeting yesterday, I said that there was another, physical number besides mathematical number. But if you only knew of the variety of number, you would have asked me about intelligible, essential, and ideal number. For number of this ⟨latter⟩ kind is truly the highest and first. Mathematical number is seen in common concepts. Physical number is found in the lowest things, things generated and divided in bodies. For the principles mixed in bodies, both in animals and plants, are physical numbers, for each of these is born, grows, and dies at determinate times. | And the philosopher should fit the appropriate numbers to the causes in nature. |

And since form is, in nature, the first and most important cause (for the being of all depends on it), thus such numbers as provide being to nature and are essential, these are connatural with forms. Physical numbers of the formal type are: all odd numbers, numbers properly called 'perfect', symmetric numbers such as multiples and superparticulars, ordered numbers such as square and cubic numbers. The beauty in numbers, which shows in their symmetry; the self-sufficiency that is apparent in perfect numbers; the generativeness seen in ⟨the numbers⟩ seven and nine; the power that is observed especially in the *tetractys*; the primacy that is found in the one; and the identity, purity, and paradigmatic character appearing in the first numbers; and the equality that may be seen in square number; all of these ⟨properties⟩ fit physical cause as form. |

Since matter is an important cause in nature, we will find it in physical numbers by taking all the opposites of the numbers we have mentioned as regards formal causes. The numbers then that are appropriate to matter are those that are even, imperfect, differentiating, dissimilar, and all others such as are in opposition to formal numbers. |

There is an efficient cause in physical numbers: one may see this in the generative numbers shown in animal generation. | And the principle of movement according to difference and inequality in numbers shows an efficient cause. | But this is especially

5 ff.; 63, 1 ff.   21–2 cf. Iambl. *Vit. Pyth.* 119, 6–7   21–4 cf. Iambl. *In Tim.* fr. 53, 6–13   22–4 cf. anon. *Theol. arith.* 1, 4 ff.   27 δὲ καὶ in Psellus can sometimes mark the beginning of an excerpt; cf. below, lines 33, 81, and, for example, *Philos. min.* nos. 2, 32   34–5 cf. below, 45 ff.   35–6 cf. below, 67 ff.   36–42 cf. Iambl. *Comm.* 61, 16–22; 64, 8–13; 73, 20–7; Syrian. *In met.* 190, 26–30; Procl. *In Eucl.* 22, 26–8; *In Tim.* III 19, 30–2

δὲ ἐπὶ τῶν οὐρανίων περιφορῶν καὶ ἀποκαταστάσεων τὸ τοιοῦτον δείκ-
νυται. καὶ οἱ τῶν ἀστέρων δὲ πρὸς ἀλλήλους σχηματισμοὶ περιοδικῶς
ἀποκαθίσταντες καὶ πάντα τὰ ἐν αὐτοῖς σχήματα καὶ αἱ δυνάμεις αὐτῶν
40 ἐν λόγοις ἀριθμῶν περιέχονται. καὶ οἱ φωτισμοὶ δὲ τῆς σελήνης καὶ
ἡ τάξις τῶν σφαιρῶν καὶ τὰ διαστήματα αὐτῶν τὰ πρὸς ἀλλήλους καὶ τὰ
κέντρα τῶν κύκλων ἐφ᾽ ὧν φέρονται, πάντα ἀριθμοῖς περιείληπται. ἔτι
τοίνυν ἡ ὑγεῖα κατὰ μέτρα ἀριθμῶν συνίσταται, καὶ αἱ τῶν νόσων κρίσεις
κατὰ ἀριθμοὺς ὡρισμένους ἐπιτελοῦνται, οἵ τε θάνατοι συμπληρούσης
45 τῆς φύσεως τὰ οἰκεῖα μέτρα τῶν κινήσεων οὕτω συμπίπτουσιν. | ἔνθεν
τοι καὶ ζῳογονικός ἐστιν ἀριθμός. ἐπεὶ γὰρ τὸ ζῷον ἐκ ψυχῆς καὶ
σώματος συνέστηκεν, οὐκ ἐκ τοῦ αὐτοῦ ἀριθμοῦ τὴν ψυχὴν συνεστάναι
λέγουσιν οἱ Πυθαγόρειοι καὶ τὸ σῶμα, ἀλλὰ τὴν μὲν ψυχὴν ἐκ κυβικοῦ
ἀριθμοῦ, τὸ δὲ σῶμα ἐκ βωμίσκου. τῆς μὲν γὰρ ἡ οὐσία ἐκ τοῦ ἰσάκις
50 ἴσου ἰσάκις καὶ συνεστάναι φασὶν ἐν ἰσότητι, τὸ δὲ σῶμα βωμίσκον
εἶναι, ὃς ἔμπαλιν συνίσταται ἐξ ἀνισάκις ἀνίσων ἀνισάκις. τὸ γὰρ
σῶμα ἡμῶν ἀνίσους ἔχει τὰς διαστάσεις· τὸ μὲν γὰρ μῆκος αὐτοῦ
μέγιστον, τὸ δὲ βάθος ἐλάχιστον, τὸ δὲ πλάτος μέσον ἀμφοῖν. ἡ μὲν
οὖν ψυχή, ὡς ἐκεῖνοί φασι, κύβος οὖσα ἀπὸ τοῦ ϛ̄ ἀριθμοῦ, ὅς ἐστι
55 τέλειος, συνίσταται ἴσος ἰσάκις ἴσος κατὰ τὸν σις̅ κύβον· ἑξάκις
γὰρ ἓξ ἑξάκις ταῦτα. τὸ δὲ σῶμα ἐξ ἀνίσων πλευρῶν ἀνισάκις ὂν
ἄνισον ἀνισάκις, οὔτε δοκὶς ἂν εἴη, οὔτε πλινθίς, ἀλλὰ βωμίσκος,
ἔχον πλευρὰς ε̄ ζ̄ ζ· πεντάκι μὲν γὰρ ἓξ λ̄, ἑπτάκι δὲ τὰ λ̄ σι̅. διὰ
ταῦτα γοῦν τὰ ἑπτάμηνα γόνιμα ἐν σι̅ ἡμέραις συμπεπληρωμένον τὸ
60 σῶμα ἔχοντα. εἰ μὲν οὖν ἡ ψυχὴ μόνη ἐγεννᾶτο, ἐν ταῖς σις̅ ἂν
ἡμέραις ἐτίκτετο, κύβου τελείου ἀποτελεσθέντος τῇ ἐκφάνσει αὐτῆς.
ἐπεὶ δὲ ἐκ ψυχῆς καὶ σώματος τὸ ζῷον ἀποτελεῖται, αἱ σι̅ ἡμέραι
εἰς συμπλήρωσιν τοῦ σώματος ἐπιτήδειοι γεγόνασι· κρατεῖ δὲ ἐπὶ
τοῦ ζῴου ἡ τοῦ σώματος γένεσις. | διὸ ἡ μὲν ψυχὴ ἰσότητος ἐφίεται,
65 τὸ δὲ σῶμα οἰκεῖον ἀνωμαλίᾳ καὶ ἀνισότητι. | τὸν δὲ βωμὸν ἔδοξε
τοῖς πάλαι κατὰ πάσας τὰς διαστάσεις ἄνισον εἶναι. |

Ἐπεὶ δὲ δοκεῖ ἡ φύσις τῇ κινήσει μάλιστα εἰδοποιεῖσθαι, δεῖ
καὶ τὸν φυσικὸν ἀριθμὸν ἐπιδεῖξαι πῶς ἔχει κίνησιν. εἰσὶν οὖν
αἴτιοι τῆς κινήσεως οἱ κατὰ τὴν δυάδα θεωρούμενοι, οἱ ἄρτιοι, οἱ
70 ἑτερομήκεις καὶ ὅσοι τοιοῦτοι (καθόλου γὰρ ὅταν ἀοριστία περὶ
τοὺς ἀριθμοὺς θεωρεῖται, τότε ἡ κίνησις ἐμφύεται), ἑτερότης δὲ
καὶ ἀνισότης | (ἡ μέν ἐστιν ὡσανεὶ σχέσις καὶ ἰδιότης ἥτις ἐστὶν
ἠρεμία, ἡ δὲ ἑτεροίωσις καὶ ἀνίσωσις καθ᾽ ἣν οὐ τὰ ἕτερα οὐδὲ τὰ
ἄνισα ἐν κινήσει, ἀλλὰ καὶ τὰ ἑτεροιούμενα καὶ ἀνισούμενα). |

38–9 cf. anon. *Prol. in Nicom.* 76, 12–14   42 cf. Iambl. *Comm.* 11, 26–7   43–4 cf.
Aristoxenus, fr. 23, p. 14, 34–5 Wehrli; anon. *Theol. arith.* 71, 10–11 (=Nicom.);
Anatolius, *De dec.* 35, 27; Theon Smyrn. *Expos.* 104, 9–12   48–64 cf. anon. *Theol.
arith.* 63, 23–64, 17 (Nicom.); Nicom. in Phot. *Bibl.* III 45 (144 b 1–4); Syrian. *In met.* 130,
34; 143, 7; 188, 1–4; Lydus, *De mens.* 32, 15–16   54–5 cf. anon. *Theol. arith.* 42, 19–
43, 2 (Anatolius); Theon, *Expos.* 45, 10–14; 101, 7–9; Iambl. *In Nic.* 34, 17–18   59 cf.

manifest in the rotations and the revolutions of the heavens. And the stars' configurations in relation to each other, their periodic revolutions, all of their shapes, their powers, are contained in the principles of numbers. And the moon's phases, 40 the order of the spheres, the distances between them, the centres of the circles which carry them, numbers contain them all. Indeed the measures of numbers determine health; crises in sickness are completed according to determinate numbers; deaths come thus also, nature having fulfilled the appropriate measures of change. | 45 Hence number is generative of animal life. For since animals are made up of soul and body, the Pythagoreans say soul and body are not produced from the same number, but soul from cubic number, body from the *bomiskos*. For, they say, ⟨soul's⟩ being is from equal times the equal equal times, coming to be in equality, 50 whereas body is a *bomiskos*, produced from unequal times the unequal unequal times. For our body has unequal dimensions: its length is greatest, its depth least, its breadth intermediate. Thus soul, as they say, being a cube from the number 6 (which is perfect), comes to be equal an equal times the equal as in the 55 cube 216, for this is 6 by 6 by 6. But body, being from unequal sides an unequal times the unequal an unequal times, is neither *dokis* nor *plinthis* but a *bomiskos*, having for sides 5, 6, 7: for 5 by 6 is 30, and 7 by 30 is 210. Thus seven-month births occur in 210 days, having a complete body. If then the soul alone were 60 generated, it would be born in 216 days, a perfect cube being completed with its coming. But since the animal is made of soul and body, 210 days are appropriate to the completion of the body: the generation of the body dominates in the animal. | Thus soul desires equality, the body relates to anomaly and inequality. | 65 The ancients thought altars should have all dimensions unequal. |

Since nature seems to form especially by change, one must show how physical number has change. The causes of change then relate to the dyad, the even, the *heteromecic* and suchlike (generally whenever indeterminateness is found in numbers, there 70 change appears), difference and inequality (one is like a relation and property, which is rest, the other a differentiating and unequalizing, such that it is not the different and unequal that are in change, but those made different and unequal). |

anon. *Theol. arith.* 51, 16–19; 64, 5–11   65–6 cf. Nicom. *Intro. arith.* 107, 22–108, 1
69 cf. Anatolius, *De dec.* 31, 3; anon. *Theol. arith.* 8, 2 ff.; 32, 13–14 (Anatolius); Theon, *Expos.* 100, 9–11; Syrian. *In met.* 5, 20–4; 131, 28–31; Procl. *In Remp.* II 137, 23–5; Lydus, *De mens.* 24, 4–21   72 cf. Plato, *Tim.* 57 e 6–58 a 2   72–4 cf. Aristot. *Phys.* 201 b 16–27; Iambl. *In Nic.* 43, 22–5; Simplic. *In Phys.* 433, 35–434, 1

75 Καὶ ἡ τοῦ ἀπείρου δὲ καὶ ἡ τοῦ περαίνοντος δύναμις καὶ ἐν
τῇ φύσει ἐστὶ καὶ ἐν τῷ φυσικῷ ἀριθμῷ. καὶ περαῖνον μὲν ἐν τῇ
φύσει τὸ ἀγαθόν, τὸ καλόν, ἡ ἰσότης, καὶ τὰ ὅμοια· τὸ δὲ ἄπειρον
τὸ ἀόριστον, τὸ ἄτακτον, τὸ ἄλογον, τὸ κακόν, τὸ αἰσχρόν, καὶ
ὅσα τοιαῦτα. | ἐν δὲ τῷ φυσικῷ ἀριθμῷ ἄπειρον μὲν ἡ κατὰ τὸ πλῆθος
80 ἀρχή, πεπερασμένον δὲ ἡ κατὰ τὸ ἓν πρώτη αἰτία. |
Ἔχει δὲ καὶ τόπον ὁ φυσικὸς ἀριθμός. εἰ γὰρ τὰ σώματα καὶ
πᾶσαν διάστασιν περιείληφεν ὁ ἀριθμός, κατὰ τὸν αὐτὸν τρόπον καὶ
τὸν συνακολουθοῦντα τοῖς σώμασι τόπον συνείληφεν ἐν ἑαυτῷ, οὐ
κατὰ ἐπαφὴν ἀλλὰ κατὰ τὴν δύναμιν ἀσώματον. | καὶ χῶραι δὲ ἑκάστου
85 ἀριθμοῦ κατὰ τὸ ἑξῆς τεταγμέναι εἰσί. τῶν γὰρ ἀριθμῶν οἱ μὲν καὶ
φύσει καὶ τάξει περιττοὶ καὶ ἄρτιοί εἰσιν, οἱ δὲ τῇ μὲν φύσει
περιττοί, τῇ δὲ τάξει ἄρτιοι. | καὶ ἔμπαλιν αἱ δὲ χῶραι πλεῖστον
ἰσχύουσιν ἐν τῇ τῶν πραγμάτων γενέσει πρὸς τὸ συνεξωμοιῶσθαι
αὐταῖς τὸ γεννώμενον. |
90 Τὸ δὲ κενὸν ἀνύπαρκτόν ἐστι καὶ ἐν τῇ φύσει καὶ ἐν τῷ φυσικῷ
ἀριθμῷ. παράδειγμα δὲ τούτου οὐκ ἂν ἄλλο τι εἴη ἢ ἀναρμοστία καὶ
ἀσυμμετρία· πεφυγάδευται δὲ ἐκ τῶν ἀριθμῶν ἡ ἀσυμμετρία, εἰ μὴ
βούλοιτό τις τὸν ἄρτιον ὡς διεχῆ λέγειν διάκενον. |
Οἶδα μὲν οὖν ὅτι βίαια ταῦτα πρὸς ἀπόδειξιν τοῦ φυσικοῦ ἀριθμοῦ.
95 ἀλλ᾽ οὖν ⟨τὰ⟩ εἰρημένα τοῖς παλαιοῖς καὶ ἡμεῖς προσιέμεθα καί σοι
τὰ πλείω ὡς ἀρέσκοντα παραδιδόαμεν. τὰ γὰρ περὶ τῆς ζῳογονίας οὐ
πάνυ τι προσιέμεθα· ἄλλοι γὰρ λόγοι ὑπάρξεως ψυχῆς καὶ συστάσεως
σώματος, δημιουργικοὶ ἀλλ᾽ οὐκ ἀριθμητικοί.

Περὶ τῆς ἠθικῆς ἀριθμητικῆς καὶ τῆς θεολογικῆς

Ὥσπερ εἰσὶν ἀριθμοὶ τῇ φύσει προσήκοντες, οὕτω δὴ καὶ τοῖς
ἤθεσι· καὶ ὥσπερ ἐστὶ φυσικὴ ἀριθμητική, οὕτω δὴ καὶ ἠθική. | ἀρχὴ
δέ ἐστι τῆς ὅλης περὶ τῶν ἠθῶν φιλοσοφίας τὸ μέτρον αὐτὸ καὶ τὸ
5 μέτριον ἐν τῇ τῶν ἀριθμῶν οὐσίᾳ, ὅπερ ἐστὶ καὶ ἀρχηγὸν ἐξαίρετον
τῆς ὅλης περὶ τὰ ἤθη κατασκευῆς. μετὰ δὲ τὴν μίαν ἀρχήν εἰσι καί
τινες ἀρχαὶ ἕτεραι τῆς ὅλης τῶν ἠθῶν φιλοσοφίας, οἷον τὸ πέρας, τὸ
τέλειον (ἡ γὰρ τελειότης ἑνοειδῶς συμπληροῖ τὸ ἄριστον μέτρον τῆς
ζωῆς)· ἐπὶ τούτοις ἡ τάξις ἡ ἐπὶ τοῖς ἀριθμοῖς προσήκει καὶ τῇ
10 ἐπὶ τοῖς ἤθεσιν εὐταξίᾳ, καὶ τὸ μονοειδὲς καὶ προσεοικὸς τῷ ἑνί,
εἴτε περὶ τὴν τετράδα εἴτε περὶ τὴν ἑβδομάδα εἴτε περὶ τὴν δεκάδα

75–80 cf. Aristot. *Phys.* 207 a 35–b1, 207 b 35; *Met.* 986 a 15 ff.   79–80 cf. Syrian.
In met. 10, 1–4; 166, 1–2   84–5 cf. Syrian. *In met.* 149, 31   85–7 Cf. Aristot.
Phys. 226 b 34–227 a 4; Simplic. *In Phys.* 641, 9–15 and 35–642, 4; 875, 11–12   90–3 cf.
Syrian. *In met.* 132, 23–9; 149, 28–31   92 cf. Iambl. *In Nic.* 91, 20   97–8 cf.
Psell. *Philos. min.* nos. 22, 23, 27

And the power of the unlimited and of the limiting is both 75
in nature and in physical number. The limiting in nature is the
good, beautiful, equality, and suchlike, the unlimited ⟨is⟩ the
indeterminate, unordered, irrational, evil, ugly, and suchlike. |
In physical number the unlimited is the cause as regards plurality, the limited
the first cause as regards the one. | 80

Physical number has place. For if number contains bodies
and all extension, in the very same way it contains in itself the
place that accompanies bodies, not as if by touch but by
incorporeal power. | And the places of each number are ordered
according to the serial ⟨order⟩. For some numbers are by nature 85
and order odd and even, whereas some are by nature odd and by
order even. | And then again places are most influential in the
generation of things in the assimilation of the generated to
them. |

Neither in nature nor in physical number is there void. Its 90
paradigm would be nothing other than lack of harmony and lack of
symmetry. But lack of symmetry is banished from numbers, unless
one wishes to speak of even number as a discontinuous gap. |

Now I know these are forceful demonstrations of physical
number. We agree with what the ancients say and pass them on to 95
you as for the most part right. For we do not accept completely
what concerns animal generation: there are other principles of soul's being
and body's making, demiurgic but not arithmetic.

On Ethical and Theological Arithmetic

As there are numbers fitting nature, so there are fitting
⟨ethical⟩ habits. And as there is a physical, so there is an
ethical arithmetic. | The principle of all ethical philosophy is
measure itself and the measured in the being of numbers, which is 5
a pre-eminent principle in all ethical ordering. After the one
principle there are other principles of all ethical philosophy,
such as limit, the perfect (for perfection unitarily completes
the best measure of life), then the order in numbers which fits
ethical good ordering, then the uniform and similar to the one, 10
such as is seen either in the tetrad, hebdomad, or decad. | There

1–2 cf. Iambl. *In Nic.* 35, 2–10; 125, 14–22; *Comm.* 88, 29–30   2 cf. Syrian.
In met. 189, 13   4–10 cf. Iambl. *Comm.* 47, 1–6; Procl. *In Eucl.* 24,
4–17   4–5 cf. Plato, *Phileb.* 66 a 6–7   6 cf. Iambl. *Comm.*
91, 28

τοῦτο θεωρηθείη. | ἔστι δὲ καὶ ἄλλο οἱονεὶ παράδειγμα τοῦ σπουδαίου τρόπου τὸ μέσον καὶ συγκρατικὸν τῆς τῶν ἀριθμῶν διαφορᾶς, ὅπερ προσήγορα πάντα ἀλλήλοις ποιεῖ, πασῶν τε ἀναλογιῶν παράγει γένεσιν,
15 καὶ τὴν ψυχὴν εὐάρμοστον ἀπεργάζεται. |

Καὶ αἱ τῆς ψυχῆς δὲ δυνάμεις ἐπὶ τὰ εἴδη τῶν ἀριθμῶν ἀναφέρονται. ἔστι γὰρ νοῦς μὲν τὸ ἓν ὡς ἑνοειδής· ἐπιστήμη δὲ τὰ δύο, διότι μετ᾽ αἰτίας γινώσκει· ὁ δὲ τοῦ ἐπιπέδου ἀριθμός, δόξα· ὁ δὲ τοῦ στερεοῦ, αἴσθησις, διότι τῶν στερεῶν σωμάτων αὕτη ἀντιλαμβάνεται. | ἡ δὲ
20 δεκὰς τὰς ἐν ἡμῖν τῶν ἠθῶν ἀρχὰς περιέχει. | ἡ δὲ κατὰ νοῦν ζωὴ πέρας ἔχει καὶ αὖθις συμφνές, τὴν ἑβδομάδα· μονοειδὴς γάρ ἐστι. καὶ ἡ ἑβδομὰς ὥσπερ ἡ νοερὰ ἐνέργεια, οὔτε γεννῶσα κατὰ πολλαπλασιασμὸν ἕτερόν τινα τὸν ἴσον τῆς δεκάδος οὔτε τικτομένη ἀπό τινος.

Εἰ δὲ ἐν μετριότητι ζωῆς καὶ τελειότητι τὸ εἶδος τῆς ἀρετῆς
25 ἀφώρισται, οἱ μέσοι ἄρα καὶ τέλειοι ἀριθμοὶ προσήκουσι τῇ φυσικῇ ἀρετῇ, οἱ δὲ ὑπερτέλειοι καὶ οἱ ἐλλιπεῖς ταῖς ὑπερβολαῖς ταύτης καὶ ταῖς ἐλλείψεσι. | καὶ τἀναντία πάντα ὧν διδόαμεν τῇ ἀρετῇ χρὴ ἀποκληροῦν τῇ κακίᾳ, τὸ ἄμετρον, τὸ ἀνάρμοστον, τὸ ἑτεροποιόν, τὸ ἄνισον, τὸ ἄπειρον, καὶ τὰ τοιαῦτα· ταῦτα γὰρ
30 πάντα τῆς κακίας ὅλης συμπληροῖ τὴν συστοιχίαν. |

Καὶ ἑκάστη δὲ τῶν ἀρετῶν ἑκάστῳ προσήκει ἀριθμῷ. ἡ μὲν γὰρ περὶ τῶν ἐνδεχομένων φρόνησις, ἤτοι ἡ πρακτικὴ εὐβουλία, τῇ τριάδι προσήκει τῇ ὡς ἐν πλάτει χρωμένῃ τοῖς λογισμοῖς· ἡ δὲ τὰ ὄντα γινώσκουσα σοφία εἰς τὴν μονάδα ἀνάγεται τὴν ἑνοειδῶς
35 ἐπιβάλλουσαν τοῖς γινωσκομένοις. καὶ κατὰ τὸ ἐναντίον ἡ ἀφροσύνη τῇ δυάδι προσήκει, ἡ ἄπειρος καὶ ἄλογος τῇ ἀπείρῳ καὶ ἀλόγῳ. καὶ ἡ ἀνδρεία δὲ κατὰ μὲν τὸ ἀρρενωπὸν εἰς τὸν περιττὸν ἀριθμὸν ἀνήκει, κατὰ δὲ τὸ μόνιμον εἰς τὸν τετράγωνον· τὸ δὲ θηλυγενὲς οἷόν ἐστιν ἡ δειλία τῷ ἀρτίῳ ἀναθετέον, καὶ τὸ ἄστατον τῷ προμήκει.
40 τῇ δὲ σωφροσύνῃ συμμετρίας οὔσῃ αἰτίᾳ ὁ ἐννέα προσήκει, ὃ ἀπὸ τῆς τριάδος πολλαπλασιαζόμενος· πάντων γὰρ τῶν τετραγώνων ἰσότητος ὄντων ποιητικῶν, οἱ ἀπὸ περιττῶν τετράγωνοι κυριώτατοι πάντων εἰσὶν [εἰσὶν] εἰς τὴν ἀπεργασίαν τῆς ἰσότητος, ὧν ἡγεῖται ὁ ἀπὸ τῆς τριάδος τετράγωνος ὁ ἐννέα, ἀπὸ δύο τελείων τοῦ τε τρία καὶ
45 τοῦ ἓξ κατὰ τὸν πρῶτον τέλεον ἀριθμὸν τὸν τρία ὅλος δι᾽ ὅλου τελεωθείς. ἡ δὲ δικαιοσύνη δύναμις οὖσα ἀνταποδόσεως τοῦ ἴσου καὶ προσήκοντος ἐμπεριέχεται ἀριθμοῦ τετραγώνου περιττοῦ μεσότητι· ὁ

---

14 cf. Plato, Rep. 546 b 7–c 1; Iambl. in Stob. Anth. I 364, 22; De myst. 17, 17   15 cf. Plato, Rep. 400 d 3, 413 e 4; Theon, Expos. 11, 9–20; Iambl. Comm. 69, 10   16 cf. Iambl. Comm. 61, 15–16   17–19 cf. Aristot. De an. 404 b 22–4; Iambl. De an. in Stob. Anth. I 364, 15–18; Simplic. In de an. 29, 2–9   20–1 cf. Aristot. Eth. Nic. 1178 a 6–7   22–3 cf. Philolaus in DK I 416, 8–10; Theon, Expos. 103, 1–3   24–7 cf. Nicom. Intro. arith. 36, 6–37, 2; Anatolius, De dec. 31, 16–18; anon. Theol. arith. 19, 12–17; Iambl. In Nic. 17, 1–2; 32, 25 ff.; 53, 6–9   30 cf. Aristot. Eth. Nic. 1096 b 6   31 cf. Iambl. Comm. 56, 8–11; In Nic. 35, 2–3   32–3 cf. anon. Theol. arith. 16, 18–21; Nicom. in

is further as a model of good character the mean which binds together the difference in numbers, making all harmonious, producing all proportions, and making the soul into something well-adjusted. | 15

Soul's powers are related to number forms. For the intellect is the one as unitary, science is 2 because it knows with cause, opinion is plane number, sensation solid number because it perceives solid bodies. | The decad contains the ethical principles in us. | Life according to intellect contains limit, 20 and, suitable also, the hebdomad, for it is unitary. And the hebdomad, like intellectual activity, neither generates another equal to the decad by multiplication nor is born of another. |

If the form of virtue is defined by a measured and perfect life, mean and perfect numbers fit natural virtue, superabundant 25 and deficient ⟨numbers⟩ ⟨fit⟩ excesses and deficiencies in relation to virtue. | And one must assign the opposites of what we give to virtue to vice: lack of measure and of harmony, the differentiating, the unequal, unlimited, and such-like. For all these fill the column of all vice. | 30

And each single virtue fits a number. For wisdom about variable matters, or practical wisdom, fits the triad which uses reasoning as if in ⟨one dimension,⟩ breadth. Wisdom which knows ⟨real⟩ beings is related to the monad which sees what is known in a unitary way. And according to the opposite, lack of wisdom 35 relates to the dyad, the unlimited and irrational to the unlimited and irrational. And courage as manliness relates to odd number, but as constancy it relates to square ⟨number⟩. What is female such as cowardice is to be fitted to even ⟨number⟩, inconstancy to oblong ⟨number⟩. Fitting temperance, cause of 40 symmetry, is 9 which is multiplied from the triad, for if all square numbers produce equality, those produced from odd numbers are the best for producing equality, and of these the first is the square from the triad, 9, which comes from two perfect numbers, the 3 and 6, according to the first perfect number, the 45 3, perfected completely and as a whole. Justice as the faculty of reciprocity of the equal and appropriate is contained by the mean

Phot. *Bibl.* III 43 (143 b 28)   32 cf. Aristot. *Eth. Nic.* 1139 a 8   33–4 cf. anon. *Theol. arith.* 4, 4–5 (Nicom.); Iambl. *In Nic.* 6, 6–7   37–9 cf. Plato, *Rep.* 442 c 1–3; *Laws* 802 d 9; Iambl. in Stob. *Anth.* III 320, 2; Syrian, *In met.* 131, 35–7   40 cf. Anatolius, *De dec.* 31, 16–18; anon. *Theol. arith.* 17, 10–12 (Anatolius); Iambl. in Stob. *Anth.* III 257, 14–258, 2; 271, 25–6   44–6 cf. Iambl. *In Tim.* fr. 53, 12–13   46–7 = anon. *Theol. arith.* 37, 2–4 (Nicom.) = Iambl. *In Nic.* 16, 16–18; cf. Anatolius, *De dec.* 31, 22–3; Iambl. *Comm.* 61, 1–3; *Pr.* 118, 1–3; Bertier *et al.* (1980), 158   47–8 cf. anon. *Theol. arith.* 29, 6–10

γὰρ τέτταρα προσήκει τῇ δικαιοσύνῃ μέσος κείμενος τῆς μονάδος καὶ τοῦ ἐννέα, καὶ ᾧ ὑστερεῖ ἀριθμῷ τοῦ ἐννέα τούτῳ
50 ὑπερέχων τῆς μονάδος. καὶ τῶν ἀπὸ μονάδος ἄχρις ἐννεάδος συγκεφαλαιουμένων ἀριθμῶν ἔνατον αὖθις ὁ πέντε μέρος ἐστί. τοιαύτη μὲν δὴ ἡ ἐν τοῖς ἤθεσιν ἀριθμητική. |

Ἰάμβλιχος δὲ ὁ φιλόσοφος καὶ κρειττόνων φύσεων ἀριθμητικὴν ἔγραψεν, οὔτε μαθηματικῶς τοὺς ἐν ταύταις ἀριθμοὺς μεταχειριζόμενος,
55 οὔτε ἀναλογίαις ἀπεικάζων τὰ κρείττονα γένη, οὔτε ὑποστατικοὺς ἀριθμοὺς ταῦτα τιθέμενος οὔτε αὐτοκινήτους οὔτε νοεροὺς οὔτε οὐσιώδεις, ἀλλά φησιν ⟨ὅτι⟩ ὥσπερ τὸ τῶν κρειττόνων γένος ἐξῄρηται πάσης οὐσίας, οὕτω καὶ ὁ ἀριθμὸς αὐτῶν ἀπόλυτός ἐστι καὶ καθ᾽ ἑαυτόν. |

Περὶ δὲ τῆς διαφορᾶς τοῦ ἀγαθοῦ λέγων καὶ τοῦ ἑνός, φησὶν ὅτι
60 ὥσπερ ἡ τοῦ ἀγαθοῦ φύσις γόνιμος οὖσα κατ᾽ αἰτίαν προηγουμένη τῶν ἀγαθῶν ὅλων ἐν ἑαυτῇ πρόεισι καὶ πληθύεται, οὕτω δὴ καὶ τοῦ ἑνὸς ἡ παντελὴς αἰτία πληροῖ πάντα ἀφ᾽ ἑαυτῆς καὶ ἐν ἑαυτῇ συνέχει τὰ ὄντα καὶ ἐν ἑαυτῇ πληθύεται. |

Καὶ ἔστι οἰκεῖον καὶ πρόσφορον τοῖς κρείττοσι γένεσι τὸ κρεῖττον
65 γένος τοῦ μαθηματικοῦ ἀριθμοῦ, οἷον τὸ ἕν, τὸ πέρας, τὸ ὡρισμένον, τὸ ἴσον, καὶ ὅσα τοιαῦτα. | ἔστι δὲ καὶ ὥσπερ τῶν φυσικῶν ἀριθμῶν φυσικὴ ἀρχή, καὶ τῶν ἠθικῶν ἠθική, οὕτω δὴ καὶ τοῦ θείου ἀριθμοῦ μονοειδής ἐστιν ἀρχὴ καὶ θεία ἡ κατ᾽ αἰτίαν προηγουμένη τῶν ἐν τοῖς ἀριθμοῖς πᾶσιν ἀρχῶν καὶ αὐτοῦ τοῦ θείου καὶ ἡνωμένου παντὸς
70 ἀριθμοῦ προϋπάρχουσα μονοειδὴς ἕνωσις. | ἔστιν οὖν τὸ πρῶτον καὶ κυρίως ἕν, ὃ δὴ φαίημεν ἂν ἡμεῖς ὁ θεός, ἑνὰς καὶ τριάς (ἡ γάρ τοι τριὰς ἀρχὴν καὶ μέσα καὶ τέλη περὶ τὸ ἕν ἀνελίσσει)· καὶ τὸ νοητὸν καὶ φανότατον τῆς μονάδος εἰς ἄκραν αἰτίαν ὑπερβαίνει, καὶ τὸ ὑπερουράνιον αὐτῆς ἀρχηγὸν διακοσμήσεως, καὶ τὸ περίγειον
75 ἀδιαίρετον ἐν τοῖς διῃρημένοις, πλῆρες ἐν τοῖς ⟨ἐν⟩δεέσιν. | ἔστι δὲ καὶ θεία δυὰς δύναμις ἄπειρος, ζωῆς πρόοδος ἀνέκλειπτος, ὑποδοχὴ τοῦ πρώτου ἑνὸς μέτρου. ἡ γὰρ δυάς ἐστι καὶ νοητὴ καὶ νοερὰ καὶ μαθηματικὴ καὶ ἔνυλος. | οὕτω δὴ καὶ τριάς· ἡ μέν τίς ἐστι νοητή, ἡ δὲ νοερά, ἡ δὲ ὑπὲρ τὸν οὐρανόν, ἡ δὲ ἐν οὐρανῷ, ἡ
80 δὲ ἐν τῷ κόσμῳ πάντῃ διαπεφοίτηκε. |

Κατὰ τοῦτον οὖν τὸν τρόπον τῆς ἐξηγήσεως τῆς θαυμασίας ταύτης ἀριθμητικῆς ἕκαστον τῶν ἐν τῷ φυσικῷ χύματι ἀριθμῶν εἰς τὰς ὑπερφυεῖς ἀνάγοις ἑνώσεις· μᾶλλον δὲ τοῦτο ὕστερόν ἐστι καὶ ἀναλογία προσῆκον. εἰ δὲ βούλοιτό τις ἀκριβέστερον τὸν θεῖον ἰδεῖν ἀριθμόν,
85 ἀπ᾽ αὐτῶν τῶν κρειττόνων γενῶν τοῦτον ἀφορίσαιτ᾽ ἄν· ἔστι γὰρ καὶ θεῖον ἓν καὶ θεία μονὰς καὶ θεία δυὰς καὶ περιττὸν καὶ ἄρτιον

49–51 cf. anon. Theol. arith. 37, 4–10; Theon, Expos. 101, 14–23; Iambl. In Nic. 16, 18–
17, 2   53–7 cf. Iambl. Comm. 63, 23–31   56 cf. Iambl. Comm. 64, 6   57–8 cf.
Iambl. De myst. 23, 15–16; 160, 1–3   59–63 cf. Iambl. Pr. 23, 21–5; Comm. 16, 10–14;
Syrian. In met. 182, 3–7   64–6 cf. Iambl. Comm. 63, 24–7; 92, 14–15; 61, 6
67–70 cf. Iambl. De myst. 261, 9–263, 7; 264, 13–265, 5; Procl. El. theol. prop. 113 (100, 5–9);

of a square odd number. For 4 fits justice, lying in between
the monad and the number 9, and the number by which it is less
than 9, by this number it is more than the monad. And 5 is the 50
ninth part of summation of the numbers going from the monad to
the ennead. Such then is arithmetic in ethics. |

The philosopher Iamblichus wrote an arithmetic of higher
natures, not treating of the numbers in them mathematically, nor
imaging the higher kinds through analogies, nor positing them as 55
hypostatic, self-moved, intellectual, or essential numbers, but
he says ⟨that⟩ as the genus of higher ⟨natures⟩ transcends all
being, so is their number absolute and of itself. |

Speaking of the difference between the good and the one, he
says that as the nature of the good is generative, being prior as 60
cause to all goods, progresses in itself, and multiplies, thus the
complete cause of the one fills all from itself, holds beings in
itself, and multiplies in itself. |

Suitable and appropriate to the higher kinds is the higher
kind of mathematical number, such as the one, limit, the 65
determinate, equal, and such-like. | As there is a physical cause
of physical numbers, an ethical for ethicals, thus of divine
number there is a uniform divine principle, prior as cause to the
causes in all numbers, a uniform unity pre-existing even all
divine unified number itself. | The first then, the one properly 70
speaking, God as *we* would say, is henad and triad (for the triad
unrolls the beginning, middle, and end around the one); and the
intelligible and brightest monad ascends to the highest cause;
and the supercelestial of the ⟨monad?⟩ leader of ⟨cosmic⟩ order;
and the earthly, indivisible in the divided, full in the 75
lacking. | There is a divine dyad, unlimited power, never failing
progression of life, receiving the measure of the first one. For
the dyad is intelligible, intellectual, mathematical, in matter. |
So also the triad: one is intelligible, one intellectual, one
supercelestial, one celestial, one penetrating the universe. | 80

In this manner then of the account of this wondrous
arithmetic you might relate each in the natural flow of numbers
to the supernatural unities. But rather this is inferior and
appropriate to analogy. If one wished to see divine number
better, one would define this from the higher kinds themselves. 85
For there is a divine one and divine monad and divine dyad, and

Theol. Plat. III 12, 10–11; 36, 13–15   71–2 cf. Plato *Laws* 715 e; Ocellus in DK I 441,
7–8; Theon, *Expos.* 100, 13–14; 46, 15; anon. *Theol. arith.* 17, 4–5 (Anatolius); Iambl. *De
myst.* 60, 1–2   72–4 cf. Syrian. *In met.* 140, 10–18   76–7 cf. anon. *Theol. arith.*
12, 10–11; Syrian. *In met.* 5, 22–3; 112, 16 and 35–113, 3; Procl. *El. theol.* prop. 152; *Theol.
Plat.* I 122, 8–10; III 45, 3–5

ἐξῃρημένα καὶ κατὰ κρείττους ἐννοίας νοούμενα. | καὶ οἶδα μὲν ὅτι
δυσχερῶς ἄν τις ταῦτα παραδέξαιτο. τοῦτο δὲ γίνεται περὶ τὴν περὶ
τὰ κρείττω ἀμελετησίαν ἡμῶν· οἷς γὰρ οὐκ ἠθίσμεθα οὐδὲ συντεθράμ-
90 μεθα, τούτων οὐκ ἂν ῥᾷστα τὰς θεωρίας παραδεξαίμεθα.

88–9 cf. Psellus, *Philos. min.* no. 29, 106, 10–11

odd and even, transcendent and thought in higher insights. And I know that one might accept these things with difficulty. This happens in our neglect of higher ⟨beings⟩. For we do not easily accept the contemplation of the unaccustomed and unfamiliar.

90

APPENDIX II

The Arabic Commentaries on the *Golden Verses* Attributed to Iamblichus and Proclus

THE existence of two Arabic manuscripts, one containing a commentary on the *Golden Verses* attributed to Proclus, the other containing another commentary attributed to Iamblichus, has been known for some time (Endres [1973], 26–7). However, the importance of the two Arabic texts could hardly be gauged so long as they remained unedited and untranslated. N. Linley's edition and translation of the commentary attributed to Proclus have now made this text accessible, and it has already been discussed in an important article recently published by L. G. Westerink (1987). Before his death Linley had also prepared a provisional incomplete typescript draft of a translation of the commentary attributed to Iamblichus. However an edition and complete translation are still lacking. In this Appendix I shall venture some remarks about the Iamblichus text and propose a few comments additional to Westerink's findings concerning the Proclus commentary. In the former case I depend on Linley's provisional and incomplete translation, and what I suggest must in consequence be regarded as tentative.

I. THE COMMENTARY ON THE *GOLDEN VERSES* ATTRIBUTED TO IAMBLICHUS

An incomplete text of this commentary survives in one manuscript of the thirteenth century now at Princeton. Linley translates its title thus: 'A Commentary, compiled from the book of Iamblichus, on the "Exhortations" of the philosopher Pythagoras'. Linley indicates (in his edition of the Proclus commentary, v) that this text, as opposed to the Proclus commentary, uses the standard Arabic translation of the *Golden Verses*. The two texts appear also otherwise to have little in common, excepting some moral platitudes, a similar exegesis at the end of their comments on verses 59–60, and some points to be mentioned shortly. In general the Iamblichus commentary does not show any close dependence either on Hierocles or on Iamblichus' exegesis in *Protrepticus*, ch. 3 (exceptions noted below), and gives the impression of being little more than a series of glosses on and paraphrases of the *Golden Verses*. Where the commentary is fuller, it gives expression to rather banal moral ideas. I do not think, however, that this text can be regarded simply as Muslim (or perhaps Christian) glossing of the *Golden Verses*, for there are signs of some dependence on Greek Neoplatonic exegesis of the *Golden Verses*.

The clearest indication of this is the articulation of the commentary into an ethical and political section, ending with the exegesis of verse 45, and a theoretical section on the divine and on man that follows. Westerink (1987), 68, has noted the occurrence of this articulation in the Arabic commentary attributed to Proclus and in Hierocles (cf. *In carm.* 84, 7–9). Another articulation is found in our Arabic Iamblichus at verses 54–8 where the exegesis marks a transition from physics to the topic of choice (προαίρεσις), a transition marked also in the corresponding part of Iamblichus' *Protrepticus* (12, 1–9), but not in Hierocles and in the Arabic Proclus commentary. One might note finally some traces in the Arabic Iamblichus text of vulgarized Neoplatonism: the conception of souls that have freed themselves from the material world as wise and divine beings (on verses 1–2)—enough is said here to indicate that the hierarchy of souls (heroic, demonic, and divine) developed by Iamblichus, Hierocles, and Proclus is in question—and emphasis on the unchanging immaterial being of the divine and on the divine intellect in man that reminds him of his superior origin and nature (on verses 46, 49–51, 61–5).

If this evidence suggests that the commentary depends ultimately on some Greek Neoplatonic original, it does not suffice, however, to determine how seriously the attribution in the title of the commentary to Iamblichus should be taken. Such an attribution is not impossible, allowance being made for many omissions and later additions in the text of the commentary. But at present at any rate there is little that could confirm the attribution.

2. THE COMMENTARY ON THE *GOLDEN VERSES* ATTRIBUTED TO PROCLUS

Another Arabic commentary on the *Golden Verses*, transmitted also by a single manuscript, consists of extracts made by Ibn aṭ Ṭayyib (eleventh century) entitled: 'The essentials of the treatise of Pythagoras known as "the Golden". Proclus' commentary'. (On the manuscript and on aṭ Ṭayyib, cf. Linley's edition.) The major points made by Westerink (1987) might be summarized as follows. (i) The commentary—a larger and much more interesting work than the Arabic commentary attributed to Iamblichus—follows a Neoplatonic Greek model, excepting some Muslim (or Christian) modifications. For it demonstrates a familiarity with Pythagoras' biography and with Plato's dialogues that goes beyond the commonplace. Westerink also shows the presence in it of specific Neoplatonic doctrines, two of which will be discussed below, namely the hierarchy of gods, demons, heroes, and souls, and a hierarchy of different kinds of number. (ii) On the question of the attribution of the commentary to Proclus, Westerink explores the various possibilities. Arabic bibliography knows of a *Commentary on the Golden Verses* by Proclus, but this information *may* be based on the text under discussion here. Greek bibliographies do not assign such a commentary to Proclus. However, the *Suda* lists as works of a certain Proclus Procleius of Laodicea a theology, a commentary on the *Golden Verses*, a commentary on Nicomachus, and various geometrical works. Westerink shows that this Proclus of Laodicea, a Neoplatonist of the end of the fourth century or slightly later, is not to be identified with Proclus the successor of Syrianus in the school of Athens. It is possible then that the author of the Greek original of the Arabic text is either of these two Procluses or perhaps another Greek Neoplatonist whose work came to be attributed to 'Proclus'.

At present it does not appear to be possible to go further than this on the question of attribution to Proclus. If the Arabic text corresponds indeed to the commentary by Proclus of Laodicea, it would constitute another example of the influence of Iamblichus' Pythagoreanizing programme. In the light of this programme the fact that this Proclus wrote on the *Golden Verses*, on Nicomachus, and on geometry does not appear to be merely coincidental. Furthermore the Arabic text contains passages of particular interest with regard to Iamblichus' Pythagoreanism. One passage (19), speaking of the hierarchy of gods, demons, and heroes, describes heroes as follows:

Heroes are souls which have passed lives as humans, and have remained with humans without becoming polluted, and were causes of their goods.

Westerink (1987), 67, compares this to Iamblichus and in particular to the unpolluted souls in Proclus. In Iamblichus, as we have seen, such pure souls are especially significant as corresponding to the great philosophical benefactors of mankind, including of course Pythagoras. However, the Arabic text does not establish this correspondence. Another interesting passage in the Arabic text (77–9) introduces numerological speculations and in particular a hierarchy of different kinds of number:

The first numbers are characteristic of the gods, the second represent the intelligible forms that are found in all that exists, the third are representations of soul . . . the fourth are representations of natural objects, in keeping with matter and its ordering by form.

Westerink refers to another such classification in Proclus. But it is already an important theme in Iamblichus' *On Pythagoreanism*, as we have seen. The Arabic commentary thus contains ideas characteristic of Iamblichus' Pythagoreanizing programme which reappear in Syrianus and in Proclus. If then the precise authorship of the Arabic commentary cannot yet be determined with certainty, it can at least be seen as further evidence of the influence of Iamblichus' revival of Pythagoreanism.

BIBLIOGRAPHY

I. ANCIENT AUTHORS

Listed below are the editions I have used in citing ancient authors (cited by page and line numbers, unless otherwise indicated). Other editions, referred to on account of the views of their modern editors, are listed in the second part of the bibliography.

ALBINUS, *Didaskalikos*, ed., transl. P. Louis, *Albinus épitomé*, Paris 1945.

ANATOLIUS, *De decade*, ed. J. L. Heiberg, *Congrès international d'histoire comparée, V^e section*, Paris 1900, 27–41 (repr. Nendeln 1972), with transl. and note by P. Tannery, 42–57.

—— *Excerpta*, ed. F. Hultsch, *Heronis Alexandrini geometricorum et stereometricorum reliquiae*, Berlin 1864, 276–80.

Anonymous, *Prolegomena in Introductionem arithmeticam Nicomachi*, ed. P. Tannery, *Diophanti Alexandrini opera omnia*, Leipzig 1895, II 73–7.

Anonymous Prolegomena to Platonic Philosophy, ed. L. G. Westerink, Amsterdam 1962.

Anonymous, [*Iamblichi*] *Theologoumena arithmeticae*, ed. V. de Falco, Leipzig 1922.

ASCLEPIUS, *In Aristotelis Metaphysicorum libros A–Z commentaria*, ed. M. Hayduck (*CAG* VI 2), Berlin 1888.

ATTICUS, *Fragments*, ed., transl. E. des Places, Paris 1977.

AUGUSTINE, *De ordine*, ed. P. Knöll, Vienna 1922.

Chaldaean Oracles, ed., transl. E. des Places, Paris 1971.

DAMASCIUS, *De principiis*, ed. E. Ruelle, Paris 1889 (transl.: cf. Combès [1986]).

—— *In Philebum*, ed., transl. L. Westerink, Amsterdam 1959.

—— *Vitae Isidori reliquiae*, ed. C. Zintzen, Hildesheim 1967.

DEXIPPUS, *In Aristotelis Categorias commentarium*, ed. A. Busse (*CAG* IV 2), Berlin 1888.

DOMNINUS, *Manual of Introductory Arithmetic*, ed. J. Boissonade, *Anecdota graeca* IV, Paris 1832 (repr. Hildesheim 1962), 413–29 (transl.: cf. Tannery [1906]).

ELIAS, *In Porphyrii Isagogen et Aristotelis Categorias commentaria*, ed. A. Busse (*CAG* XVIII), Berlin 1900.

EUNAPIUS, *Vitae Sophistarum*, in *Philostratus and Eunapius The Lives of the Sophists*, ed., transl. W. Wright, London 1922.

EUSEBIUS, *Historia ecclesiastica*, ed. E. Schwartz, Leipzig 1908.

HERMIAS, *In Platonis Phaedrum Scholia*, ed. P. Couvreur, Paris 1901, repr. with additions by C. Zintzen, Hildesheim 1971.

HERMOGENES, *Progymnasmata*, ed. H. Rabe, Leipzig 1913.

HIEROCLES, *In Aureum Pythagoreorum carmen commentarius*, ed. F. Köhler, Stuttgart 1974 (transl.: cf. Köhler [1983]).

IAMBLICHUS, (?) *Commentary on the Pythagorean Golden Verses*, typescript of provisional incomplete English translation by N. Linley (communicated by L. G. Westerink).

—— *De mysteriis*, ed. G. Parthey, Berlin 1857 (repr. Amsterdam 1965) (transl.: des Places [1966]).

—— *Fragments: Commentaries on Plato*: cf. Dillon (1973); *Commentaries on Aristotle*: cf. Larsen (1972); *De anima*: cf. Stobaeus; *Letters*: cf. Stobaeus.

—— *On Pythagoreanism*:
  Book I. *De Vita Pythagorica* (= *Vit. Pyth.*), ed. L. Deubner (1937), repr. Stuttgart 1975 (transl.: cf. von Albrecht [1963], Montoneri [1973]);
  Book II. *Protrepticus* (= *Pr.*), ed. L. Pistelli (1888), repr. Stuttgart 1967 (transl. Schönberger [1984], des Places [1986]);
  Book III. *De communi mathematica scientia* (= *Comm.*), ed. N. Festa (1891), repr. Stuttgart 1975;
  Book IV. *In Nicomachi Arithmeticam introductionem* (= *In Nic.*), ed. H. Pistelli (1894), repr. Stuttgart 1975.

JEROME, *Epistula adversus Rufinum*, ed. P. Lardet, *S. Hieronymi . . . Opera III 1*, Turnhout 1982.

LYDUS, *De mensibus*, ed. R. Wünsch, Leipzig 1898.

MARINUS, *Commentarius in Euclidis data*, in *Euclidis Opera omnia*, ed. I. Heiberg and H. Menge, vol. VI, Leipzig 1896.

—— *Vita Procli*, ed. J. Boissonade, Leipzig 1814, repr. Amsterdam 1966 (transl.: cf. Masullo [1985]).

MAXIMUS OF TYRE, *Orationes* (*Philosophumena*), ed. H. Hobein, Leipzig 1910.

MENANDER, *De laudationibus*, ed. L. Spengel, *Rhetores graeci*, vol. III, Leipzig 1856.

NICOMACHUS, *Introductio arithmetica*, ed. R. Hoche, Leipzig 1866 (transl.: cf. D'Ooge [1926], Bertier [1978]).

—— *Manuale harmonicum*, ed. K. von Jan, *Musici scriptores graeci*, Leipzig 1895, repr. Hildesheim 1962, 237–65.

NUMENIUS, *Fragments*, ed., transl. E. des Places, Paris 1973.

PHILOPONUS, *In Aristotelis Physica commentaria*, ed. H. Vitelli (*CAG* XVI–XVII), Berlin 1888.

—— *In De anima*, ed. M. Hayduck (*CAG* XV), Berlin 1897.

—— *In Nicomachum*, ed. R. Hoche, Program Wesel 1864–7.

PHOTIUS, *Bibliotheca*, ed., transl. R. Henry, Paris 1959–77.

PLOTINUS, *Enneads*, ed. P. Henry, H. R. Schwyzer, Bruxelles–Paris–Leiden 1951–73 (transl.: cf. Armstrong [1966 ff.]).

PLUTARCH, *De procreatione animae*, ed., transl. H. Cherniss, *Plutarch's Moralia* XIII 1, Cambridge, Mass. 1976.

PORPHYRY, *De abstinentia*, ed., transl. J. Bouffartigue and M. Patillon, Paris 1977–9.

— *De philosophia ex oraculis haurienda*, ed. G. Wolff, Berlin 1856, repr. Hildesheim 1962.

— *Epistula ad Anebo*, ed. A. R. Sodano, *Porfirio Lettera ad Anebo*, Naples 1958.

— *Opuscula Selecta*, ed. A. Nauck, Leipzig 1886, repr. Hildesheim 1963.

— *Quaestiones Homericae ad Iliadem*, ed. H. Schraeder, Leipzig 1880–2.

— *Vie de Pythagore, Lettre à Marcella*, ed., transl. E. des Places, avec Appendice d'A.-Ph. Segonds, Paris 1982.

— *Vita Plotini*, edited at head of Plotinus' *Enneads*.

PROCLUS, *Commentary on the First Alcibiades of Plato*, ed. L. G. Westerink, Amsterdam 1954 (transl.: cf. O'Neill [1965], Segonds [1985–6]).

— *Commentaria in Parmenidem*, in Proclus, *Opera inedita*, ed. V. Cousin, Paris 1864 (transl.: cf. Morrow and Dillon [1987]).

—(?) *Commentary on the Pythagorean Golden Verses* (Extracts made by Ibn aṭ-Ṭayyib), ed. transl. N. Linley, Buffalo 1984.

— *Institutio Physica*, ed., transl. A. Ritzenfeld, Leipzig 1912.

— *Hypotyposis astronomicarum positionum*, ed. C. Manitius, Leipzig 1909.

— *In Platonis Cratylum commentaria*, ed. G. Pasquali, Leipzig 1908.

— *In Platonis Rempublicam*, ed. W. Kroll, Leipzig 1899 (transl.: cf. Festugière [1970]).

— *In Platonis Timaeum*, ed. E. Diehl, Leipzig 1903 (transl.: cf. Festugière [1966–8]).

— *In Primum Euclidis Elementorum librum commentarii*, ed. G. Friedlein, Leipzig 1873, repr. 1967 (transl.: cf. Morrow [1970]).

— *The Elements of Theology*, ed., transl. E. R. Dodds, 2nd edn., Oxford 1963.

— *Théologie Platonicienne*, ed., transl. H.-D. Saffrey and L. G. Westerink, Paris 1968 ff.

— *Tria opuscula* (*De providentia, libertate, malo*) ed. H. Boese, Berlin 1960 (transl.: cf. Erler [1978], [1980]).

MICHAEL PSELLUS, *Chronographia*, ed., transl. E. Renauld, Paris 1926.

— *Philosophica minora*, ed. J. M. Duffy, D. J. O'Meara, vol. II, ed. D. J. O'Meara, Leipzig 1988.

SIMPLICIUS, *In De anima*, ed. M. Hayduck (*CAG* XI), Berlin 1882.

— *In De caelo*, ed. I. Heiberg (*CAG* VII), Berlin 1894.

— *In Categorias*, ed. C. Kalbfleisch (*CAG* VIII), Berlin 1907.

— *In Aristotelis Physicorum libros*, ed. H. Diels (*CAG* IX–X), Berlin 1882–95.

STOBAEUS, *Anthologium*, ed. C. Wachsmuth–O. Hense, Berlin 1884–1912.

Stoicorum veterum fragmenta, ed. H. von Arnim, Leipzig 1905–24, repr. Stuttgart 1978.

SYRIANUS, *In Hermogenem*, ed. H. Rabe, Leipzig 1892.

— *In Metaphysica commentaria*, ed. W. Kroll (*CAG* VI), Berlin 1902.

THEMISTIUS, *In Aristotelis Physica Paraphrasis*, ed. H. Schenke (*CAG* V 2), Berlin 1900.

THEON, *Progymnasmata*, ed. L. Spengel, *Rhetores graeci*, vol. II, Leipzig 1854.

THEON OF SMYRNA, *Expositio rerum mathematicarum ad legendum Platonem utilium*, ed. E. Hiller, Leipzig 1878 (transl.: cf. Dupuis [1892]).

TIMAEUS LOCRUS, *De natura mundi et animae*, ed. W. Marg, Leiden 1972.

2. MODERN AUTHORS

This bibliography includes some titles not cited in this book but of relevance to its subject. Articles which have been reprinted are cited in the notes according to the year of first publication and the pagination of the reprint.

ALBRECHT, M. VON (1963). *Iamblichos Pythagoras*, Zurich.

—— (1966). 'Das Menschenbild in Iamblichs Darstellung der pythagoreischen Lebensform', *Antike und Abendland* 12, 51–63.

ALLEN, R. E. (1970). *Plato's 'Euthyphro' and the Earlier Theory of Forms*, New York.

ANNAS, J. (1976). *Aristotle's Metaphysics Books M and N*, Oxford.

ANTONELLI, M. (1969). 'L'idea di matematica in Giamblico', *Arts libéraux et philosophie au moyen âge*, Montréal–Paris, 1007–21.

ARMSTRONG, A. H. (1966 ff.). *Plotinus* (English transl.), London and Cambridge, Mass.

—— (1967). Ed., *The Cambridge History of Later Greek and Early Medieval Philosophy*, Cambridge.

AUBENQUE, P. (1962). *Le Probleme de l'être chez Aristote*, Paris.

AUJAC, G. (1975a). *Géminos Introduction aux phénomènes*, Paris.

—— (1975b). 'Michel Psellos et Denys d'Halicarnasse: le traité sur la composition des éléments du langage', *Revue des études byzantines* 33, 257–75.

AUJOULAT, N. (1976). 'Sur la vie et les oeuvres de Hiéroclès, Problème de chronologie', *Pallas* 23, 19–30.

—— (1986). *Le Néo-Platonisme Alexandrin: Hiéroclès d'Alexandrie*, Leiden.

BALTES, M. (1978a). Review of Kobusch (1976), *Gnomon* 50, 256–61.

—— (1978b). *Die Weltentstehung des Platonischen Timaios nach den antiken Interpreten* II, Leiden.

BEIERWALTES, W. (1961). 'Eine Reflexion zum Geist-Begriff des Proklos', *Archiv für Geschichte der Philosophie* 43, 119–27.

—— (1963), 'Der Begriff des "unum in nobis" bei Proklos', *Miscellanea Medievalia*, ed. P. Wilpert, 2, 255–66.

—— (1969). 'Neoplatonica', *Philosophische Rundschau* 16, 130–52.

—— (1972). 'Andersheit', *Archiv für Begriffsgeschichte* 16, 166–97.

—— (1979). *Proklos Grundzüge seiner Metaphysik*, 2nd revised edn., Frankfurt.

—— (1985). *Denken des Einen*, Frankfurt.

BENAKIS, L. (1964). 'Doxographische Angaben über die Vorsokratiker im unedierten Kommentar zur "Physik" des Aristoteles von Michael Psellos', *XAPIΣ (K. I. BOYPBEPH)*, Athens, 345–54.

BERTIER, J. (1978). *Nicomaque de Gérase Introduction arithmétique*, Paris.

—— *et al.* (1980). *Plotin Traité sur les nombres (Ennéade VI 6[34])*, Paris.

BEUTLER, R. (1953). 'Porphyrios', *RE* 22, 1, 275–313.

—— (1957). 'Proklos', *RE* 23, 186–247.

BIDEZ, J. (1913). *Vie de Porphyre*, Ghent, repr. Hildesheim 1964.

—— (1919). 'Le philosophe Jamblique et son école', *Revue des études grecques* 32, 29–40.

—— (1928). *Catalogue des manuscrits alchémiques grecs* VI, Brussels.

BIELER, L. (1935). *ΘΕΙΟΣ ANHP. Das Bild des "göttlichen Menschen" in Spätantike und Frühchristentum*, Vienna.

BIELMEIER, P. (1930). *Die neuplatonische Phaidrosinterpretation*, Paderborn.

BLUMENTHAL, H. J. (1975). 'Plutarch's Exposition of the *De anima* and the Psychology of Proclus', *De Jamblique à Proclus*, Vandœuvres–Geneva, 123–51.

—— (1978). '529 and its sequel: What happened to the Academy', *Byzantion* 48, 369–85.

—— (1981). 'Plotinus in Later Platonism', in *Neoplatonism and Early Christian Thought*, ed. H. J. Blumenthal and R. Markus, London, 212–22.

—— (1982). 'Proclus on Perception', *Bulletin of the Institute of Classical Studies* (University of London) 29, 1–11.

—— (1984). 'Marinus' Life of Proclus: Neoplatonist Biography', *Byzantion* 54, 469–94.

—— (1986a). 'John Philoponus: Alexandrian Platonist?', *Hermes* 114, 314–35.

—— (1986b). 'Body and Soul in Philoponus', *The Monist* 69, 370–82.

BOESE, H. (1985). *Wilhelm von Moerbeke als Übersetzer der Stoicheiosis Theologike des Proclus*, Heidelberg.

BOISSONADE, J. (1838). *Michael Psellus de operatione daimonum*, Nürnberg, repr. Amsterdam 1964.

BORGHORST, G. (1905). *De Anatolii fontibus*, Berlin diss.

BOWER, C. (1978). 'Boethius and Nicomachus: an Essay concerning the Sources of the *De institutione musica*', *Vivarium* 16, 1–45.

BRETON, S. (1969). *Philosophie et Mathématique chez Proclus*, Paris.

BRISSON, L., *et al.* (1982). *Porphyre: la vie de Plotin*, Paris.

BROWNING, R. (1975). 'Enlightenment and Repression in Byzantium in the Eleventh and Twelfth Centuries', *Past and Present* 69, 3–23.

BRUNSCHVICQ, L. (1929). *Les Étapes de la philosophie mathématique*, Paris.

—— (1937). *Le Rôle du Pythagorisme dans l'évolution des idées*, Paris.

BURKERT, W. (1961). 'Hellenistische Pseudopythagorica', *Philologus* 105, 16–43, 226–46.

—— (1972). *Lore and Science in Ancient Pythagoreanism*, Cambridge, Mass.

CARDULLO, L. (1985). *Il Linguaggio del Simbolo in Proclo*, Catania.

CHADWICK, H. (1981). *Boethius: the Consolations of Music, Logic, Theology, and Philosophy*, Oxford.

CHARLES, A. (1967). 'Sur le caractère intermédiaire des mathématiques dans la pensée de Proklos', *Les Études philosophiques* 22, 69–80.

—— (1969). 'La raison et le divin chez Proclus', *Revue des sciences philosophiques et théologiques* 53, 458–82.

—— (1971). 'L'imagination, miroir de l'âme selon Proclus', *Le Néoplatonisme*, Paris, 241–8.

—— (1982). *L'Architecture du divin. Mathématique et philosophie chez Plotin et Proclus*, Paris.

CHERNISS, H. (1976). Cf. Plutarch, *De procreatione animae*.

COMBÈS, J., WESTERINK, L. G. (1986). Ed., transl., *Damascius Traité des premiers principes*, Paris.

COX, P. (1983). *Biography in Late Antiquity. A Quest for the Holy Man*, Berkeley.

CRAPULLI, G. (1969). *Mathesis universalis. Genesi di un'idea nel XVI secolo*, Rome.

CUMONT, F. (1922). 'Alexandre d'Abonotichus et le Néo-Pythagorisme', *Revue de l'histoire des religions* 86, 202–10.

DELATTE, A. (1915). *Études sur la littérature pythagoricienne*, Paris.

DES PLACES, E. (1966). *Jamblique: Les mystères d'Egypte*, Paris.

—— (1986). *Jamblique: Protreptique*, Paris.

DEUBNER, L. (1935). 'Bemerkungen zum Text der Vita Pythagorae des Jamblichos', *Sitz. d. König. preuss. Akad. d. Wiss., Philos.-hist.-kl.*, 612–90, 824–7.

DEUSE, W. (1973). *Theodoros von Asine*, Wiesbaden.

—— (1983). *Untersuchungen zur mittelplatonischen und neuplatonischen Seelenlehre*, Wiesbaden.

DIELS, H. (1879). *Doxographi graeci*, Berlin.

DILLON, J. M. (1969). 'A Date for the Death of Nicomachus of Gerasa?', *Classical Review* NS 16, 274–5.

—— (1973). *Iamblichi Chalcidensis in Platonis dialogos commentariorum fragmenta*, Leiden.

—— (1976). 'Image Symbol and Analogy: Three Basic Concepts of Neoplatonic Allegorical Exegesis', *The Significance of Neoplatonism*, ed. R. B. Harris, Norfolk VA, 247–62.

—— (1977). *The Middle Platonists*, London.

DODDS, E. R. (1960). 'Tradition and Personal Achievement in the Philosophy of Plotinus', *Journal of Roman Studies* 50, 1–7.

DÖRRIE, H. (1944). 'Der Platoniker Eudorus von Alexandreia', *Hermes* 79, 25–38 = *Platonica minora*, Munich 1976, 297–309.

—— (1955). 'Ammonios, der Lehrer Plotins', *Hermes* 83, 439–77 = *Platonica minora* 324–49.

—— (1963). 'Der nachklassische Pythagoreismus', *RE* 24, 268–77.

—— (1973a). 'Platons Reisen zu fernen Völkern', *Romanitas et Christianitas* (Festschrift J. H. Waszink), ed. W. den Boer *et al.*, Amsterdam, 99–118.

—— (1973b). 'L. Kalbenos Tauros', *Kairos* 15, 24–35 = *Platonica minora*, 310–23.

—— (1976). *Von Platon zum Platonismus. Ein Bruch in der Überlieferung und seine Überwindung*, Opladen.

D'OOGE, M. L., *et al.* (1926). *Nicomachus of Gerasa: Introduction to Arithmetic*, New York.

DUHEM, P. (1914). *Le système du monde*, Paris.

DUPUIS, J. (1892). *Théon de Smyrne philosophe platonicien*, Paris, repr. Brussels 1966.

EBBESEN, S. (1981). *Commentators and Commentaries on Aristotle's Sophistici Elenchi* I, Leiden.

EECKE, P. VER (1948). *Proclus de Lycie, Les commentaires sur le premier livre des Eléments d'Euclide*, Bruges.

ELTER, A. (1910). 'Zu Hierokles dem Neuplatoniker', *Rheinisches Museum* 65, 175–99.

ENDRES, G. (1973). *Proclus Arabus*, Beirut.

ERLER, M. (1978). *Proklos Diadochos. Über die Existenz des Bösen*, Meisenheim.

—— (1980). *Proklos Diadochos. Über die Vorsehung, das Schicksal und den freien Willen*, Meisenheim.

EVANS, G. R. (1980). 'Boethian and Euclidean Axiomatic Method in the Theology of the Later Twelfth Century', *Archives internationales d'histoire des sciences*, 30, 36–52.

EVRARD, E. (1960). 'Le maître de Plutarque d'Athènes et les origines du néoplatonisme athénien', *L'Antiquité classique* 29, 108–33, 399–406.

FARAGGIANA DI SARZANA, C. (1985). *Proclo I Manuali*, Milan (with long introduction by G. Reale).

FESTUGIÈRE, A. J. (1937). 'Sur une nouvelle édition du *De vita Pythagorica* de Jamblique', *Revue des études grecques* 50, 470–94 = *Études de philosophie grecque*, Paris 1971, 437–61.

—— (1950–4). *La Révélation d'Hermès Trismégiste*, Paris.

—— (1963). 'Modes de composition des commentaires de Proclus', *Museum Helveticum* 20, 77–100 = *Études de philosophie grecque*, 551–74.

—— (1966–8). *Proclus Commentaire sur le Timée*, Paris.

—— (1969). 'L'ordre de lecture des dialogues de Platon aux V/VIe siècles', *Museum Helveticum* 26, 281–96 = *Études de philosophie grecque*, 535–50.

—— (1970). *Proclus: Commentaire sur la République*, Paris.

FINAMORE, J. (1985). *Iamblichus and the Theory of the Vehicle of the Soul*, Chico CA.

FOWDEN, G. (1982). 'The pagan holy man in late antique society', *Journal of Hellenic Studies* 102, 33–59.

FRITZ, K. VON (1971). *Grundprobleme der Geschichte der antiken Wissenschaft*, Berlin.

GALPERINE, M.-C. (1980). 'Le temps intégral selon Damascius', *Les Études philosophiques*, 35, 325–41.

GAUTIER, P. (1977). 'Michel Psellos et la Rhétorique de Longin', *Prometheus* 3, 193–203.

GELZER, T. (1966). 'Die Epigramme des Neuplatonikers Proklos', *Museum Helveticum* 23, 1–36.

GERSH, S. (1973). *ΚΙΝΗΣΙΣ ΑΚΙΝΗΤΟΣ: A Study of Spiritual Motion in the Philosophy of Proclus*, Leiden.

—— (1978). *From Iamblichus to Eriugena*, Leiden.

GLUCKER, J. (1978). *Antiochus and the Late Academy*, Göttingen.

GRAESER, A. (1987). Ed., *Mathematics and Metaphysics in Aristotle*, Bern.

GRONDIJS, L. H. (1960). 'L'Ame, le Nous et les hénades dans la théologie de Proclus', *Mededelingen der Kon. Nederlanske Akad. van Wetenschappen*, Letter-kunde 23. 2, 29–42.

HADOT, I. (1978). *Le Problème du néoplatonisme alexandrin. Hiéroclès et Simplicius*, Paris.

—— (1979). 'Ist die Lehre des Hierokles vom Demiurgen Christlich be-einflusst?' *Kerygma und Logos* (Festschrift C. Andresen), ed. A. Ritter, Göt-tingen, 258–71.

—— (1984). *Arts libéraux et philosophie dans la pensée antique*, Paris.

—— (1987*a*). 'Les Introductions aux commentaires exégétiques chez les auteurs néoplatoniciens et les auteurs chrétiens', *Les Règles de l'interprétation*, ed. M. Tardieu, Paris, 99–122.

—— (1987*b*). 'La Vie et l'œuvre de Simplicius d'après des sources grecques et arabes', *Simplicius. Sa Vie, son œuvre, sa survie*, ed. I. Hadot, Berlin, 3–39.

HADOT, P. (1968). *Porphyre et Victorinus*, Paris.

—— (1974). 'L'Harmonie des philosophies de Plotin et d'Aristote selon Porphyre dans le commentaire de Dexippe sur les Catégories', *Plotino e il neoplatonismo in oriente e occidente*, Rome, 31–47.

—— (1979). 'Les divisions des parties de la philosophie dans l'Antiquité', *Museum Helveticum* 36, 201–23.

—— (1987). 'Théologie, exégèse, révélation, écriture, dans la philosophie grecque', *Les Règles de l'interprétation*, ed. M. Tardieu, Paris, 13–34.

HÄGG, T. (1975). *Photios als Vermittler antiker Literatur*, Uppsala.

HARDER, R. (1926). *Ocellus Lucanus*, Berlin.

HARTMANN, N. (1909). *Des Proklus Diadochus philosophische Anfangsgründe der Mathematik*, Giessen, repr. Berlin 1969 (transl. in Breton [1969]).

HATHAWAY, R. (1982). 'The Anatomy of a Neoplatonist Metaphysical Proof', *The Structure of Being*, ed. R. B. Harris, Norfolk VA, 122–36.

HEATH, T. (1921). *A History of Greek Mathematics*, Oxford.

—— (1956). *Euclid: The Thirteen Books of the Elements*, New York.

HEIBERG, J. L. (1882). *Literargeschichtliche Studien über Euklid*, Leipzig.

—— (1925). *Geschichte der Mathematik und Naturwissenschaften im Altertum*, Munich.

HOFFMANN, P. (1979). 'Simplicius: Corollarium de loco', *L'Astronomie dans l'antiquité classique* (colloque Toulouse–Le Mirail 1977), Paris, 143–61.

—— (1980). 'Jamblique exégète du pythagoricien Archytas: trois originalités d'une doctrine du temps', *Les Études philosophiques* 35, 307–23.

HULTSCH, F. (1905). 'Domninos', *RE* 5, 1521–4.

HUNGER, H. (1978). *Die Hochsprachliche profane Literatur der Byzantiner* I, Munich.

HYLDAHL, N. (1966). *Philosophie und Christentum*, Copenhagen.

IMBACH, R. (1978). 'Le (Néo-)Platonisme médiéval, Proclus latin et l'école dominicaine allemande', *Revue de théologie et de philosophie* 110, 427–48.

JEAUNEAU, E. (1963). 'Mathématiques et Trinité chez Thierry de Chartres', *Miscellanea medievalia*, ed. P. Wilpert, 2, 289–95.

KENNY, A. (1978). *The Aristotelian Ethics*, Oxford.

KERN, O. (1922). *Orphicorum fragmenta*, Berlin.

KLEIN, J. (1968). *Greek Mathematical Thought and the Origin of Algebra*, transl. E. Brann, Cambridge, Mass.

KOBUSCH, T. (1976). *Studien zur Philosophie des Hierokles von Alexandrien*, Munich.

KÖHLER, F. W. (1983). *Hierokles Kommentar zum Pythagoreischen goldenen Gedicht* (transl.), Stuttgart.

KRÄMER, H. J. (1964). *Der Ursprung der Geistmetaphysik*, Amsterdam.

KREMER, K. (1961). *Der Metaphysikbegriff in den Aristoteles-Kommentaren der Ammonius-Schule*, Münster.

KRIARAS, E. (1968). 'Psellos', *RE* suppl. 11, 1124–82.

KUSTAS, G. (1973). *Studies in Byzantine Rhetoric*, Thessaloniki.

LAMBERTON, R. (1986). *Homer the Theologian*, Berkeley.

LARSEN, B. D. (1972). *Jamblique de Chalcis. Exégète et philosophe*, Aarhus.

LEEMANS, E. A. (1937). *Studie over den wijsgeer Numenius van Apamea*, Brussels.

LEMERLE, P. (1977). *Cinq études sur le XIᵉ siècle byzantin*, Paris.

LEVIN, F. (1975). *The Harmonics of Nicomachus and the Pythagorean Tradition*, University Park, Pa.

LEWY, H. (1956). *Chaldaean Oracles and Theurgy*, Cairo; new edn. Paris 1978.

LOHR, C. (1986). 'The Pseudo-Aristotelian *Liber de causis* and Latin Theories of Science in the Twelfth and Thirteenth Centuries', *Pseudo-Aristotle in the Middle Ages*, ed. J. Kraye *et al.*, London, 53–62.

LOWRY, J. (1980). *The Logical Principles of Proclus' ΣΤΟΙΧΕΙΩΣΙΣ ΘΕΟ-ΛΟΓΙΚΗ as Systematic Ground of the Cosmos*, Amsterdam.

MADIGAN, A. (1986). 'Syrianus and Asclepius on Forms and Intermediates in Plato and Aristotle', *Journal of the History of Philosophy* 24, 149–71.

MAHNKE, D. (1937). *Unendliche Sphäre und Allmittelpunkt. Beiträge zur Genealogie der mathematischen Mystik*, Halle (Saale).

MANSFELD, J. (1971). *The Pseudo-Hippocratic Tract* Περὶ ἑβδομάδων *ch. 1—11 and Greek Philosophy*, Assen.

MARG, W. (1972). *Timaeus Locrus: De natura mundi et animae*, Leiden.

MASI, M. (1983). *Boethian Number Theory. A Translation of the De institutione arithmetica*, Amsterdam.

MASULLO, R. (1985). *Marino di Neapoli: Vita di Proclo*, Naples.

MÉAUTIS, G. (1922). *Recherches sur le pythagorisme*, Neuchâtel.

MERLAN, P. (1960). *From Platonism to Neoplatonism*, 2nd edn., revised, The Hague.

—— (1965), 'Zur Zahlenlehre im Platonismus (Neuplatonismus) und im *Sefer Yezira*', *Journal of the History of Philosophy* 3, 167–81.

MEWALDT, J. (1904). *De Aristoxeni Pythagoricis Sententiis et Vita Pythagorica*, diss. Berlin.

MEYER, H. (1969). *Das Corollarium de Tempore des Simplikios und die Aporien des Aristoteles zur Zeit*, Meisenheim am Glan.

MOERBEKE, *Proclus, Commentaire sur le Parménide de Platon. Traduction de Guillaume de Moerbeke*, I: *Livres I à IV*, ed. C. Steel, Leiden–Louvain 1982; II: *Livres V à VII*, Leiden 1985.

MONTONERI, L. (1973). *Giamblico: Vita pitagorica*, Rome–Bari.

MORAUX, P. (1985). 'Porphyre, commentateur de la *Physique* d'Aristote', *Aristotelica* (Mélanges M. de Corte), ed. A. Motte, C. Rutten, Brussels–Liège, 227–39.

MORROW, G. R. (1970). *Proclus. A Commentary on the First Book of Euclid's Elements* (transl.), Princeton.

——, DILLON, J. (1987). *Proclus' Commentary on Plato's Parmenides* (transl.), Princeton.

MUELLER, I. (1970). 'Aristotle on Geometrical Objects', *Archiv für Geschichte der Philosophie* 52, 156–71.

—— (1974). 'Greek Mathematics and Greek Logic', *Ancient Logic and its Modern Interpretations*, ed. J. Corcoran, Dordrecht, 35–70.

—— (1987a). 'Iamblichus and Proclus' Euclid Commentary', *Hermes* 115, 334–48.

—— (1987b). 'Mathematics and Philosophy in Proclus' Commentary on Book I of Euclid's *Elements*', *Proclus lecteur et interprète des anciens* (colloque international du C.N.R.S.), ed. J. Pépin, H.-D. Saffrey, Paris, 305–18.

NAUCK, A. (1884). *Iamblichi de Vita Pythagorica liber*, St. Petersburg, repr. Amsterdam 1965.

O'BRIEN, D. (1981). '"Pondus meum amor meus": Saint Augustin et Jamblique', *Revue de l'Histoire des Religions* 198, 423–8.

O'MEARA, D. J. (1975). *Structures hiérarchiques dans la pensée de Plotin*, Leiden.

—— (1976). 'Being in Numenius and Plotinus', *Phronesis* 21, 120–9.

—— (1981). 'New Fragments from Iamblichus' *Collection of Pythagorean Doctrines*', *American Journal of Philology* 102, 26–40.

— (1986). 'Le problème de la métaphysique dans l'antiquité tardive', *Freiburger Zeitschrift für Philosophie und Theologie*, 33, 3–22.

— (1988). 'Proclus' First Prologue to Euclid: The Problem of its Major Source', *Gonimos*. Festschrift L. G. Westerink, ed. J. Duffy, J. Peradotto, Buffalo, N.Y., 49–59.

O'MEARA, J. (1959). *Porphyry's Philosophy from Oracles in Augustine*, Paris.

O'NEILL, W. (1965). *Proclus: Alcibiades I* (transl.), The Hague.

OPPERMANN, H. (1929). Review of Anonymous [Iamblichi] *Theologoumena arithmeticae*, ed. de Falco, *Gnomon* 5, 545–58.

PISTELLI, E. (1888). 'Dei manoscritti di Giamblico e di una nuova edizione del Protreptico', *Museo italiano di antichità classica* 2, 457–70.

PRAECHTER, K. (1903). Review of *Syrianus In met.*, ed. Kroll, *Gött. Gelehr. Anz.* 165, 513–30 = *Kleine Schriften*, ed. H. Dörrie, Hildesheim 1973, 246–63.

— (1910). 'Richtungen und Schulen im Neuplatonismus', *Genethliakon für C. Robert*, Berlin, 105–56, = *Kleine Schriften*, 165–216.

— (1913). 'Hermias', *RE* 8, 732–5.

— (1926). 'Das Schriftenverzeichnis des Neuplatonikers Syrianos bei Suidas', *Byzantinische Zeitschrift* 26, 253–64 = *Kleine Schriften*, 222–33.

— (1932). 'Syrianos', *RE* II, 8, 1728–75.

PUECH, H.-C. (1934). 'Numénius d'Apamée et les théologies orientales au second siècle', *Mélanges Bidez*, Brussels, 745–78.

RENAULD, E. (1920). *Étude de la langue et du style de Michel Psellos*, Paris.

RICHARD, M. (1950). '*ΑΠΟ ΦΩΝΗΣ*', *Byzantion* 22, 191–222 = *Opera minora* III, Turnhout–Louvain 1977, No. 60.

RIST, J. M. (1967). *Plotinus: the Road to Reality*, Cambridge.

ROBBINS, F. E. (1920). 'Posidonius and the Sources of Pythagorean Arithmology', *Classical Philology* 15, 309–22.

— (1921). 'The Tradition of Greek Arithmology', *Classical Philology* 16, 97–123.

ROCCA-SERRA, G. (1971). 'La lettre à Marcella de Porphyre et les Sentences des Pythagoriciens', *Le Néoplatonisme*, Paris, 193–9.

ROMANO, F. (1985). *Porfirio e la fisica aristotelica*, Catania.

ROSÁN, J. (1949). *The Philosophy of Proclus*, New York.

RUELLE, C. E. (1883). 'Texte inédit de Domninus de Larissa sur l'arithmétique', (with note by J. Dumontier) *Revue de philologie* 7, 82–94.

SAFFREY, H. D. (1967). 'Une collection méconnue de 'symboles' Pythagoriciens', *Revue des études grecques* 80, 198–201.

— (1968). '*ΑΓΕΩΜΕΤΡΗΤΟΣ ΜΗΔΕΙΣ ΕΙΣΙΤΩ*. Une inscription légendaire', *Revue des études grecques* 81, 67–87.

— (1971). 'Abamon, pseudonyme de Jamblique', *Philomathes* (Festschrift P. Merlan), ed. R. Palmer, R. Hamerton-Kelly, The Hague, 227–39.

— (1975). 'Allusions antichrétiennes chez Proclus le diadoque platonicien', *Revue des sciences philosophiques et théologiques* 59, 553–63.

SAFFREY, H. D. (1976). 'Théologie et anthropologie d'après quelques préfaces de Proclus', *Images of Man* (Festschrift G. Verbeke), ed. F. Boissier *et al.*, Louvain, 199–212.

—— (1984). 'La Théurgie comme phénomène culturel chez les néoplatoniciens (IVᵉ–Vᵉ siècles)', *KOINΩNIA* 8, 161–71.

—— (1987a). 'La *Théologie Platonicienne* de Proclus et l'histoire du néoplatonisme', *Proclus et son influence*, ed. G. Boss, G. Seel, Zurich, 29–44.

—— (1987b). 'Comment Syrianus, le maître de l'école néoplatonicienne d'Athènes, considérait-il Aristote?', *Aristoteles Werk und Wirkung* (Festschrift P. Moraux), ed. J. Wiesner, Berlin–New York, 205–14.

SAMBURSKY, S. (1962). *The Physical World of Late Antiquity*, London.

—— (1965). 'Plato, Proclus and the Limitations of Science', *Journal of the History of Philosophy* 3, 1–11.

——, PINES, S. (1971). *The Concept of Time in Late Neoplatonism*, Jerusalem.

SCHÖNBERGER, O. (1984). *Iamblichos' Aufruf zur Philosophie*, Würzburg.

SCHRIMPF, G. (1966). *Die Axiomenschrift des Boethius (De hebdomadibus) als philosophisches Lehrbuch des Mittelalters*, Leiden.

SCHULTZE, W. (1978). *Zahl Proportion Analogie. Eine Untersuchung zur Metaphysik und Wissenschaftshaltung des Nikolaus von Kues*, Münster.

SCHWYZER, H.-R. (1978). Review of Hierocles, *In Carm.*, ed. Köhler, *Gnomon* 50, 251–6.

—— (1983). *Ammonius Sakkas der Lehrer Plotins*, Rheinisch-Westfälische Akad. der Wiss., Geisteswiss. Vorträge G 260.

SEGONDS, A. (1985–6). Ed., transl., *Proclus sur le premier Alcibiade de Platon*, Paris.

—— (1987). 'Philosophie et astronomie chez Proclus', *Proclus et son influence*, 159–77.

SHAW, G. (1985). 'Theurgy: Rituals of Unification in the Neoplatonism of Iamblichus', *Traditio* 41, 1–28.

SHEPPARD, A. (1980). *Studies on the 5th and 6th Essays of Proclus' Commentary on the Republic*, Göttingen.

—— (1982). 'Monad and Dyad as Cosmic Principles in Syrianus', *Soul and the Structure of Being in Late Neoplatonism*, ed. H. Blumenthal and A. Lloyd, Liverpool, 1–14.

SICHERL, M. (1960). 'Michael Psellos und Iamblichus de mysteriis', *Byzantinische Zeitschrift* 53, 8–19.

SMITH, A. (1974). *Porphyry's Place in the Neoplatonic Tradition*, The Hague.

SOLIGNAC, A. (1958). 'Doxographies et manuels dans la formation philosophique de saint Augustin', *Recherches augustiniennes* 1, 113–48.

SONDEREGGER, E. (1982). *Simplikios: Über die Zeit*, Göttingen.

SORABJI, R. (1983). *Time Creation and the Continuum. Theories in Antiquity and the Early Middle Ages*, London.

—— (1987). Ed., *Philoponus and the Rejection of Aristotelian Science*, London.

STAEHLE, K. (1931). *Die Zahlenmystik bei Philon von Alexandria*, Leipzig and Berlin.

STECK, M., SCHÖNBERGER, P. (1945). *Proklus Diadochus Kommentar zum ersten Buch von Euklids "Elementen"*, Halle (Saale).

STEEL, C. (1978). *The Changing Self. A Study on the Soul in Later Neoplatonism: Iamblichus, Damascius and Priscianus*, Brussels.

—— (1986). 'Proclus: Filosofie en mythologie', *Tijdschrift voor filosofie* 48, 191–206.

—— (1987). 'L'anagogie par les apories', *Proclus et son influence*, 101–28.

SZLEZÁK, T. (1972). *Pseudo-Archytas über die Kategorien*, Berlin.

—— (1979). *Platon und Aristoteles in der Nuslehre Plotins*, Basle and Stuttgart.

TANNERY, P. (1884). 'Domninos de Larissa', *Mémoires scientifiques* II, Paris 1912, 105–17.

—— (1885a). 'Sur l'Arithmétique Pythagoricienne', *Mémoires scientifiques* II, 179–201.

—— (1885b). 'Notes critiques sur Domninos', *Revue de philologie* 9, 128–37.

—— (1887). *Pour l'histoire de la science hellène*, ed. A. Diès, Paris 1930.

—— (1906). 'Le manuel d'introduction arithmétique du philosophe Domninos de Larissa', *Mémoires scientifiques* III, Paris 1915, 255–81.

TARÁN, L. (1969). *Asclepius of Tralles: Commentary to Nicomachus' Introduction to Arithmetic*, Philadelphia.

—— (1974). 'Nicomachus of Gerasa', *Dictionary of Scientific Biography* 10, 112–14.

—— (1981). *Speusippus of Athens*, Leiden.

TAYLOR, T. (1816). *The Theoretic Arithmetic of the Pythagoreans*, London, repr. Los Angeles 1934.

THESLEFF, H. (1961). *An Introduction to the Pythagorean Writings of the Hellenistic Period*, Åbo.

—— (1965). *The Pythagorean Texts of the Hellenistic Period*, Åbo.

TROUILLARD, J. (1957). 'Le sens des médiations proclusiennes', *Revue philosophique de Louvain* 55, 331–42.

—— (1959). 'La monadologie de Proclus', *Revue philosophique de Louvain* 57, 309–20.

—— (1965). *Proclus: Eléments de Théologie, traduction, introduction et notes*, Paris.

—— (1972). *L'Un et l'âme selon Proclus*, Paris.

—— (1983). 'La puissance secrète du nombre selon Proclus', *Revue de philosophie ancienne* 2, 227–41.

VERBEKE, G. (1981). 'Aristotle's Metaphysics viewed by the Ancient Greek Commentators', *Studies in Aristotle*, ed. D. J. O'Meara, Washington, 107–27.

VINCENT, M.-A. (1971). 'Syrianus et le Politique d'Aristote', *Le Néoplatonisme*, Paris, 215–26.

VOGEL, C. J. DE (1966). *Pythagoras and Early Pythagoreanism*, Assen.

VOLLENWEIDER, S. (1985). *Neuplatonische und christliche Theologie bei Synesios von Kyrene*, Göttingen.

WAERDEN, B. VAN DER (1979). *Die Pythagoreer*, Zurich.

—— (1980). 'Die gemeinsame Quelle der erkenntnistheoretischen Abhandlungen von Iamblichos und Proklos', *Sitz. Heidelb. Akad. d. Wiss.*, Phil.-hist. kl. 12.

WALLIS, R. T. (1972). *Neoplatonism*, London.

WASZINK, J. H. (1964). *Studien zum Timaioskommentar des Calcidius* I, Leiden.

—— (1966). 'Porphyrios und Numenios', *Porphyre*, Vandœuvres–Geneva, 35–83.

WEDBERG, A. (1955). *Plato's Philosophy of Mathematics*, Uppsala.

WESTERINK, L. G. (1959). 'Exzerpte aus Proklos' Enneadenkommentar bei Psellos', *Byzantinische Zeitschrift* 52, 1–10 = Westerink, *Texts and Studies in Neoplatonism and Byzantine Literature*, Amsterdam 1980, 21–30.

—— (1971). 'Damascius, Commentateur de Platon', *Le Néoplatonisme*, Paris, 253–60 = Westerink, *Texts and Studies*, 271–8.

—— (1987). 'Proclus commentateur des *Vers d'or?*', *Proclus et son influence*, 61–78.

WHITTAKER, J. (1967). 'Moses Atticizing', *Phoenix* 21, 196–201.

—— (1974). 'Parisinus graecus 1962 and the Writings of Albinus', *Phoenix* 28, 320–54.

WINDEN, J. C. M. VAN (1971). *An Early Christian Philosopher*, Leiden.

WOLSKA-CONUS, W. (1979). 'L'école de droit et l'enseignement du droit à Byzance au XIe siècle: Xiphilin et Psellos', *Travaux et mémoires* 7, 1–107.

ZIMMERMAN, A. (1983). Ed., *Mensura. Mass, Zahl, Zahlensymbolik im Mittelalter* (Miscellanea Medievalia 16), Berlin.

INDEX